Global Flow Security

A New Security Agenda for the Transatlantic Community in 2030

Erik Brattberg and Daniel S. Hamilton
Editors

Center for Transatlantic Relations
Paul H. Nitze School of Advanced International Studies
Johns Hopkins University

Erik Brattberg and Daniel S. Hamilton, eds. *Global Flow Security: A New Security Agenda for the Transatlantic Community in 2030*

Washington, DC: Center for Transatlantic Relations, 2014.

Center for Transatlantic Relations
The Paul H. Nitze School of Advanced International Studies
The Johns Hopkins University
1717 Massachusetts Ave., NW, Suite 525
Washington, DC 20036
Tel: (202) 663-5880
Fax: (202) 663-5879
Email: transatlantic@jhu.edu
http://transatlantic.sais-jhu.edu

ISBN 13: 978-09907720-1-9

Cover image: Anton Balazh

Contents

Part I
Setting the Scene: Global Flows and Global Trends

Part II
Perspectives on Global Flow Security 2030

Introduction

In this age of accelerating globalization, the true security of our societies, or its citizens, economy and state institutions, is to a very large extent a function of the security of the flows across borders, of the securities of all of those flows of persons, goods, capital, energy, information, whether it be digital or otherwise, that flows across nations, regions and the globe; that is the core of the process of globalization. To secure all of these flows all the way naturally requires a high degree of collaboration; national security is no longer enough.

—Carl Bildt, former Foreign Minister of Sweden, speech at the International Institute for Strategic Studies, London, December 1, 2010.

In a world increasingly interconnected and interdependent, no country or region is necessarily immune to developments occurring elsewhere across the globe. Global "megatrends" such as globalization, geopolitical power shifts, rapid urbanization, energy transformation, technological innovation and climate change are all certain to reverberate locally—whether the "local" is Stockholm, Shanghai, São Paulo or San Francisco. Different trends may also interact to generate unanticipated effects. Decision makers across the world are challenged to understand these trends and the ways they may intersect to influence the societies in which they live.

A closer look at global megatrends reveals the interconnected nature of contemporary challenges. Transboundary arteries carrying people, ideas, money, energy, goods and services criss-cross modern societies and contribute significantly to economic growth and prosperity. They are essential sinews of open societies, daily communications, and the global economy. Yet they are also susceptible to intentional or accidental disruption. Growing interdependencies have also facilitated the growth of trafficking in people, drugs, arms and many other illicit products and services that can disrupt and undermine the resiliency of societies. The mutual vulnerabilities of interconnected societies, in turn, can amplify the cascading effects of such disruptions, further impairing the ability of our societies to function.

Just as governments traditionally protect their territory, so too must they protect their connectedness—the networks that bind them and their citizens with the rest of the world. Safeguarding *critical global flows*—e.g. transboundary arteries that constitute the essence of open societies, daily communications and the global economy, as well as the prevention of illicit flows states—constitutes a growing strategic imperative for policymakers and security providers. Global mega-trends may not only enhance dependency on many of these global flows; they may add new vulnerabilities. Conversely, activities in individual societies may also potentially ripple back across the rest of the world. The 2014 Ebola outbreak is a reminder that diseases that were once local scourges can have global range. Understanding the interaction between deep global trends and critical global flows is necessary to address the changing needs and nature of societal security.

Unfortunately, many decision makers are not yet adequately equipped to take on this task. While the notion of "national security" has evolved considerably since the Cold War, a more 'hyper-interdependent' world requires decision makers to marry traditional goals of ensuring territorial integrity and national sovereignty with new and innovative efforts to secure a society's critical functions.

With this in mind, this volume looks at how future global trends are likely to affect ''flows" critical to the security and prosperity of the Euro-Atlantic region in 2030. Led by a team of researchers at the Swedish Institute of International Affairs (UI) and the Center for Transatlantic Relations (CTR) at Johns Hopkins University's School of Advanced International Studies, the main objective of this project is to assist Euro-Atlantic policymakers in their strategic thinking about what seemingly distant and abstract global trends may mean for operational efforts to enhance societal security closer at home. Strategic planning and foresight are required to ensure that competencies and operational capabilities are developed to cope with a range of diffuse and multidimensional security threats—some of which are old, some new, and some newly important.

Section I of this volume offers a foundation for ensuing contributions. In Chapter 1, Tomas Ries sets forth a theoretical framework in which to understand the evolving nature of global flow security. In Chapter 2, Erik Brattberg presents a number of key global trends, synthesized from a range of government and non-governmental studies across different countries.

In Section II our authors examine a number of discrete global flows and their likely interaction with other global trends with a view towards 2030, and draw conclusions for societal security in Europe and North America. Authors were asked to address a number of questions. How will global megatrends affect the critical flows upon which Europe and the United States will continue to depend? How will specific Euro-Atlantic dependencies and vulnerabilities be affected by these long-term trends? How can public and private decision makers work to ensure the resilience of critical flows and safeguard the critical functions of our societies?

We provide an Executive Summary that distills our core findings, and we offer a set of recommendations for action by policy makers and private sector actors. Our recommendations draw on the authors' insights, and in some cases are a direct reflection of their suggestions, but responsibility for advancing these views rests with the editors alone. We have profited greatly from our authors' contributions and thank them for their time and energy.

We would also like to thank Miriam Cunningham of the Center for Transatlantic Relations; Mark Rhinard of the Swedish Institute of International Affairs; and Mat Burrows and Lars Hedström. We thank Carin Kaunitz and Bengt Sundelius and the Swedish Civil Contingencies Agency (MSB) for their encouragement and support of this project.

All authors write in their personal capacity, and none of the views expressed here represent those of the Swedish Civil Contingencies Agency or any government or institution.

Erik Brattberg
Daniel S. Hamilton

Executive Summary

Part I. Global Trends and Global Flows

Global Flow Security: A Conceptual Framework

Critical economic, technological and human flows upon which our societies depend are diffusing and spreading so that for the first time they now transcend the state on a significant scale, in terms of both volume and power; and global ecological flows for the first time are critically affected by human activity. The scale and complexity of "critical flows," as well as the dependency of many societies of such flows, have increased dramatically. Securing these global flows is emerging as the primary existential interest of all major globalizing actors, be they state or non-state. Transnational actors who direct or influence these flows are emerging as new power brokers—transnational corporations, civil society, organized crime, transnational revolutionary networks.

As long as global flows function and major state actors not only benefit but also depend on them (and realize this dependence), there is a good chance that the focus of security policy could shift from protecting and promoting state sovereignty to protecting and promoting shared critical transnational flows. But we are not yet there. "Territory"-oriented security and "flow" security agendas coexist uneasily.

Global Megatrends Likely to Impact Global Flows

Six global trends are likely to impact global flows to 2030:

1. the changing distribution of global power toward a "G-Zero World";

2. the diffusion of state power to transnational actors leading to a more "Liquid World";

3. global technological diffusion likely to generate "More Human Power";

4. growing population and resource scarcity causing a "Shrinking World";

5. the empowerment of individuals amidst rising social vulnerabilities, a "Global Awakening";

6. climate change and environmental degradation leading to a more "Extreme World".

Part II. Perspectives on Global Flow Security 2030

Flow Security in the Digital Age

As digital modality comes to affect most aspects of life, cyber flows are becoming essential for the proper functioning of the overall system of flows that transports goods, people, and information across the globe. Cyber flows highlight a new vision of world order based as much on the geopolitics of milliseconds as on strategy based on geographies. At the same time, geography still matters; nation-based identities will likely continue to provide central and identifying organizing concepts, and the cyber flow world is not "flat," but uneven—its contours are influenced by decisions made by state actors. Thus countries are increasingly caught between state-centric and flow-centric security models. Decision makers are challenged to develop appropriate conditions to identify and establish access points to positive global flows while ameliorating the negative of illicit shadow flows. Global cyber flows are also affecting sub-regions within countries. New political and economic dynamics may emerge as sub-regions or certain societal strata within countries perceive that their prosperity and security of their region may be more related to the vibrancy, prosperity and security of sub-regions or social groupings outside their country than to regions within their own country. Businesses and the communities in which they are based are increasingly dependent on assured, and often instantaneous, access to regular flows of materials and resources. These flows are rearranging the map via new economic and political models that can affect people's daily lives. They require secured access points and sustained capacity to tap into the flow, which in turn require interoperable technologies that pose demands for regional infrastructure, education, and societal organization. Effective cyber security must be rooted in an understanding that digital flows are embedded in interrelated human communities of practice.

Global Energy Flows

Global energy flows will be affected by several global megatrends. First, individual empowerment, demographic changes, and new patterns of production and consumption are shifting demand from the West to the East. This trend is already apparent and will continue well into and beyond 2030. Second, the Atlantic Basin in emerging as a major energy reservoir for the world; in future the Pacific is largely going to be the world's primary energy consumer and the Atlantic the world's primary energy provider. Already the Atlantic Basin supplies some 35% of total world petroleum imports—the same percentage of world imports coming from the Middle East. To 2030, over nearly 60% of the increase in oil production will come from the Atlantic Basin. For the first time in modern history, the growing source of energy supply could be located beyond the Eurasian landmass. Third, although oil currently dominates global energy flows as well as the global material flow map, by 2050 internationally trade in energy is likely to double and will be increasingly dominated by liquid movements of gas, even as climate change and new innovation generate additional pressures and opportunities to shift to renewables. Climate change is also likely to have profound effects on global shipping and resource extraction—in particular, by opening the Arctic to these kinds of activities. Fourth, since global energy trade remains the single most important global flow on the seas, both in terms of size and centrality to economic and geopolitical interests, the "global energy seascape" will remain the most strategic dimension of the 'global flow map,' and these megatrends will reinforce the importance of securing sea lanes and choke points. Global energy flows are also likely to boost the importance of "low-latitude" sea lanes such as the Straits of Hormuz and Malacca, but also 'high-latitude' passages such as the Cape of Good Hope linking the Atlantic Basin with the Indian Basin and Northern routes via the Arctic. The Bering Strait will achieve a significance rivaling that of the Panama Canal on the global energy flow map. Ocean basins—with their new and evolving interfaces between ocean and "maritime rimlands"—are becoming a new nexus of geoeconomics, geopolitics and transnational environmental collaboration and key governance frames to address strategic challenges.

Global Flows of Materials

Three threats challenge regular, secure and sustainable flows of materials: functional threats of price volatility and peaks; political threats from new players and fragile countries; and managing ecological threats resulting from environmental pressures. Global drivers can overshadow local drivers in the management of common pool resources such as river basins management and agriculture. On top of this, increasing connectivity allows local turbulence to spread rapidly, with unintended side-effects on other resources and regions. Local and regional stress factors are likely to hit critical nerves of global supply chains, and might transform strong systems into fragile ones.

Global flows of materials (especially natural resources) will be affected a great deal by on-going megatrends. First, the diffusion of power means that security of supply will increasingly be an issue as more powerful states vie for the same finite resources. Second, population growth, rapid urbanization and the emergence of a global middle class will alter the geography of commodity trade; increase and tighten resource markets; and very likely lead to intensified and volatile competition for resources. The increasingly important challenge will be to manage materials flows in a sustainable manner. Third, increased risks for regional instability will continue to produce new forms of illicit flows of materials. Finally, climate change and extreme weather will exacerbate the "global resource nexus," i.e. increasing inter-linkages across the use of a number of resources. Even though these inter-linkages are at the heart of global flow security, most public and private strategies tend to be either predominantly supply-oriented ("raw materials strategy," "unconventional fuels") *or* demand oriented ("resource efficiency," "sustainable consumption and production"). They must expand their focus to hybrid forms of public-private governance and more holistic "life-cycle" approaches that relate sustainable global material flow security to the global resource nexus.

Global Financial Flows

More than six years after the collapse of Lehman Brothers, the United States remains at the center of the global financial universe, backed by one of the largest and most resilient economies in the world. The global appeal of the U.S. dollar remains relatively strong, while the eurozone crisis has diminished investor appetite for the euro. Meanwhile, developing nations—despite having over $10 trillion at their disposal in the form of international reserves—have failed to use their financial firepower effectively to stave off a cyclical economic slowdown, let alone marshal their massive savings to fundamentally remake the global financial order.

But past is not prologue. Global megatrends are likely to accelerate the emergence of a more multi-polar financial world by 2030, with the United States and the U.S. dollar likely to remain first among equals. The international role of both the euro and the Chinese renminbi (RMB) will expand, but the process will be gradual and deliberate. To what extent the euro emerges as a world reserve currency will be determined by Europe's attempts to forge a banking union and create pan-European capital markets that would pool and allocate capital more efficiently and effectively. China's renminbi is growing in importance, recently replacing the euro as the second most heavily used currency in international trade finance. Yet for China's currency to remotely challenge the reign of the dollar, China has to first modernize and open its financial sector and make the RMB convertible.

Global Technology Flows

Global technology flows will change dramatically in the next two decades. First, rising hyper connectivity will enable developing countries and small companies alike. Second, global economic power shifts mean that Asia will increasingly be a source of technological innovation. The flow of ideas, knowledge, and intellectual property related to technical advancements and innovations will not only increase in volume and speed, it will be increasingly dispersed within and among developed and emerging economies. The speed of this movement will depend on the availability of human and financial capital in the developing countries; rules of law to protect intellectual property rights; and the general desire of developing-economy companies to grow and be globally competitive. Third, *automation* from a particularly interesting set of electro-mechanical and information technologies, stimulated by hitherto unthinkable volumes of data, is poised to drive major disruption in industries, government services, and elements of our social lives in the next twenty years.

Key building blocks for advances in automation include artificial-intelligence (AI) software; mobile and broadband networks; cloud services; sensors; power, motion, and manipulation technologies; the evolving internet of things; and user interfaces that mediate people's relationships with computers, cars, entertainment electronics, office automation, technology in public spaces, and handheld devices. People will engage in increasingly natural modes of interaction with machines. When integrated together, these building blocks create a wide range of new automation functions, systems, and capabilities that will transform the ways government and industry conduct business and how individuals conduct their lives. These include telepresence and teleoperation; industrial robots; additive manufacturing (3D printing); nonindustrial or personal robots; remote-controlled and autonomous—unmanned—vehicles; collaborative machines; pervasive computing; and automated knowledge-work tasks.

For Europe and North America the impacts of advanced automation flows in the next 20 years will be particularly acute: advanced automation will affect the competitive dynamics of many industries, the work tasks done by humans in both product-manufacturing and knowledge-worker organizations, and how we personally interact with our physical environments and each other. Dramatic changes can be expected for financial services, healthcare, and retail.

- **Financial services.** Major EU-U.S. flow impacts from future automation in financial services include increased capital flows within and between regions because of better products and services from financial services companies located in the regions, the increased use of information-technology services by financial services institutions, the delivery of services by those institutions to customers, and the movement of talent, expertise, and intellectual property among regions to fill the changing needs. Employment in financial sectors and across consumer finance will be negatively impacted.

- **Healthcare.** Automation technology flows will have a very large impact because of the urgent needs in developed countries for improved operational efficiency, lower cost, reduced labor requirements, and demand for greater personalization or choice. Until now, healthcare economic systems have been mostly national with small cross-border flows. Automation technology could change that in a major way. The internationalization of healthcare is likely to face challenges from national regulatory and professional bodies. The major flows impacts from healthcare automation will be functional global economic flows and global technology flows. Flow circuits will primarily involve the United States and Europe, but developing countries could play a role in custom manufacturing (China) or software and services (India).

- **Retail.** Automation innovations in retail in response to market needs will be implemented rapidly in both Europe and North America, resulting in significant economic and social change. E-commerce—and its sibling m-commerce—will quite probably be responsible for a large percentage of total retail sales. Social networks may function as a portal through which those transactions occur, and automation will make any retail experience highly personalized. Product delivery and logistics will be transformed. These changes will have both positive and negative impacts on developed-world economies as private-sector competitive environments adjust; as governments try to implement new information management, policy setting, regulatory, and public safety functions and capabilities; and as people adjust to new personal environments.

Europe and North America are well positioned to lead the development of automation technologies and systems and supply the companies that will serve the new markets. On the other hand, both regions are already invested in current ways of doing things; changes to meet future societal needs for connectedness, adjust labor markets, and to remain industrially competitive will be difficult because they will require almost everyone to acquire new skills and live their lives differently. There will be many costs in making these changes.

Inter-Industry Flows

In recent years we have witnessed numerous cascading "crashes" of industrial activity, in which a small and local breakdown in the flow of physical goods or finance triggers a shutdown of systems across the world. While analysts point to international industrial integration and the rise of "just-in-time" and "lean" production techniques as relevant factors responsible for these cascading, cross-border industrial crashes, the more fundamental source of fragility is the geographic concentration of keystone production capacity critical to many industries—more than half of industrial companies depend on single sources of supply for key inputs. Many industrial production activities that a few years ago were spread around the world are increasingly concentrated in a few keystone factories, in one or another of the world's main industrial nations. This is the one factor that is entirely new; we have never before seen such high degrees of concentration of vital capacity. In many instances, the entire world supply of some keystone component now takes place in a single industrial zone, even a single factory. This concentration of capacity, in turn, concentrates physical risk and financial risk, and an "inherent magnification effect" on shocks. If a critical capacity is shut down or disabled, production managers are left with little or no ability to respond to even predictable disruptions. This new global industrial commons is characterized by numerous single points of failure, innumerable active tectonic and political fault lines, and by extremely "tight coupling." The fragility of these systems derives not from the fact that production is located outside a country's boundaries, but from the fact that all production of many keystone components is located in one or a couple places only. The key to ensuring the resiliency of our international production systems is to build up real-time redundancy by physically distributing the capacity to produce keystone components, be they electronics, chemicals or information. This, in turn, leads to all sorts of pragmatic, practical rules and laws—for instance regarding sourcing transparency or competition policies—that would ensure the resiliency of vital systems while avoiding protectionism.

Global Illicit Flows

Keeping borders open for legal trade and travel, while attempting to deter, detect, and interdict clandestine flows of items that are prohibited, stolen or counterfeit, is and will remain an inherently cumbersome and frustrating task. The difficulties are particularly evident in efforts to manage growing transactions between developed and less developed regions of the world, for instance across the southern and eastern edges of Europe or the southern edges of the United States. In the next decade and a half or so we are not likely to see some sort of fundamental shift in the illicit global economy. Illicit flows will persist, as they always have—but their location, organization, method, and content will vary.

The most important global trends are all going to impact illicit trade. The rise of non-state actors, conflict regions, increased ethnic and sectarian violence, displacement of populations, economic disparity, climate change are all going to impact the nature of illicit trade in the developed countries of North America and Europe through the displacement of people, the need for individuals to survive and the absence of legitimate opportunities. The decline of state power, the retreat of the state, and the embedding of non-state actors in the power and governance structures of many regions suggest a different organization of power in the future that will make many countries outside the affluent states of Europe and North America unable to control the illicit trade at its origin. In addition, many states' integrity and capacity where these problems are most pronounced have been compromised by corruption; they are not capable of opposing illicit actors.

An entangled threat of crime, corruption, and terrorism will require more attention from the leadership of North America and Western Europe because of its endemic nature in many diverse regions of the world, especially in conflict regions; the financial success and extensive influence of non-state actors on governments, often by means of corruption; the increasing economic role of criminals and terrorists both as employers and participants in the local and global economy; the deleterious impact of crime and terrorism on communities and the political order; and the incapacity of state and multinational organizations to successfully challenge transnational criminals and terrorists at the national, regional, and global levels.

Global technological innovation and diffusion will enable smuggling and the production of new types of illicit products—such as new synthetic drugs, DNA theft, illicit cloning or 3D printing of illicit arms—while also improving government capacity to track and police the cross-border flow of people, cargo, money, and information. Finally, the diffusion of power away from the United States is likely to have important consequences for policing illicit flows as policing preferences become more varied, priorities change, and coordination becomes more cumbersome. In this regard, the rise of China and other potential regional challenges in coming years may erode the hegemony of U.S.-sponsored international crime control initiatives and approaches. At the same time, U.S. policing influence may outlast its waning power. Some U.S.-backed international initiatives, such as the anti-money laundering efforts of the Financial Action Task Force, have taken on a life of their own and generated their own momentum. Major international agreements that the United States played an instrumental role in creating have built on and reinforced each other and provided models for future agreements.

These developments will contribute to (and necessitate) the continued, yet likely uneven, growth of international policing cooperation, most developed in Europe and in U.S.-EU relations. Ever-thickening cross-border law enforcement networks have become a crucial—even if often overlooked—dimension of transatlantic relations and regional and global governance. Declining U.S. leadership may present new opportunities for the EU to play a bigger global, and not just regional, role in this realm. "At-the-border" inspections are likely to be supplemented where possible by procedures that "push the border out" through prescreening, preclearance, new technologies and new cooperative procedures, but will also generate new frictions among authorities due to different legal customs, rules and regimes. Policing cyberspace will continue to develop as a new frontier of law enforcement that coexists and intermingles with traditional terrestrial policing. This will no doubt also continue to provoke intense political battles and concern over privacy and civil liberties issues, both domestically and internationally.

Global Flows of Ideas

The 21st century international system is becoming "Copernican"—the United States is not at the center of the system; it is part of a more diffuse system of countries, each with its own orbit and own sources of influence, interests, identities, and domestic politics. A "global marketplace of ideas" is emerging, marked by three main dynamics: (1) greater doubts about Western models at both the international system and national domestic levels; (2) increasing affirmation across the non-Western world for ideas rooted in one's own history, culture and identity, as well as one's own national and regional politics; and (3) technology as a driver of a profoundly different discourse and competition of ideas enabled by a digital infrastructure that increasingly connects everyone to everyone. The global marketplace of ideas means that the competition is on for the appropriate norms to guide the international system, and for what constitutes a capable state. If the West is to adapt the international system to better fit these deeper trends of power diffusion and new nationalism of this Copernican world, it must engage proactively, and to be more open to a range of political-economic models beyond traditional Western ones so long as they have genuine legitimacy in the eyes of their own people.

Transnational Revolutionary Movements

Islamic, democratic, nationalist secessionist, and even authoritarian Marxist revolutions are the most likely varieties of revolution to occur between now and 2030, though the possibility of other types cannot be ruled out. Transnational revolutionary movements are political movements that arise in several countries either at the same time or in relatively close proximity to one another. They may be understood as flows that interact with other flows and are influenced by deeper global trends. The changing distribution of global power, for instance, can give rise to revolution. It should not be surprising that the American withdrawal from Iraq and Afghanistan, combined with American and European reluctance to undertake major military interventions, appears to be leading to another upsurge of revolutionary activity. The diffusion of state power to transnational actors may also contribute to the perception that states are becoming weaker, and thus more susceptible to revolution, but it is also possible that the growing influence of transnational actors may result in new types of revolutionary movements that focus their efforts not on overthrowing the state, but damaging or destroying the transnational actors that they find particularly objectionable. Global technological diffusion, especially in the realms of communications technology and social media, has already provided revolutionary movements with highly important advantages. Still, the ability of technically-capable counter-revolutionary regimes such as China to limit or deny their opponents access to these new technologies while at the same time taking advantage of them should not be underestimated. Growing population and resource scarcity, where

Our survey of the interrelationship among deep global trends and key global flows underscores the importance of norms and standards when it comes to efforts to promote societal resilience. The EU and United States are central nodes in global networks, yet the diffusion of power could mean that the window of opportunity for the West to be standard-setters, rather than standard-takers, could be closing. And being able to adopt common normative postures, when the normative identity of many rising powers is in flux, constitutes a comparative advantage in a world shaped by relative power.[2]

This insight applies directly to issues related to upholding open, common areas of freedom, security and justice. The rules of the road for the regulation of cyberspace, for instance, will prove a contentious issue, one on which autocratic and democratic societies will stake out different positions. If the United States and Europe can agree on basic international norms and standards, such measures will likely provide the basis for global arrangements. If the United States and Europe fail to agree or diverge in their approaches, however, in a world of diffuse power no such global standards are likely to emerge—or both sides could be faced with standards and norms set by others.[3]

These trends demand a reoriented approach to EU-U.S. security cooperation with regard to a challenging spectrum of hazards, risks and threats. We believe the U.S.-EU partnership needs to focus efforts to advance transatlantic resilience in a common area of freedom, justice and security. Unfortunately, there is a mismatch between the nature of our challenges and the institutional frameworks, strategic-action capacity, and practical tools at our disposal to achieve this goal.

We recommend action in four areas:[4]

---

[2]Giovanni Grevi and Richard Youngs, "What Norms for a New-Order Transatlantic Relationship? European Perspectives," in Daniel Hamilton and Kurt Volker, eds., *Transatlantic 2020: America and Europe in a Changing World* (Washington, DC: Center for Transatlantic Relations, 2011); G. John Ikenberry, "The Rise of China and the Future of the West," *Foreign Affairs*, January/February 2008; G. John Ikenberry, "The Future of the Liberal World Order," *Foreign Affairs*, May/June 2011.

[3]For more on this issue, see Jason Healey, "Breakthrough or Just Broken? China and Russia's UNGA Proposal on Cyber Norms"; UK Foreign Minister William Hague, "Security and Freedom in the Cyber Age—Seeking the Rules of the Road," Munich Security Conference, February 4, 2011; "Nations call on UN to discuss cyber security," *China Daily*, September 14, 2011.

[4]Some recommendations draw from and build on Daniel S. Hamilton, ed., *Shoulder to Shoulder: Forging a Strategic U.S.-EU Partnership* (Center for Transatlantic Relations, Washington, DC,

- Strengthen EU-U.S. cooperation to enhance societal security;
- Develop compatible societal security capabilities;
- Invest in global supply chain security;
- Project resilience outward.

Strengthen EU-U.S. Cooperation to Enhance Societal Security

Europe and the United States do not lack for institutional frameworks: transatlantic cooperation takes place amidst a veritable alphabet soup of mechanisms and institutions. Many observers focus first on NATO, which remains an essential transatlantic security institution. But NATO is neither equipped, nor always the most appropriate vehicle, to take the lead on what must become a core goal in EU-U.S. relations: building transatlantic resilience. Many areas of law enforcement, domestic intelligence, civil security and disaster response are well beyond NATO's area of competence, and are better handled in other venues. NATO could—and should—complement such efforts, for instance by helping (as it has already done) with security for mass public events, dealing with the consequences of various natural disasters, or coping with a catastrophic terrorist event, particularly one involving agents of mass destruction. But in most of these areas NATO would be at most a supporting player, not the lead actor.

The EU-U.S. relationship is increasingly the vehicle for pursuing common goals related to societal resilience. That relationship, especially when seen to encompass the relations the United States maintains with the EU's 28 member states as well as its Brussels-based institutions, is among the most complex and multi-layered economic, diplomatic, societal and security relationship that either partner has. Not only does cooperation run broad and deep—a critical consideration when designing resilience-enhancing initiatives across the policy

2010); Daniel Hamilton and Mark Rhinard, "All For One, One For All: Towards A Transatlantic Solidarity Pledge," in EUISS, *The U.S.-EU Security and Justice Agenda in Action* (Paris, 2012), http://transatlantic.sais- jhu.edu/publications/articles/Chapter_4_Hamilton_Rhinard_All_for_ one_one_for_all.pdf; as well as Patryk Pawlak and Erik Brattberg, "Equipping the EU for Future Security Challenges Through Strategic Planning," *UI Occasional Paper No 20* (Stockholm: Swedish Institute of International Affairs, 2013).

spectrum—but the two sides are also enmeshed in security interdependencies. Add to this the fact that the EU is increasingly the institution that European governments use to coordinate their own policies and action in the interrelated realms of societal security and "flow" security, and it is hard to deny that the EU will be America's essential partner in many of the areas beyond NATO's purview and capacities.

Yet the U.S.-EU relationship has never been properly framed in strategic terms. The United States has no link to European partners in the EU that is equivalent to its link through NATO, even though most of those partners are members of both organizations. There is insufficient understanding in many (but not all) Washington circles about the rising role of the EU not only in justice and home affairs matters but in protecting citizens and critical infrastructures more broadly. The EU shoulders some of the blame: the nature of its bureaucratic structures, and the division of national-supranational competences, makes strategic dialogue difficult. Former U.S. Secretary of State Hillary Clinton touched upon this reality when she noted to her European colleagues, "the system is designed so we can't have a strategic dialogue."[5] A strategic partnership would encompass regular, shared assessments of key security threats; the ability to deal create a common operational picture of risks, hazards and threats; the facility to manage daily grind of immediate policy demands while pursuing long-term priorities related to ensuring security, prosperity and values; and the capacity to harness the full range of resources in building complementary responses to common challenges. Today, we do not have that relationship.[6]

EU-U.S. working and expert groups already exist in such areas of transportation security, cybercrime and cyber security. For the most part, however, this dimension of the transatlantic security agenda has fallen victim to ad hoc, reactive responses that are not commensurate with the challenges at hand or the depth of our interdependencies. There is no overarching vision to guide and benchmark on-going work between agencies and bureaucracies. And although we understand the thick web of functional interdependencies between us, we

---

[5]Cited in Daniel Hamilton, ed., *Shoulder to Shoulder*, op. cit.
[6]Ibid.; also Ronald D. Asmus, "New Plumbing, New Purposes—Rebuilding the Transatlantic Alliance," *The American Interest*, November/December 2008.

have limited tools at our disposal in only a scattered number of policy areas (e.g. container security, data exchange, terrorist financing). Considering the mutual damage that could be done if the vital arteries crossing the Atlantic were to be disrupted, more needs to be done.

We propose framing our joint efforts towards building transatlantic resilience in a common area of freedom, justice and security. We define the concept of resilience as the ability at international, national, regional and local levels to deter, prevent, detect, respond to and absorb disruptive challenges to the critical functions of society, and to regain functionality swiftly should such disruptions occur.[7] Achieving resilience requires heterogeneity in systems, processes and responses and an improved understanding of how those systems work. It is not simply a matter of dealing with consequences; anticipation and prevention are crucial. A strategy of resiliency seeks to ensure that the basic structures and critical functions of our interconnected societies remain strong and can continue even in the face of natural or man-made disasters.[8] This suggests advanced work to strengthen, and/or build redundancies, into transatlantic arteries operating at the technical, social and even political levels. Initiatives at each level must be integrated into a comprehensive strategy with a clearly identifiable goal: achieving transatlantic resilience in a common area of freedom, justice and security.

Adopt a Transatlantic Solidarity Pledge

While Europe and the United States will be even more dependent on global flows by 2030, the thickest web of dependencies will still be across the Atlantic. Given these prospects, the United States and the EU should seek to supplement their traditional focus on military

---

[7]See Daniel S. Hamilton, "Transatlantic Society Security. A New Paradigm for a New Era," in Anja Dalgaard-Nielsen and Daniel S. Hamilton, *Transatlantic Homeland Security* (London: Routledge, 2006), pp. 181-182; David Omand, "The International Aspects of Societal Resilience: Framing the Issues," in Esther Brimmer, *Five Dimensions of Homeland and International Security* (Washington, DC: Center for Transatlantic Relations, 2008), pp. 15-28.

[8]Mark Rhinard and Bengt Sundelius, "The Limits of Self-Reliance: International Cooperation as a Source of Resilience," in *Designing Resilience: Preparing for Extreme Events*, edited by Louise Comfort, Arjen Boin and Chris Demchak (Pittsburgh: Pittsburgh University Press, 2010); Arjen Boin, "Enhancing Societal Security in the Face of Transboundary Crises: Pointers for Transatlantic Cooperation," unpublished paper prepared for Center for Transatlantic Relations/PACER, January 2009.

threats through their transatlantic military alliance, NATO, with an additional focus on the security of critical societal functions. NATO's Article 5 may be relevant for non-traditional security threats—after the September 11, 2001 attacks, Article 5 was indeed invoked for the first time in the alliance's history. But when it comes to many other non-military threats (both man-made and accidental), it is the EU and not NATO that has both the competences and capacities to respond. Consequently, the United States and the EU should adopt a joint political declaration to assist each other in a spirit of solidarity in the event of a major crisis such as a terrorist attack or man-made or natural disaster. The pledge should also include a declaration to work in common to prevent attacks from occurring the first place as well as to protect democratic institutions and civilian populations in the event of an attack. A similar pledge already exists as a part of the EU's Lisbon Treaty,[9] but it is now time to widen the scope to include both sides of the Atlantic. If the EU and the United States can agree on such a solidarity pledge, it could help pave the way for similar commitments with other parts of the world as well.

A Transatlantic Solidarity Pledge would fill an important gap in the transatlantic community's deep and integrated relationship. At the moment, the only commitment Americans and Europeans have to each other is through NATO, and that commitment is defined in the North Atlantic Treaty as response to "armed attack." Yet the types of disruptive challenges we face today do not fall easily under traditional definitions of "armed attack." In addition, most of these challenges are more civilian than military. Moreover, the United States and the EU have no equivalent commitment to each other. If the relationship is truly to be strategic and effective, the partners would also underpin their activities with a binding sense of common purpose. European Commissioner Cecilia Malmström has made the case clearly and directly: "an attack on Baltimore is as much an attack on Berlin or

---

[9]The treaty's Solidarity Clause (Art. 222) obliges EU member states to mutual support in the face of a range of new threats; to jointly assess new threats; to coordinate closely in the event of an attack or disaster; and to provide mutual assistance to a stricken state. See Sara Myrdal and Mark Rhinard, "Empty Letter or Effective Tool? Implementing the EU's Solidarity Clause," *UI Occasional Paper*, No. 2 (Stockholm: Swedish Institute of International Affairs, 2010).

Brussels. Our societies are so open and interlinked that no matter if an attack occurs in Europe or the US we will both pay the price."[10]

If political leaders on both sides of the Atlantic adopted such a pledge, they would signal an appreciation of the complexity of modern threats, the interconnectedness of European and American societies, and the determination of the EU and United States to stand together in a shifting world. They would signal mutual recognition of the need for democratic societies to complement traditional approaches geared to protecting territory with high-priority efforts to protect critical functions of society. More specifically, a Transatlantic Solidarity Pledge would create key preconditions for advancing overall resilience: political impetus, bureaucratic guidance and operational mechanisms towards that goal.

Implementation of a Transatlantic Solidarity Pledge would require U.S. and European actors to work together on a common threat assessment (such as the one required by the EU's Solidarity Clause) and would require EU and U.S. officials to acknowledge, evaluate and prioritize threats to the shared arteries spanning the Atlantic. Threat assessment could be used as a guide for on-going capacity building in the form of advanced planning and prevention in line with a resilience approach. Yet the Pledge would also require both partners to work through operational response requirements in the event of a major transatlantic breakdown. Issues around Host Nation Support capacities would need to be addressed promptly to transform such a political pledge into an operational reality when it is needed.

Agreement on a Transatlantic Security Pledge would boost political impetus across the spectrum and recalibrate security cooperation towards a clear purpose: building resilience into transatlantic infrastructures. A high-profile pledge of this nature would help rebuild a sense of common cause across the Atlantic and set priorities to prevent or prepare for any future crisis. This impetus could carry over into diplomatic initiatives in the alphabet soup of transatlantic cooperation frameworks directed at improving coherence through strategic direction.

---

[10]Cecilia Malmström, "The EU Internal Security Strategy—What Does It Mean for the United States?" Speech to the Center for Transatlantic Relations, Johns Hopkins University SAIS, December 8, 2010.

At the bureaucratic level, a Transatlantic Solidarity Pledge could set the framework for improved technical cooperation among European and U.S. agencies and departments. This level of cooperation, which currently takes place but needs new bearings, should focus on the key transatlantic infrastructures most susceptible to attack and/or disruption.[11] Focus must be placed on the ways these arteries can be made not just more robust—but also more resilient—in the face of disruptions. A focus on these arteries—including how to enhance resilience and manage complicated cross-over disruptions—could guide work related to implementing a Transatlantic Solidarity Pledge.

Toward that end, a renewed focus on coordination could be placed on relations between EU and U.S. operation centers—with the task of providing early warning, situational awareness and crisis coordination support. Such centres could include the DHS National Operations Center (NOC), FEMA's National Response Coordination Center (NRCC), the EU's European Response Coordination Centre (ERCC), and the EU Situation Room in Brussels. These objectives would require regular exercises between EU and U.S. officials to familiarize themselves with procedures and protocols in working together. Other needs include joint investigation teams, including Europol and Eurojust, to cooperate on cases that cross international borders; enhanced cooperation between the U.S. Coast Guard and related agencies with Frontex, the EU border protection agency; collaboration on resilience-related research for instance between the program of Horizon 2020 for European Security Research and similar U.S. efforts; and development of a EU-U.S. Critical Vulnerabilities Security Action Plan to generate mutually supporting strategies to address their own critical foreign vulnerabilities.

A Transatlantic Solidarity Pledge would generate new impetus for the public and private sectors to work together to advance overall

---

[11]See, for instance, Dalgaard-Nielsen and Hamilton, op. cit.; Brimmer, op.cit; Antonio Missiroli, ed., "Disasters, Diseases, Disruptions: A New D-Drive for the EU," *Chaillot Paper* No. 83 (Paris: EU Institute for Security Studies, 2005); Robert Whalley, "Improving International Co-ordination and Co-Operation on Homeland Security/Societal Security and Resilience Issues," unpublished paper prepared for Center for Transatlantic Relations/PACER, January 2009; Jonathan M. Winer, "An Initial International Cooperation Agenda on High Consequence Events for the Obama Administration," unpublished paper prepared for Center for Transatlantic Relations/PACER, January 2009.

resilience. The private sector owns most of critical infrastructures binding the two sides of the Atlantic—both actual facilities and networks—yet has its own views of protection that can differ from those of governments. As these connections deepen, it is critical that the private sector be engaged as an active partner.

For example, various chapters in this volume underscore that global movement systems are integrally linked in today's highly networked and interconnected global economy. The drive to improve efficiency has made these global movement systems more vulnerable not only to attack by terrorists, but to cybercrime and even natural disasters and extreme weather. A EU-U.S. public-private Global Movement Management Initiative (GMMI) could offer an innovative governance framework to align security and resilience with commercial imperatives in global movement systems, including shipping, air transport, and even the internet.[12] And if the EU and the United States could achieve agreement, the norms and standards that would emerge could provide a framework for global arrangements.

Energy is another topic that should be covered by a Transatlantic Solidarity Pledge. In the case of a serious disruption on either side of the Atlantic, Europe and America should be committed to assisting one another to help offset potential shortages. In Europe, the issue of energy security has become a top political priority after the 2014 crisis in Ukraine, which has highlighted the continent's heavy dependence on Russian gas. A Transatlantic Solidarity Pledge could push each side to work through ways to tackle legal and technical barriers (e.g. bans on gas exports and rudimentary energy infrastructure) and develop concrete policies to implement such a pledge in practice.

A EU-U.S. Transatlantic Resilience Council—operating at a similar level as the Transatlantic Energy Council—could be formed to operationalize this initiative, integrating the discussion on societal security, justice and freedom across all sectors and serving as a cross-sector

---

[12]This idea is drawn from a report by IBM Global Business Services, "Global Movement Management: Commerce, Security, and Resilience in Today's Networked World," and a 2005 paper entitled "Global Movement Management: Security the Global Economy," available through www.ibm.com/gbs/government. See also Stephen E. Flynn and Daniel B. Prieto, *Neglected Defense: Mobilizing the Private Sector to Support Homeland Security* (New York: Council on Foreign Relations, 2006).

forum for strategic deliberations about threats, vulnerabilities, and response and recovery capacities that cut across sectors and borders. This group would complement existing professional work within established but stove-piped fora, such as the Policy Dialogue on Borders and Transportation Security. Although we recognize that new institutions are not the first imperative for building resilience, we are convinced that some degree of structured oversight between both blocs is needed to provide strategic perspective on where EU-U.S. cooperation is working and where more attention is needed.

In sum, a Transatlantic Solidarity Pledge, coupled to a concerted package of focused initiatives, would generate the necessary political attention, administrative direction, and operational mechanisms to bind the transatlantic relationship tighter in a time of increasing threat complexity and global flux. It would reaffirm the continued vibrancy of the transatlantic partnership, yet tune it to new times and new challenges. It would guide bureaucracies and balance the traditional focus on "pursue and protect" strategies with a greater focus on prevention and response. The need to prepare for resilience in advance while being ready for effective, joint crisis response is the essence of the initiative and is unlikely to generate significant political opposition on either side of the Atlantic. It signals the need—and the pathway—for two historical partners to renew and reenergize their relationship for a new global context. Our ultimate goal should be a resilient Euro-Atlantic area of justice, freedom, and security that balances mobility and civil liberties with societal resilience.

Develop Joint EU-U.S. Strategic Planning

Crafting a White Paper on Societal Security could be a useful internal exercise to address U.S.-EU differences and commonalities with regard to ways to address societal security threats. In addition to developing the common intellectual ground for joint and complementary strategies, the EU and the United States should also make sure that their long-term strategic assessments are in sync—as this will help determine their ability to cooperate on security threats in the future. Fortunately, on both sides of the Atlantic initiatives to enhance our understanding of and strategic planning for key future trends have been undertaken in recent years. In the United States, the National

Intelligence Council (NIC) has regularly provided a *Global Trends* report for the incoming U.S. President. This report assesses critical drivers and scenarios for global trends, looking approximately fifteen years ahead. In Europe, since 2010 the inter-institutional initiative European Strategy and Policy Analysis System (ESPAS) has provided EU institutions with assessments of the long-term political and eco-nomic environment shaping the EU over the next twenty years. While these kind of separate assessments are useful, there is also a growing need to think "transatlantically" about global trends and what these may mean for EU and U.S. security. Better connecting government strategic foresight initiatives such as NIC and ESPAS and involving the think-tank communities on both sides of the Atlantic would be a good place to start in this regard. In order for the EU and the United States to develop their security cooperation, it is not sufficient to agree on threats and risks today—fostering common understanding of the likely future security environment is equally important.

Develop Compatible Societal Security Capabilities

Invest in Civilian Security Capabilities and "Whole Of Society" Approaches

Many of the emerging societal security challenges identified in this volume require closer cooperation between a variety of societal actors to work towards similar if not identical objectives when it comes to crisis management and disaster response. This includes both civilian (e.g. law enforcement, emergency response, border management, urban planners) and military. Too often, however, different actors' working methods and time frames are different. Increasingly, civilian actors will be required to perform tasks that were previously reserved for military or law enforcement agencies overseas. For instance, in case of an outbreak of epidemics, health care experts may be posted in other parts of the world in order to contain the spread of epidemics and perform a *de facto* homeland defense function. Another example is the quasi-military tasks performed by humanitarian aid and crisis response agencies, as in case of the tsunami off the eastern coast of Japan in 2011, which included experts in logistics, radiology and nuclear technology who, in close cooperation with Japanese authori-ties, coordinated the storage, transport and distribution of assistance

2020 program and in future multiannual framework programs. EU-U.S. cooperation in the field of security research have made progress, but could be expanded further. In particular, the EU-U.S. agreement on security research cooperation should be supplemented with more concrete substance about the type of collaboration between the Commission and DHS in the field of homeland security. The EU and the United States should also, to the extent possible, coordinate their approaches to third countries when it comes to security research cooperation so as to avoid duplication and unnecessary redundancies.

Finally, the EU and the United States should consider initiatives to further bind their respective "homeland security industries" closer together. First, European stakeholders should engage their American counterparts in seeking to produce commonly accepted standards without prejudice to anyone's industrial base. The current negotiations over the Transatlantic Trade and Investment Partnership (TTIP) are an excellent opportunity to address these issues. It is crucial that security industry associations in the EU and United States also engage with each other directly as a part of these negotiations. In particular, EU and U.S. authorities should undertake efforts to foster general interoperability of solutions and common standards for next-generation security solutions. This includes promoting interoperability at the European level among the 28 member states and interoperability of systems used by federal, state and local end-users in the United States. Finally, the EU and the United States should consider co-organizing an annual forum, bringing together key institutions, stakeholders and end-users (at technical and operational level, rather than high political level) to discuss opportunities for partnership, information sharing, market trends analysis, better understanding of key requirements, customer preferences, as well as the operating constraints and regulatory environments.

Strengthen Joint Transatlantic Disaster Response

Given the possibility for increased disruptions due to state and non-state actors and mother nature, EU-U.S. cooperation on disaster response should be given more attention. U.S. bilateral arrangements between individual EU member states remain important, but they should be supplemented by multilateral EU-U.S. agreements to reduce policy divergences, both within Europe itself but also between the EU and the United States. Transatlantic cooperation on disaster response is relevant both in the Euro-Atlantic region but also when jointly responding to disasters overseas. EU-U.S. cooperation on disaster response has grown in scope in recent years. The Federal Emergency Management Agency (FEMA) and the EU Commission already have signed an agreement on mutual disaster management cooperation. This agreement encompasses cooperation on disaster risk reduction, resilience and response to disasters. Further strengthening transatlantic disaster response cooperation should be a top priority as we look towards 2030.[14]

Going forward, the EU and the United States should seek to strengthen their operational readiness to respond jointly to disasters. This would include testing systems on a regular basis, including carrying out joint training and exercises. When holding joint training, full participation from all relevant actors in the Euro-Atlantic space is essential. Moreover, both sides should each second at least one staff member to each other on a permanently rotating basis. The EU Commission and FEMA should also undertake efforts to enhance interoperability between European and American disaster response capabilities and capacities. Interoperability and standardization of technology are key in this regard.

Additionally, the EU and the United States should seek to strengthen operational exchange of information. Although such cooperation is already quite extensive, it could be made even stronger. As the EU has developed its own Emergency Response Coordination Centre (ERCC) within the EU Commission's Humanitarian Aid and Civil Protection directorate (DG ECHO) as well as a Situation Room within the European External Action Service (EEAS), there is a need to connect these to relevant U.S. operations centers—especially the DHS National Operations Center (NOC), FEMA's National

---

[14]Transatlantic disaster response assistance is not unprecedented. Following both Hurricane Katrina and the 2010 Deepwater Horizon accident, several EU member states contributed actively. See Anne C. Richard, *Role Reversal: Offers of Help from Other Countries in Response to Hurricane Katrina* (Washington, DC: Center for Transatlantic Relations, 2006); Mark Rhinard and Bengt Sundelius, "The Limits of Self-Reliance: International Cooperation as a Source of Resilience," Louise Comfort, Arjen Boin and Chris Demchak, eds., *Designing Resilience for Extreme Events* (Pittsburgh: Pittsburgh University Press, 2010); U.S. Department of State website: http://www.state.gov/r/pa/prs/ps/2010/06/143127.htm

Response Coordination Center (NRCC). Better linking these centers together would assist EU and U.S. officials to detect and identify risks and threats. It is equally important that these information-sharing activities are supplemented with regular exchanges of situation awareness reports and through interactive regular training activities workshops and joint exercises to enhance prospects for situational awareness and effective coordination in real events in the transatlantic area. Additionally, efforts aimed at exchanging experiences and lessons learned should be put in place.

In addition to transatlantic disaster response in the Euro-Atlantic region, the EU and the United States should also step up cooperation on responding to disaster occurring elsewhere in the world. This includes both sharing of information and best practices as well as coordination in the events of large-scale international disaster requiring extensive EU and U.S. assistance. Better strategic dialogue between USAID and the EU Commission's DG ECHO as well as other relevant institutions for emergency relief and preparedness, including the U.S. State Department and the EU's External Action Service, should also be a priority. Ways of strengthening NATO's role in disaster response and its cooperation with the EU should also be explored in this regard. Additionally, Europe and the United States should consider developing more pre-established agreements built around "lead partner" criteria for different parts of the world.

Invest in Global Supply Chain Security

Address Shortcomings in the Global Industrial System

The United States and the European Union will not be able to completely shield themselves off from global supply chains. But they should both be very concerned about the prospects for industrial crashes. The structural flaws in the industrial system will likely continue to get worse. In order to avoid a truly catastrophic scenario, the EU and the United States should take the lead on addressing the inherent shortcomings in the current system by investing in building more resilient structures. One notable way of accomplishing this is by taking coordinated steps to limit extreme concentrations of risk by redistributing capacity and risk in order to ensure resilience.

Develop Coordinated EU-U.S. Management of Material Flows

When it comes to natural resources, reliance on domestic extraction or partially withdrawing from global material flows is not an option in either Europe or America. At the same time, investing in resource efficiency strategy may look smart, but faces an uphill battle as long as international market distortions prevail. Consequently, both regions are likely to be affected if other major world regions face stress resulting from food, water and material flow security. Thus the direct implications are risks and threats for supply chain security for manufacturing companies and economies in the transatlantic space and elsewhere. To address these challenges, the EU and the United States should strive to integrate supply and demand strategies. Good governance of commodity markets will comprise more transparency with better information in the extractive industries and downstream, stringent resource efficiency efforts, and empowerment and measures to turn natural endowments into opportunities for the world's poor. The EU and the United States should also seek to improve knowledge for managing global material flows and the resource nexus—for instance by establishing an international data hub along with expert groups on foresight and disseminating best practices for principles of stewardship and metals recycling. Finally, despite current tensions resulting from the energy price gap and competitiveness concerns as well as from a number of political difficulties, there is a rationale for a coordinated EU-U.S. management of material flows. Further steps could include the establishment of a transatlantic multi-stakeholder forum on material flows security that actively promotes the inclusion of G20 and other countries.

Foster Global Mutual Recognition of Supply Chain Security Standards

The EU and the United States have taken considerable steps toward mutual recognition of each other's diverse security standards. In June 2012, the U.S. Transportation Security Administration and the EU Commission reached an unprecedented agreement to recognize each other's air cargo security regimes. This agreement is intended to eliminate unnecessary duplication of security controls and the need to implement divergent regimes depending on the destination of the air cargo in question, which could lower cargo operators' costs and to air, land, and sea security with equipment, logistics, training, and technical support; joint trainings and exercises, and early warning systems. They should also promote international standardization and interoperability in doctrine, equipment, and procedures in a range of areas, such as maritime security assistance or cyber security. The OECD principles for risk management offer a solid template from which to work. Such principles offer the EU and the United States an opportunity to widen the body of good practice to a broader circle of OECD members and beyond.

Finally, the EU and the United States, as well as NATO allies, should work to enhance vulnerable countries' societal resilience to resist corruption, psychological warfare and disruptions in cyber, financial and energy networks and other critical infrastructure. The latter set of activities is especially pertinent in the post-Ukraine security environment and will be of growing relevance in the future as the risk of "hybrid warfare" grows.

Part I

Setting the Scene:
Global Flows and Global Trends

Chapter 1

Global Flow Security: A Conceptual Framework

Tomas Ries

Globalization And Flows

We are currently in the turbulent midst of what American futurist Alvin Toffler once referred to as the "Third Wave." This post-industrial revolution is generating a paradigm shift of the human condition, with two deep consequences as a result. First, technology is shrinking the world, both ecologically and socially. Ecologically the world has for the first time become palpably finite and severely damaged in a number of ways. Social communications technology has shrunk the world into a global village, but a village in which deep socioeconomic tensions also generate violent revolutionary pressures. Second, and closely linked to the above, technology is making the human condition more fluid in every respect. The critical economic, technological and human flows on which our societies depend on are diffusing and spreading from within the boundaries of the state to the transnational global sphere beyond individual state control. These transnational "mega-flows" are now the vital life systems on which the well-being and survival of globalizing societies depend.

Emerging Actors in the Global Arena

Transnational actors who direct or influence these flows are emerging as new power brokers alongside the traditional state. They do not have the broad range of power of leading states, but they are increasingly influential, and in some cases even dominant, in certain domains. These non-state actors can be grouped into three broad categories and six types:

- First, two "alpha" actors—transnational corporations and leading urban nodes. These actors need states and often share vital interests with them, but they operate beyond any single state's boundaries and increasingly function parallel to them. In addition, they are replacing the state as core economic, technological and scientific drivers. States can still dictate the rules of the road, but they are no longer in the economic and scientific driver's seat.

- **Second, civil society, morphing as two "rainbow" actors— either as political clouds (voters where that is possible, or rioters where not) or as economic clouds (consumers).** Both of these actors are empowered by the grass-roots mass communications that emerged for the first time with the dawn of the Internet.

- **Third, two "black" actors—global organized crime and transnational revolutionary networks—**with agendas actively threatening the interests of states and alpha actors. As a result, the center of political gravity is shifting from state structures to transnational flows.

Each of these three types of actors has a distinct impact on global flows. Together with nation-states they generate, shape and/or damage global flows in a variety of ways.

Methodological implications: When considering global flow security it is essential to keep these six non-state actors in mind in addition to the state. It is important to identify the particular role and influence each exerts and how they impact on global flows. Alpha cities and global organized crime tend especially to be overlooked, despite the fact that both exert considerable influence in specific ways. The particular importance of cities as leading emerging actors is crucial.

The Place of Flows

The importance of economic, technological and human flows is not a recent phenomenon, yet two aspects are new. First, these human flows for the first time now transcend the state on a significant scale, both in terms of volume and power. Second, global ecological flows are now for the first time critically affected by human activity.

Our dependence upon human-created flows is not new, but in the past their scale was far less significant. Local flows of people, goods and services were important for agricultural society, but critical flows were generally limited geographically. During the industrial age, the range of critical economic flows expanded, but the economic core activities on which industrial societies depended remained essentially national and confined within individual state boundaries. The name of the Westphalian game was to protect that what was inside the borders of the state, or to expand those borders, but transactions taking place beyond the borders were only of importance to the extent that they affected the interests of the state. They did not yet have an intrinsic value and power per se, and with few historical exceptions—such as the Hanseatic League—they were run by states and did not create a power base for independent non-state actors.

Similarly, the global ecosystem—which is a massively complex "flow of flows"—has always been essential for our survival, but until about one hundred years ago it was largely unaffected by human activity. It was both self-sustaining and offered unlimited natural resources. Moreover, it was an infinite public good that humans could take for granted and exploit seemingly limitlessly.

From Borders to Flows

Both of the flow conditions described above changed in the late industrial age, causing both new opportunities and challenges. On the one hand, the surge of post-industrial communications technology boosted flows exponentially:

- First, the **scale** of "critical flows" on which advanced societies depend has increased massively, both in terms of geographic range, volume of transaction and multitude of flows.

- Second, the **complexity** of critical flows—and especially the complex synergies between different flows—is multiplying.

- Third, the **dependency** of the world's societies—especially of the richest societies—on transnational global flows has increased massively.

The world's leading actors—including all the major state powers—now depend critically on these functional flows that transcend the borders and control of individual states. This gives those leaders who are aware of this dependence and who prioritize it a powerful incentive to collaborate to promote these flows.

On the other hand, the global ecosystem came under increasing strain in the late industrial age. By the middle of the 20th century, technological power had multiplied the number of people inhabiting the planet, and multiplying their power to consume, pollute and manipulate their natural environment. As a result, today we find ourselves in a world with a finite global ecosystem characterized by severely damaged flows and whose condition is likely to continue to deteriorate markedly for the foreseeable future. Although it is highly uncertain how steep or fast the descent may be, even the most positive forecasts indicate that things will get very bad. Here it is important to emphasize, however, that this negative technological impact was largely the product of crude industrial-age technology. Today's post-industrial revolution is providing technology that offers vital solutions to the global ecological crisis. Our growing ecological crisis is thus largely a residual effect of the industrial era, whereas post-industrial technology represents one important part of the solution to the eco-crisis.

Methodological implications: How does the rise of flows impact on the way in which we traditionally have understood "international" relations? Will transnational actors and flows supersede state and inter-state relations?

Two Fundamental Megaflow Systems

When speaking of flow security we thus speak of two interacting but distinct types of global megaflows:

Global Functional Flows

The economic, social and technological flows created by humans and on which the most advanced, prosperous and powerful societies of the world depend. If these functional flows crash they will bring down with them both the political world order that has emerged since the end of the Cold War, and almost all human societies in the world, from the richest to the poorest. These functional flows can be divided into three interactive subcategories:

- **Global economic flows** are now the lifeblood of all globalizing societies. Our dependence upon them is immediate, constant and considerable, and their importance is constantly increasing.

- Global economic flows in turn rest on vast networks of **global technological flows** without which they would crash instantly. A mere slowdown of either of these two flows will have immediate and massive consequences for our societies, with potentially severe political consequences. The implications of a sudden breakdown of these would be immensely severe, with potentially existential consequences within days.

- **Global social flows** of humans are both an essential part of our economic flows and a critical element in our political security. The challenge here is on the one hand to optimize the human flows needed for our functional requirements (e.g. human migration, information, etc.) while on the other hand controlling and filtering these same flows against various threats. Managing these human flows is our third major security priority.

Global Ecological Flows

The global ecosystem and the massive eco-services on which the functional flows depend. As these ecological flows deteriorate—which they certainly will do—they place the functional flows under increasing strain, which in turn will lead to increasingly violent stresses within societies and between leading global political actors. And if we reach a drastic ecological tipping point the entire human edifice of the anthropogenic age could crumble.

From a human functional perspective the global ecosystem can in turn be perceived in terms of providing two interacting basic functions:

- **Habitat.** First, an ecosystem that is compatible with human biological needs (i.e. providing a favorable biotope for humans) is essential for the survival and comfort of humans. "Climate Change" is the catchword for the challenge we face in this respect. And the increasing turbulence facing us—of which we have so far only seen the beginning—will severely strain our social, economic and technological flows.

- **Resources.** Secondly, the ecosystem has historically provided us with a self-sustaining platform on which we have built our functional activities—from agriculture to mining to settlements to transport. These foundations remain unchanged. What has changed, however, is that the global ecosystem is now for the first time in planetary history becoming critically depleted and disrupted by human activity. Under current trends this will have catastrophic consequences for both humans and the planet alike. It is therefore critical that humans now—as James Lovelock noted four decades ago—for the first time in history take active responsibility for sustaining global ecosystem flows on a large scale. This means that not only protecting, but also actually servicing, the global ecosystem is now becoming an increasingly urgent task for humanity.

The net result is that the significance of these transnational flows for human survival has grown to the point where **securing these global flows is emerging as the primary existential interest of all major globalizing actors, be they state or non-state**. This gives all major globalizing actors a powerful and concrete shared interest in non-zero sum cooperation to ensure these functional flows flourish.

Methodological implications: When analyzing flow security it is essential to keep this big picture in mind. First, to include all the critical dots (holistic perspective). Second, to place them correctly in terms of their relations with each other (structured perspective). Third, to keep in mind the ways in which they do or can interact (synergistic perspective). Fourth, to understand their order of priority (hierarchic perspective).

But Yesterday's Ghosts Still Haunt Us

The nascent joint interest in collaborating to protect vital global commons, however, shares the stage with a competing and more divisive agenda. It is now clear that the visions of a liberal international world order envisioned two decades ago[1] were premature. Yesterday's Westphalian agenda of inter-state competitive power politics is not over. The world's major states remain the principal global actors, authoritarian regimes of varying degrees of ruthless brutality remain in power (including in states of global significance) and the potential for major violent conflicts among great power states is becoming more apparent.

At the same time, these same great powers all depend, to varying degrees, on their shared transnational functional and ecological flows for their survival. On the fringes of globalization, some of the more primitive major state regimes—such the Putin "conglomerate" running Russia—do not realize it entirely, while others, more deeply embedded in globalization—such as the Communist Party leadership of the People's Republic of China—are acutely aware of it. We thus currently have a tense overlap between yesterday's residual Westphalian zero-sum competition between state "islands" and the nascent globalizing imperatives for non-zero sum cooperation to promote shared transnational flows.

As long as global flows function and major state actors not only benefit but also depend on them (and realize this dependence), there is a good chance that the trend towards increasing non-zero sum cooperation will continue. In this case the focus of security policy could shift from protecting and promoting state sovereignty to protecting and promoting shared critical transnational flows transcending the boundaries of any single state or group of states. This would in turn entail a shift over time of the center of gravity from borders to cross-border flows. Under such conditions, power would gradually drain from the "Lords of Territory" to the "Lords of Flows," in much the same way as the industrial revolution shifted power from the rural lords of arable land to the urban lords of industry.

We are not yet there, however. The relationship between yesterday's and tomorrow's security agendas is balanced on a very unstable tightrope. It can be toppled by a host of factors. Political instability within leading global states can shift policies, and functional flows can break down either from deliberate attack from revolutionary networks or hostile states, corrode from the ravages of organized crime, or col-

---

[1]See, for example, Francis Fukuyama, *The End of History and the Last Man* (New York Avon Books, 1992).

lapse from simple mismanagement of flawed design. In fact, the only two genuinely existential threats that the world has faced since the end of the Cold War have been due to the last factor: the Y2K "Millennium bug" (e.g. flawed design) and the near financial meltdown of 2008-2009. Finally, ecological shocks (e.g. pandemic) or environmental stresses (e.g. scarcity and turbulence) will strain and could knock out our functional flows.

As we see from both of the two major global multilateral agendas—the Doha Round and the succession of global ecological summits—efforts to address the two main transnational challenges posed by the global economy and the global ecosystem face huge difficulties. This is compounded by growing multipolarity in the global system—as seen, for instance, in the recent diversification of the leading global state actors from the G7 to the G20. The agenda to protect and promote our global functional and ecological flows thus faces daunting challenges. Yet, it is crucial that we face up to the challenge.

Methodological implications: The tensions between the Westphalian "island" agenda and the globalizing flow agenda are becoming crucial. What interests drive them, how do they interact, what sort of syntheses can emerge that affect global flows and what are their respective future prospects. Normatively, how can we promote a non-zero flow cooperation agenda over zero-sum power politics?

Flow Security

What Is A Flow?

Before we can assess global flows, we must first consider that all flows share three essential characteristics:

- First, **all flows are circuits**. A flow is never linear, always cyclical. From a limited perspective it may appear linear as if one watches one single stretch of a river. However, the more one broadens and deepens the perspective the more the whole circuit becomes apparent. For instance, a river is merely part of a complex hydrological cycle involving condensation, rain, rivers, evaporation, clouds, rain again and so forth. A flow that is not circular dies.

- Second, **all flows involve transformation**. That which flows, and the means of flow themselves, both evolve dynamically during the flow process. If the transformation is restricted, the flow suffers.

- Third, **all flows are integral parts of other flows**, with complex synergies and multiple spinoffs interacting with other flows. Flows are always part of complex systems of complex systems. The more harmoniously a flow is integrated with its surrounding flows the more efficient, secure and cost-effective it is.

Understanding complex multidimensional synergies and managing these will be a second major security challenge in the 21st century.

Methodological implications: The above two factors mean that in coming decades we will increasingly have to take into account the full cyclical and multi-systems context of our critical flows. While specialized microscopic analysis remains important, it will mean very little unless it can be placed into context in the Big Picture. However, Big Picture analysis (or consilient analysis, to use Edward O. Wilson's term) with its unavoidable "fuzziness" calls for a very different mind-set from that of traditional political science methodology. Moreover, specialized analysis of selected flows will have to be integrated with broader consilient analysis of the broader systems context.

Components of the Flow Circuit

A flow circuit consists of five distinct parts, all of which are essential:

- First, "**the flower**," or the object which is flowed. Examples of flowers are water or iron ore or a given manufactured product, humans, etc.

- Second, **the streams**, or the medium or the context in which the flow takes place. These do not need to be physical channels—i.e. narrow and solid. For instance, the atmosphere in which evaporated water rises, or currents in a river are also media in which flows take place.

- Third, **the nodes**, or, to be more precise, the transformation conditions under which the flower is transformed and shifts to a new stream, and in the case of human-created flows is directed and perhaps propelled onwards. Examples are factories, harbors, cities, etc.

- Fourth, **propulsion**, moving the flower and the dynamics of the stream in which it moves—for instance gravity in the case of rain or liquid water, or an engine in the case of a boat.

- Fifthly **a directing factor**, which keeps the flow coherent. In the case of natural or ecological flows this directing factor is multi-systemic, i.e. a decentralized and dispersed interaction of the entire system or systems. In the case of human-created flows the directing factor is far more limited, and generally centralized at some point, even if post-industrial technology allows for increasingly automated decentralized systemic flows at the lower levels of the flow chain. Nevertheless the human directing factor is ultimately also influenced by several tangential systems outside its immediate parameters.

Methodological implications: Understanding these five components of the flow cycles individually and as they interact will become an increasingly vital requirement in coming years, creating a new high-technology market revolving around the integrated management of multiple systems. Of particular importance is the hitherto largely overlooked role of the nodes—especially the urban nodes.

What Do Flows Need?

For flows to flow optimally, each of the above five component parts must interact harmoniously, creating a self-sustaining cycle of transformation of "the flower" with unending momentum. In addition the flow must be considered in its systemic context. Thus a flow that is inherently vigorous may have damaging spinoff effects that need to be taken into account. An example would be a river that floods its surroundings.

For human-created flows this requires four support functions:

- First, **maintenance**. The flow must be kept running. This is essentially a logistical task involving servicing and repairs.

- Second, **direction**. The flow must be directed to go where one wants it to go, and its volume and speed must be tuned so it neither overwhelms the system nor starves it. This is essentially a control function, involving all aspects of Command, Control, Communications and Intelligence (C3I). As post-industrial technology, especially nanotechnology, becomes more refined, the demand for products in this sector will increase enormously.

- Third, **development**. The flow system may be improved for more optimal inherent performance with reduced spinoff effects. This is essentially a design task, involving science and holistic systems analysis.

- Finally, **protection** against inherent breakdowns or damage from external factors. This involves both shielding against external threats and filtering against internal threats. This security requirement is increasing massively as the vulnerability of our societies to breakdowns in critical flows increases.

Additionally, one might add a fifth factor, which is likely to become increasingly important in future, namely integrating the flow with the surrounding environment so that it can operate as smoothly as possible and benefit as much as possible from its surroundings while damaging the surrounding flows as little as possible.

Generic Threats to Flows

From the above, it follows that there are three generic types of threats to flows:

- First, "**rusting**," when lack of maintenance leads to failing channels and nodes with effects such as blockages, leaking, loss, degradation, contamination, etc. The source here can be either human insufficiency (e.g. incompetence, indifference, incapacity) or functional weaknesses (e.g. faulty engineering, weak components).

- Second, **inherent systems failure**, when the flow system as a whole overheats or starves as a result of too much or too little flow. In human-created flows this is essentially a problem of basic design or C3I once in operation.

- Third, **damage from an external factor** not part of the inherent flow cycle, such as a grain of sand in a clock, or a missile against an aircraft. Here the source can be either a deliberate hostile human intent or else a significant external event—ecological or social—tangentially disrupting the flow system.

In all cases, the absolutely most severe threats are those where one or more of the three security dimensions (social, functional and ecological) overlap. This increases both the intensity but also the complexity of the crisis, which makes it more difficult to deal with than when taking place in a single dimension. Crises in multiple overlapping security dimensions increase the danger exponentially.

Types of "Flowers"

The globalizing world involves three basic human generated flow security categories ('flow security concerns'):

- Light—desirable flows (e.g. trade, investments, tourism, information)

- Gray—swing flows. With potential for both good and bad impacts (e.g. migration, attitudes of civil society)

- Dark—undesirable flows, directly damaging in various ways (e.g. crime, terrorism, anarchy).

Methodological implications: How to map these flows per se? How to map their interactions? Can we map the overlap between functional types of flows and flow security concerns? A critical security task will be to maintain and protect desirable flows at an optimal rate while filtering out undesirable flows. This is already done, for instance, in airports, harbors, etc., but now on a global and far more pervasive scale. What are the implications for freedom and integrity?

Threats To Flows Under Globalization

The Three Vital Interests of Globalizers in the Post-Westphalian World

Physical threat is a function of the interaction of two factors: first, the essential subjective operational objectives of a given entity, generally termed vital interests; and second, the objective obstacles in the world around us that lie in the way of achieving those objectives.

When these present an active danger to vital interests, they are generally termed a threat. In today's globalized world, the three generic threat dimensions outlined above translate into three primary vital interests and three distinct sources of threat.

Our most immediate and constant vital interest is our functional security—i.e. the critical life systems upon which globalized society depend. These are the transnational economic, technological and social flows on which we depend for our daily existence. These critical "transboundary arteries" are the center of gravity of the globalizing world. If they were to collapse, human civilization would collapse almost instantly. Maintaining functional security is the core vital interest of "the globalizers."

Our second vital interest is the political order on which the functional life systems of the globalizing world depend. These threats tend to grab news media headlines but are essentially a secondary danger, because, first, the political system is no longer the center of gravity, but rather serves as a buffer for the new functional center; and second, because the globalizers" political order has more resilience and capacity to manage challenges than functional life systems. The political order can be stretched and battered far more than our functional base and we can still survive and work towards solutions. This is the second layer vital interest of the globalizers in terms of immediacy.

Our third vital interest is the harmonious functioning of the ecological system upon which we as humans depend and upon which our functional and political foundations depend. This is placed third because dangers to this dimension are emerging the most slowly, but they are also the most profound and basic. If this fails, then everything else fails. Safeguarding the global ecosystem is in humanity's deepest vital interest. This is a third layer of vital interests in terms of immediacy, but at the same time also the most fundamental vital interest we have in the long term. The paradox is that while it does not yet manifest itself as overwhelmingly immediate existential threats today, it will do so in the long term. Yet unless we address it today, its long term momentum will become so great that we cannot redress it later.

Three Essential Sources of Threat to "The Globalizers"

As a corollary, sources of threat arise in three dimensions.

- **Political threats** arise from conflicts between human beings, the "dialectic of opposing wills using violent force to resolve their difference," as André Beaufre expressed it.[2] The key lever here is the will of the opposing party or parties. This threat dimension remains very much subject to the principles explored by Machiavelli and Clausewitz—i.e. the way humans react to the use of violence—even if the actors and tools have changed radically.

- **Functional threats** arise from the malfunctioning of the critical life systems upon which a society depends. These problems are essentially internal—malfunctions due to the breakdown of the system itself. In this case the lever is primarily technical and the solutions are essentially engineering ones.

- **Ecological threats** result from our ecosystem. They can be either first-order threats, such as a Hurricane Katrina, or else the source of second-order problems, such as political friction generated by competition for scarce resources, refugee flows, etc.

This has two major implications. First, in the globalizing world the threats come at us from more directions. While our attention during the Modern Age came to be focused primarily on the political dimension—and during much of the Cold War on the even narrower military-technological sphere—we now need to broaden our perspective. This is because now all three dimensions can generate catastrophic existential threats.

Cutting-edge security analysis—and the security industries—must now broaden the threat perspective to include all three dimensions mentioned above. This is what we may call an holistic security perspective. The need for an holistic perspective holds true even if one continues to focus on a given part of the security spectrum and produce specialized products for that sector, for these products will have to be baked into larger systems and broader holistic strategies. Those who understand the holistic security environment and are prepared to

---

[2]For details see André Beaufre as quoted by Julian Lider, in *Military Theory-Concept, Structure, Problems* (Gower Publishing Company Ltd., England, 1983), p. 6.

develop holistic response strategies will be better able to provide the sort of solutions that will be needed.

Second, the three threat dimensions interact intimately, creating new complex synergistic threats. In all cases the most complex and severe threats arise when the three threat dimensions overlap. For instance, if hostile intent (e.g. political threat) results in deliberate attack against the functional base of an opponent requiring a complex combination of political and technical responses, which our existing stovepiped state structures have difficulty coping with. In the future, security policy will increasingly be based on synergistic threat analysis and response. This calls for a new synergistic capability on the part of all involved actors.

The Flow Security Agenda

This means that the tomorrow's security agenda will increasingly focus on three major areas:

- **Ecological security.** Protecting our ecological foundation, maintaining and reviving the global ecological flows.

- **Functional security.** Protecting the functional foundations of the globalizers, ensuring that our technological and economic flows function and can evolve.

- **Political security.** Protecting our ecological and functional foundations from human threats, whether they are driven by political, criminal or other motives.

Each of these three dimensions presents a challenge in its own right. On the one hand, in terms of the distinct basic nature and characteristics of each dimension, which will require a strategic approach adapted to the conditions in that dimension. On the other hand, in terms of the sheer volume of specific challenges within that dimension. These three dimensions will be the new focus of evolving security policies.

In addition, however, the three dimensions overlap and thus create complex synergies among these essentially different environments. This in turn generates a second major challenge, which is to pull together the strings of these three very different yarns and to understand how they interact, and especially to discern which radically new security consequences this can generate. This calls for a very general and broad epistemological approach coupled to a increased emphasis on systems analysis. We largely lost this broad type of approach during the Modern Age, when the essential focus was on increasingly narrow specialization.

There will be an increasing need for a new holistic and synergistic approach, capable of dealing with the interaction of complex systems. This "consilient" approach, in the terms of Edward O. Wilson,[3] is beginning to emerge in the business and the intelligence communities, notably in the United States.

A Flow Security Perspective

The above three dimensions (i.e. political, functional, and ecological) and their interaction leads to eight major areas of potential threat requiring more concerted security analysis. These eight areas, in turn, each encompass several specific security agendas within their own area.

Political Dimension

The political dimension includes two main areas, of which the second—external security—currently includes six key agendas.

1. **Internal stability.** The new challenges that globalization present to the domestic stability of the world's leading societies. This includes both the established elite states and the rapidly emerging transitional societies.

2. **External security.** This includes one traditional agenda and five new ones.

   - First, to develop a synergistic relationship between the state, as yesterday's established power centers, and the emerging new power centers around the transnational corporations (TNCs).

   - Second, the need for the globalizing community—including the club of globalizing states, transnational corporations and other key non-state actors—to deepen their joint understanding of the new globalizing secu-

---

[3]Edmund O. Wilson, *Consilience* (London. Little, Brown and Co, 1998).

rity environment, and develop a joint strategy for dealing with it under a unified leadership.

- Third, to welcome the rapid transition economies (RTEs) into the world's elite state community, and integrate them among the stakeholders of globalization.

- Fourth, to support those states and societies that are attempting to join economic globalization but that have varying degrees of difficulty in doing so. This is perhaps the most critical and urgent political security challenge that we face under current conditions. This is essentially an economic development challenge, but intimately linked to political and social developments over which we have very little influence.

- Fifth, to manage those regimes that are alienated from or actively hostile to globalization. An extreme example is North Korea, but others include Iran, Venezuela and most significantly Russia. Where this challenge becomes acute it essentially calls for a traditional *Realpolitik* and power-political response, but now in increasingly asymmetric forms.

- Sixth, the need to alleviate the misery of the world's poorest societies. Here the main danger is not—yet—one of confrontation but rather of implosion. This is essentially a problem of socio-economic development. While not as time-urgent as the fourth item listed above, it still presents the same dangers in the long run.

Functional Dimension

Security in this dimension essentially involves two basic objectives.

3. **Protecting our global technological base.** Ensuring that the intricate global technological networks and flows on which the globalizing economy and its societies depend continue to function. This is the deepest functional foundation on which the entire globalizing era rests.

4. **Protecting our global economic base.** Ensuring that the globalized transnational economy continues to thrive and evolve. This is the second deepest functional foundation on which the globalizing era rests. If this were to crash, then all else, including our political order, would crash.

Protecting this functional base constitutes the single most important foundation of the globalizers. If this crashes then everything else in the globalizing world would crash. We may suffer severe political setbacks and defeats, but provided our technological and economic globalization continues to thrive we can recover. This imperative has not yet received the political recognition it requires, but it will do so with a vengeance after our first serious global functional crisis. At this point if not before, the political will to deal with this challenge will emerge. Those business sectors that have made preparations to enter this sector will then be in an extremely powerful position.

It is also important to note that the task of protecting our functional base will of necessity entail a very close cooperation between state and transnational corporate actors, since much of today's transnational functional activity on which the lead states depend is actually run—and owned—by such actors.

Ecological Dimension

The ecological dimension involves our basic natural environment on which we depend to survive and upon which our functional base rests. This applies both to our technological base (energy, communications, urbanization, etc.) and our economic base (raw materials, renewable resources) as well as our sheer ability to function biologically. Four major and closely interwoven threats have emerged in this domain.

5. **Depletion.** The depletion of vital non-renewable resources on which we depend. A possible example would be oil, though this is contested. More fundamental and severe is diminishing biodiversity, the consequences of which we are not even aware.

6. **Degradation.** The degradation of renewable resources, such as potable water, fish stocks (thirteen of the worlds fifteen major oceanic fish spawning areas are currently overfished), arable land, regional flora and fauna, etc.

7. **Disruption.** The disruption of the global ecosystem, with consequences such as climate change, leading to a chain reaction from global warming to rising sea levels to increasingly extreme climatic conditions (increasingly severe heat waves alternating with extreme rainfall and flooding, stronger storms and hurricanes, etc.) to the potential reversal of oceanic conveyor belt currents, etc.

8. **Unnatural Disaster.** The potential for more extreme, widespread and devastating man-made ecological catastrophes. Cher-

nobyl and other lesser industrial accidents (oil spills, poisonous spills, etc.) are examples. The most severe are probably to come in the form of potential biogenetic mistakes or the release (accidental or otherwise) of contagious diseases or other autonomously generating agents upsetting the eco-balance.

Conclusion

Protecting and supporting the three major flow dimensions and dealing with the eight key generic threats outlined above will be the core of our principal future security agenda. The future security nexus will have the following characteristics:

- First, the center of gravity of our security will be the Functional Flows. As the Ecological crisis deepens these flows will gradually assume a parallel importance.

- Second, our security response should ideally focus on managing the complex interaction between the three dimensions. This synergistic, consilient approach should ideally dominate our security thinking, strategies, operations and tools. All of these will increasingly be baked into a broad multidimensional security network.

This, however, is an ideal situation. In practice the short-term security challenges and political imperatives facing major states will dominate, as we see from the ongoing trade and climate negotiations. How we can manage these pressing concerns while at the same time focusing on the existential structural and long-term issues is one of the big practical challenges we face. Nothing new here, but in our present circumstances the long term trends are so devastating that the issue is of existential importance.

The focus of further research needs to be on the more specific interaction between the Functional Dimension and the Political and Ecological Dimensions and the concrete threats this new synergy can generate. This can provide the basis for more focused studies of the sorts of synergistic response strategies, organizations and instruments that will emerge.

Our secondary security concern will be to protect the multitude of functional and social globalization flows that we depend upon and that are buffeted by the above three dimensions. This will provide a niche for more specialized flow defense strategies and products. However these will also need to be conceived of within the context of the broad threat environment and synergistic integrated responses.

Chapter 2

Overview of Global Megatrends— Key Trends and Takeaways[1]

Erik Brattberg

In an increasingly complex and uncertain global environment, it is ever more critical to develop a good understanding of long-term strategic trends. It is not surprising, therefore, that various governments, international organizations and private actors today devote substantial resources to developing their foresight capacities. Despite their obvious limitations these studies generally offer a useful framework for discussing and planning for alternative futures. This chapter offers a brief cursory overview of global trends identified in various studies—including the *Global Trends 2030* report of the U.S. National Intelligence Council; its EU equivalent drafted in the framework of the ESPAS project (European Strategy and Policy Analysis System); and the World Economic Forum Global Risk report. Relevant scholarly works and notable non-governmental reports by private sector corporations and civil society groups are also taken into consideration. While by no means intended to be a comprehensive discussion of global trends, this chapter sets the scene for the following chapters on the impact of global trends on critical global flows in 2030. The six different megatrends in this section were selected by because of their relevance in the context of discussing the future of critical global flows in 2030:

- **Trend 1**: *G-Zero World*—Changing distribution of global power [Geopolitics]
- **Trend 2**: *Liquid World*—Diffusion of state power to transnational actors [Global power diffusion]
- **Trend 3**: *More Human Power*—Global technological diffusion: creating a level playfield? [Technology]

---

[1]This chapter draws on Patryk Pawlak and Erik Brattberg, "Equipping the EU for Future Security Challenges Through Strategic Planning', UI Occasional Paper No 20 (Swedish Institute of International Affairs, Stockholm, June 2013).

- **Trend 4:** *Shrinking World*—Growing population and resource scarcity [Demography, Sustainability]
- **Trend 5:** *Global Awakening*—Empowerment of individuals and social vulnerabilities [Demography]
- **Trend 6:** *Extreme World*—Climate Change and Environmental Degradation [Environment & Sustainability]

Trend 1: G-Zero World— The Changing Distribution of Global Power

The distribution of global power is undergoing a "megashift." Whether in terms of GDP, military spending, or R&D investments, by 2030 significant portions of global power will have shifted from the West to the "Rest," especially to countries like China, India or Brazil— but also "middle powers" such as Indonesia, Turkey, and South Africa.[2] Although power is a notoriously hard concept to measure, the U.S. National Intelligence Council's power index, which uses four traditional power variables (i.e. economic, demographic, military, and technology), unambiguously predicts that the global power shift is underway. The NIC's assessment is that China will be more powerful than Europe by 2015-2020 and the United States by 2030. Likewise, India will surpass both the EU (in the mid-2030s) and the United States (in the mid-2040s). Regardless of the accuracy of these specific projections, the big picture is crystal clear: global power is increasingly evaporating in the West and moving Eastward—and it is doing so rather quickly.

At the same time, the NIC Global Trends 2030 report also points out that the global power shift will not be as rapid if one also takes into account a broader set of factors such as health, education and governance indicators—areas where industrialized nations will remain superior. Furthermore, it should be noted that this global power shift does not denote an absolute shift but a relative one. For example, Western countries will remain far wealthier per capita than the rising powers in the East far beyond 2030. Finally, the impact of globalization, and the extremely high level of economic interdependence that

---

[2]According to Goldman Sachs, the "Next Eleven" consists of Bangladesh, Egypt, Indonesia, Iran, Mexico, Nigeria, Pakistan, The Philippines, South Korea, Turkey, and Vietnam. See "Beyond the BRICs: A Look at the Next 11" (Goldman Sachs, April 2007).

comes with it, suggests that the world is hardly a zero-sum game since rising powers in the East and South will also remain heavily dependent on the West for their own economic growth.

In Transition: Globalization's Center of Gravity

Economic power shifts are perhaps the easiest to spot. While the 2008 financial crisis exacerbated the ongoing shift from the West to the East and South, it is important to note that even prior to the crisis many emerging economies already had significantly higher growth rates than the West. Although growth rates in several emerging economies are currently showing signs of slowing down somewhat, the overall trend will persist over the next two decades, though perhaps not at the same pace as seen during recent years. Asia's share of global exports is expected to nearly double by 2030 to 39%. In particular, China's economy is expected to bypass that of the United States during the next decade. Even if China's growth rate slows down, it will still surpass the United States as the world's largest economy by 2030. China is also projected to have twice the share of global trade as the United States, and will be the world's largest creditor.[3] But China will not be unrivalled at the top. India is expected to begin to catch up or even be on par with China by 2030 in some economic terms.[4] Both China and India are projected by the World Bank to maintain high growth rates by 2030, combined with high R&D expenditures.[5] This could lead to a tripling of India's GDP per capita by 2030. But other middle powers are also growing in relevance. Consulting firm PWC estimates that the "E7," comprised of the four BRICs plus Indonesia, Mexico and Turkey, will surpass the G7 in economic performance already by 2017. By 2030, the gap between the traditional economies and the new up-comers will be even greater as emerging markets will account for an even bigger share of global economic growth.[6] The

---

[3]"China 2030: Building a Modern, Harmonious, and Creative Society" (The World Bank, Washington, DC, 2013), p.7.

[4]*Global Trends 2030* (National Intelligence Council, 2012), p.15

[5]Charles, Wolf Jr., et al. "China and India, 2025: A Comparative Assessment" (Rand Corporation, 2011); 2013 R&D Magazine Global Funding Forecast, available online: http://www.rd-mag.com/digital-editions/2012/12/2013-r-d-magazine-global-funding-forecast

[6]"World in 2050: The BRICs and Beyond: Prospects, Challenges and Opportunities," *PWC Economics*, January 2013.

Figure 1. Real GDP Growth 2017

World Bank estimates that "by 2025, global economic growth will predominantly be generated in emerging economies."[7] The figure above shows how the fastest growth rates will predominantly occur in Southeast and East Asia and Sub-Saharan Africa.

But growth in countries like China and India and in other emerging economies cannot be taken for granted. Many of these countries still face massive internal challenges on multiple fronts—for instance in the governance sector. So while the overall trend points toward a global economic power shift, such a development is also contingent on the successful implementation of needed reforms in many of these states. Both China and India also face a realistic risk of ending up in a "middle income trap." As China increasingly seeks to move beyond an export-led growth to a domestic consumption-led one, it might also become more prone to economic nationalism and protectionism, which in turn can undermine its global competitiveness, causing other

---

[7]"Global Development Horizons 2011: Multipolarity: The New Global Economy" (The World Bank, Washington, DC, 2011).

countries to replace China as a cheap destination for manufacturing. Furthermore, technological advancements and the potential for lower energy costs could prompt a return of manufacturing to developed countries (for example, both the shale gas revolution in North American and advances in 3D printing technology could be drivers of such a development).[8] Yet, even with gradually slower growth rates, the major trend towards the rise of China as a major global economic superpower is not expected to alter course significantly. The only thing that could possibly offset this trend would be a major disruption within China (e.g. widespread domestic political instability) bringing growth to a halt. Such a scenario, while certainly a possibility, remains distant and especially hard to predict.

Moreover, while China might surpass the United States in terms of economic strength, it will still have a long way to go before it is the global dominant player in research and innovation. Although China emerged as the second largest aggregate R&D spender in 2010, the United States still spends about a third of the global total. Moreover, Chinese R&D expenditure as a percentage of GDP (1.97%) remains significantly lower than that of the United States (2.7%). Still, China is on track to surpass the EU around 2020 in terms of R&D spending. But while the Chinese government is increasing its spending, Chinese companies are still trailing behind their Western competitors. In 2013, there were 527 companies in the EU and 658 companies in the United States with R&D investment above €22.6 million, while the equivalent number for China and India was merely 93 and 22, respectively.[9] That said, the share of Chinese R&D companies among the top 1000 global innovation companies is steadily rising.[10] R&D spending aside, a major question mark is whether China will successfully establish a truly competitive market environment with strong intellectual property rights in promotion of higher innovation.[11] Another challenge is that the actual quality of Chinese R&D outputs

---

[8]"China-US Cooperation: Key to the Global Future" (Atlantic Council, Washington, DC, 2013).

[9]The 2013 EU Industrial R&D Investment Scoreboard.

[10]Barry Jaruzelski et al. "The Global Innovation 1000: Navigating the Digital Future," *Strategy + Business, Booz & Co*, Issue 73, Winter 2013, p.38.

[11]"China 2030: Building a Modern, Harmonious, and Creative Society" (The World Bank, Washington, DC, 2013).

still tends to be significantly below that of North America, Europe and Japan. Growing economic performance among emerging countries may also translate into more political influence over the global economy. While the "next eleven" (or N-11) countries[12] may not be powerful enough by themselves to exert global influence, when acting together they can still have significant clout, possibly even surpassing Europe and Japan in global influence. It is questionable, however, whether such a disparate group could, in fact, work in concert. Nonetheless, emerging powers are showing increasing signs of growing assertiveness on the international stage.

Together, these developments will pave the way for a far more multipolar world order in which there is no longer one dominating superpower but rather a group of major global powers. This shift in global power distribution has been interpreted as either a move towards "no one's world"[13] or a "polycentric world"[14] in which no single country will be in a hegemonic position. With the evolving global environment, the concepts that laid the foundations for the "liberal international order" are increasingly becoming subject to renegotiation, including debates over values, sovereignty issues, global responsibility, and international institutional arrangements.[15] International organizations such as the United Nations and the Bretton Woods institutions will probably have to be reformed to remain relevant. Some experts even believe that the two most dominant states—the United States and China—will be forced to strike some kind of "grand bargain" in which they would work out their differences within the context of a rules-based international order.[16] We have already witnessed the gradual replacement of the previous G7 "dynasty" with the significantly broader G20 arrangement. The trend towards a "G-Zero" world, characterized by a more diverse composition of global power, will cer-

---

[12]These are Bangladesh, Egypt, Indonesia, Iran, Mexico, Nigeria, Pakistan, the Philippines, Turkey, South Korea and Vietnam. The term was originally coined by Goldman Sachs economist Jim O'Neill.

[13]Charles A. Kupchan, *No One's World: the West, the Rising Rest and the Coming Global Turn* (New York: Oxford University Press, 2012).

[14]ESPAS Report "Global Trends 2030—Citizens in an Interconnected and Polycentric World" (European Union Institute for Security Studies, Paris, 2010).

[15]Steven Weber and Bruce, Jentleson, *The End of Arrogance* (Harvard University Press, 2010).

[16]John G. Ikenberry, *Liberal Leviathan: The Origins, Crisis, and Transformation of the American World Order* (Princeton University Press, 2011.)

tainly continue in the coming decade.[17] As a result, current international institutions and global governance mechanisms will either have to evolve or else may risk falling into irrelevance. It is already clear that many of the rising powers do not share the same basic assumptions about how the world should be organized.

Maintaining Free and Open "Global Commons"[18]

In a world of diffuse global power, one critically important factor is whether "global common goods" will continue to be provided for by the international system. One particularly vital such "global public good" is the global "maritime commons." As both global trade and competition over resources grow,[19] the importance of maritime security grows as well. The maritime commons faces an uncertain future. First, the ongoing diffusion of global maritime power stemming from the "rise of the rest" could alter the geostrategic maritime balance. New and rising powers are challenging existing rules of the game and are pressing for a "re-territorialization" of the seas as well as a revision of existing maritime legal norms. In this emerging global maritime context, developments in faraway maritime regions will increasingly reverberate throughout the world, and national rivalries and resource competition may gradually encroach on the international freedom of navigation. China's recent claim over the air defense zone (ADIZ) in the South China Sea should therefore be viewed against this background.

Second, other maritime threats are also lurking on the horizon. Global maritime flows are increasingly connected to criminal activities (e.g. human smuggling, drug trafficking, and pirates) and, in some cases, terror-related activities (e.g. WMD proliferation, hijacking, terrorist attacks). Ungoverned maritime spaces along major sea lanes already pose a major threat as a refuge for armed maritime groups, especially pirates, and a safe-haven for illicit activities. Piracy remains a considerable threat to maritime trade in various regions, including

---

[17]Ian Bremmer, *Every Nation for Itself: What Happens When No One Leads the World* (Portfolio, 2012).

[18]This part draws on the report *The Maritime Dimension of CSDP: Geostrategic Maritime Challenges and their Implications for the European Union* (European Parliament, Brussels, 2013).

[19]The flows of goods, mainly from Asia to Western markets are intensifying, as are the flows of raw materials and strategic resources to the sites of production. For example, maritime commerce today represents 90% of world trade and some 60% of petroleum exports.

the Gulf of Aden, the Strait of Malacca and the Gulf of Guinea. Piracy has also proven to be a global and adaptable phenomenon in recent years that has sought to exploit weaknesses in the international security architecture wherever they arise. This means that localized action often does not suffice to address the wider challenge, as pirate activities shift in line with international attention.

Until now, the U.S. Navy has taken the lead responsibility to provide for security of maritime supplies across the oceans—a task it inherited from Britain after World War II. This role is less certain as we look towards 2030. Faced with economic pressures at home and rising and resurging powers abroad, the United States has adopted a bleak reading of its military and economic capabilities. As a result, Washington is gradually withdrawing from long-term overseas commitments that were characteristic of the post-Cold War era, and moving slowly towards a more modest vision of commanding access to the global commons and securing attendant global flows.[20] This may cause friction with emerging powers mistrustful of U.S. policies. China, Russia, India and Brazil are all in the process of developing their own naval capabilities to project power beyond their own territorial waters. At the same time, the development of new anti-access and area-denial (A2/AD) capabilities has raised questions about the future viability of large surface fleets, further blunting the conventional superiority of the U.S. Navy and potentially posing a raft of localized threats to the freedom of navigation.

Of course, a decline of Western naval power does not have to be a challenge to the global maritime security environment. On the contrary, if employed to strengthen international regimes it has the potential to reinforce the security and safety of international shipping. However, paired with growing geopolitical competition in especially the Asia-Pacific and Indian Ocean regions, the global shift in maritime power harbors some potential for conflict and confrontation; whether in terms of low-intensity conflicts and proxy wars between middling

---

[20]The 2010 US National Security Strategy (NSS) defined the "Safeguarding the Global Commons" as one of the "Key Global Challenges" that require the attention of both the United States but also the international community as a whole. In a similar vein, the 2010 U.S. Quadrennial Defense Review (QDR), the 2011 US National Military Strategy (NMS) and most recently the 2012 review "Sustaining U.S. Global Leadership" (SUSGL) have all highlighted the growing importance of the Global Commons.

powers or, less likely, great power confrontation. By raising the costs of any future maritime confrontation, this diffusion of maritime power away from the West may strengthen the ability of new and rising powers to challenge the existing legal order over territorial claims and exclusive economic zones.

The Changing Global Distribution of Military Power

Military power is also shifting, although somewhat less rapidly than economic power. Today, Chinese spending on defense is second only to that of the United States. This gap is expected to shrink further over the next decade. According to the U.S. Defense Department's Annual Report to Congress on China, the People's Liberation Army "is on track to achieve its goal of building a modern, regionally-focused military by 2020."[21] The quality of Chinese military capabilities is also improving. One reliable estimate suggests that the quality of the Chinese military in 2030 will be on par with European nations, albeit behind the United States. In particular, China is investing in improving its naval capabilities, which are seen by Beijing as crucial for projecting power in the Asia-Pacific region and protecting vital Chinese security interests. China has also already surpassed the UK as a world's fifth largest arms exporter in terms of volume. But aside from China, India's military power will soon also rival those of European states such as the UK.[22] For example, India plans to have 30 submarines by 2030, although this goal can prove tough to reach.[23] Asia as a whole is already outspending Europe on defense.[24] At the same time, Russia is also investing heavily in building up and modernizing its defense sector, although this upgrade will depend on the sustainability of the Russian economy.

---

[21]"Annual Report to Congress: Military and Security Developments Involving the People's Republic of China 2011," U.S. Department of Defense, Washington, DC, 2011. Of course, this also depends on the future development of U.S. defense spending under sequestration and budget cuts.

[22]"From R&D Investment to Fighting Power, 25 Years Later," *McKinsey on Government*, Spring 2010, p.72.

[23]"India Responds to China Navy," *The Diplomat*, August 23, 2010.

[24]Sam Perlo-Freeman et al. "Trends In World Military Expenditure 2012," *SIPRI Fact Sheet* (SIPRI, Stockholm, 2013).

Meanwhile, while many countries are investing heavily in their militaries, the general trend in Europe and North America is one of shrinking defense budgets. Since the end of the Cold War, European NATO countries" defense spending has fallen by close to 20% even though their combined GDP has risen by nearly 55%. It is also a fact that military spending among European countries has steadily declined from around 2% of GDP in the year 2000 to 1.74% in 2009, despite ongoing operations in Afghanistan. As of 2013, the United States accounted for 73% of all NATO defense spending. Only 4 out of 28 NATO member states (Britain, Greece, Estonia and the United States) fulfilled the alliance requirement to spend 2% or more of national GDP on defense. Despite pledges to increase spending—most recently at the September 2014 summit in Wales—planned and ongoing cuts in defense budgets are projected to be substantial and widespread, affecting the capabilities of many countries.

Small But Growing Potential for Regional Tension and Conflict

Although most studies tend to agree that conflict between major powers is unlikely, simply because too much is at stake, the changes in the global distribution of power nevertheless heighten the level of uncertainty and the risk of miscalculation. Hence, the possibility of great power conflict cannot be entirely dismissed in the future. Nor can the risk for increased regional tension, especially in East Asia and the South China Sea where border and maritime disputes between China and its neighboring states are already a reality and in Europe where Russia's invasion and annexation of Crimea and support to rebels in eastern Ukraine has raised concerns about the durability of the post-Cold War security order in Europe. While economic interdependence and globalization have significantly reduced the likelihood of conflict between great powers, history has shown that this alone is not a sufficient condition to prevent conflict from breaking out. In fact, power transitions have historically been rather tumultuous moments in time.[25] As economic nationalism and protectionism fester, seemingly peripheral incidents and localized disputes will also have the potential to escalate into broader conflicts. However, the huge

---

[25]Charles A. Kupchan, *Power Transitions: The Peaceful Change of International Order* (United Nations University Press, 2001).

costs attached to any such conflict and the low probability of an outright victory will continue to act as a strong deterrent.

While any direct confrontation between the United States and China therefore appears unlikely, this does not preclude the possibility of clashes between middling powers, proxy wars, or low-intensity and covert conflicts. With both China and the United States vying for allies around the Asia-Pacific region, this might also encourage brinkmanship behavior by smaller states eager to exploit the backing of one of the great powers to bolster their own territorial claims (who, except North Korea, would expect Chinese support for territorial claims/and who are China's allies in Asia). Similarly, great powers might attempt to use proxies in order to change the strategic balance in certain regions, while avoiding direct confrontation.

Clashes between rising powers can therefore not be excluded within the foreseeable future. For example, China's attempts to widen its influence in the Indian Ocean puts it starkly at odds with a rising India and have fueled competitive dynamics. As China becomes increasingly dependent on natural resources, its presence is being felt in regions beyond the Asia-Pacific, such as Central Asia, Africa, the Middle East and Latin America. And as the sea ice continues to melt in the Arctic, China will also have a growing stake in the region's shipping and resources. At some point, China may even feel the need to expand its military presence in the Arctic to protect security of supply should it grow increasingly dependent on the region's resources and shipping routes for its economy.[26]

Besides China, Russia is also on a worrisome path at the moment. Although it is still much too difficult to predict where this country will be in 2030—or even in 2020—the current trajectory is one towards more authoritarianism at home and aggressiveness abroad, especially in the post-Soviet space. Unresolved border issues in Europe's periphery, combined with Moscow's neo-imperialist tendencies, do not bode well for regional stability in the next decade. Moreover, Russia's preference to use both direct military force (as in Georgia 2008) and

---

[26]Russia has already taken steps towards boosting its military presence in the Arctic and is likely to continue on a similar path. Still, most experts do not foresee rising geopolitical tensions in the Arctic anytime in the near future, especially since regional cooperation frameworks (such as the Arctic Council) are already in place to help manage disputes.

hybrid warfare tactics (as in Crimea in 2014) raises new concerns about its potential to destabilize other countries it views as part of its traditional sphere of influence. Ultimately, Russia seems to have little desire to be part of a Western-led security order. Instead, it actively seeks to undermine NATO and Western unity and to bolster its own great power status. To what extent Russia will be successful in challenging Western power remains to be seen. While Moscow has made attempts to solidify its relationship with Beijing, including signing a landmark deal with supply China with gas, the China-Russia relationship is far from certain as we look towards 2030.

Although relative power certainly is diffusing it does not necessarily mean global power is shifting from the West to the "Rest" in a clear-cut way. The term multipolar world implies the existence of coherent "poles" that can be identified. However, while the West remains a fairly coherent group of nations with political, military and economic structures firmly in place, there is no such "Eastern" equivalent. While China and other emerging powers will certainly continue to grow in importance, they are yet to form a coherence bloc challenging the West. Given the enormous differences among each other, it is therefore quite unlikely that we will see such different poles in place in 2030.

Trend 2: Liquid World— Diffusion of State Power to Transnational Actors

Non-state actors, particularly national and transnational civil society networks and private corporations, will increasingly have a significantly larger imprint on global policies. Enabled by the spread of communication technologies, the influence of these "micro-powers"[27] will in some cases even exceed that of many traditional states, possibly even giving rise to new forms of governance.[28] The weakening of the traditional state's grip and the rising imprint of networked non-state actors produces a two-fold consequence: it democratizes international politics by bringing in voices previously silenced, but potentially also

---

[27]Moises Naim, *The End of Power: From Boardrooms to Battlefields and Churches to States, Why Being In Charge Isn't What It Used to Be* (Basic Books, 2013).

[28]ESPAS Report "Global Trends 2030—Citizens in an Interconnected and Polycentric World" (European Union Institute for Security Studies, Paris, 2010), p.19.

facilitates the operations of transnational criminal networks and terrorist groups.

New Mega-Companies in the Global Economy

The growing role of corporations in the global economy is already apparent, and is likely to be a defining feature over the next two decades. In 2009, 44 of the 100 largest economic entities were corporations.[29] The annual revenue of one single company, Wal-Mart Stores, surpassed the GDP of 174 countries. If Wal-Mart were a country, it would be the 22nd largest economy in the world. Other multinational corporations such as Apple and Google also have an annual turnover surpassing the GDP of several smaller states. While the role of multinational corporations (MNCs) is predicted to increase further, the make-up of the world's largest corporations will also change drastically. In particular, more companies from developing nations will be among the top global economic entities in 2030.[30] The McKinsey Global Institute estimates that by 2025 nearly half of the Fortune 500 companies will be from the developing world—up from 5% in 1990 and 17% in 2010. The report also points out that out of the 5,000 new large companies, 40% will be based in China. To further illustrate this, in 2010, there were 8,000 companies with $1 billion or more in revenue. In 2025, this number will have nearly doubled to 15,000 companies—the bulk of which will come from emerging states. McKinsey further predicts that this shift will "be profound because large companies have an outsized impact on their home economies and even on the global economy through their role in trade flows."[31] This geographic rebalancing of global companies will have major implications for economic competitiveness, including the race for resources and talented workforces, standard setting, innovation, and economic growth. In a more general sense, the growing influence of MNCs will

---

[29]See "Corporate Clout: The Influence of the World's Largest 100 Economic Entities," Strategy Dynamics Global Limited. Available online: http://www.globaltrends.com/images/stories/corporate%20clout%20the%20worlds%20100%20largest%20economic%20entities.pdf

[30]See "The Universe of the Largest Transnational Corporations" (United Nations, New York and Geneva, 2007).

[31]Dobbs, Richard, et al., "Urban World: The Shifting Global Business Landscape" (McKinsey Global Institute, 2013).

also fundamentally transform societies, both in the developed and developing world. We are likely to see more interdependence between corporations, governments and their citizens. From a policy perspective, this means that strengthening relationships among these actors and partnering to address joint challenges will be a key imperative.

The Rise of Megacities

Another aspect of diminishing state power stems from within states themselves, and has to do with the growing role of cities as major players in the global economy—especially so-called "megacities."[32] As we look towards 2030, the relative importance of global megacities is projected to grow. Global population and urbanization patterns aid this trend. In 2010, for the first time in history, more than half of the world's population (3.3 billion people) lived in urban areas. The UN expects this number to reach five billion, or 60% of the world's total population in 2030 (see graph below).

Although the growth in the number of cities with one million of more inhabitants will slow over the coming decade, the general trend towards increased urbanization will persist well into and beyond 2030.[33] By 2050, it is predicted that 6.3 billion people out of a global population of 9 billion will dwell in cities, which would be about ten times the size of the total world population in 1950. The bulk of this population growth will take place in cities located in developing nations. This trend will help lift millions out of poverty around the world. In both Asia and Africa, a majority of citizens are expected to live in urban areas by 2030. As a result, the rise of a global "consuming class" by 2030 means that the developing world will increasingly serve as engines of global GDP growth. It is expected that the developing world will spend $20 trillion by 2025.

---

[32]See Beaverstock, J.V., Faulconbridge, J.R. and Hoyler, M., "Globalization and the City," in A. Leyshon, R. Lee, L. McDowell and P. Sunley, eds., *The SAGE Handbook of Economic Geography* (SAGE, London, 2011); M. Castells, *The Urban Question* (Arnold, London, 1977); Lévy, J. *L'Europe, une géographie* (Paris: Hachette, 1997); Saskia Sassen, *The Global City* (Princeton University, Princeton, 1991); Taylor, P. J., *World City Network: A Global Urban Analysis* (Routledge, London, 2004).

[33]United Nations, Department of Economic and Social Affairs, Population Division, *World Urbanization Prospects, the 2011 Revision* (United Nations, New York, 2011).

Figure 2. Global population growth and urbanization rate in 2030

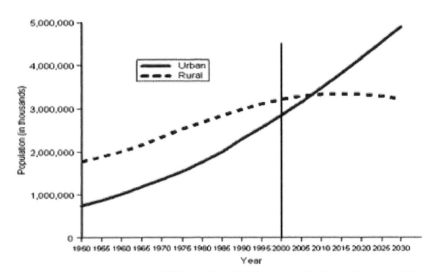

Source: http://web.worldbank.org/WBSITE/EXTERNAL/NEWS/0,,contentMDK%3A20149913~menuPK%
3A34457~pagePK%3A64003015~piPK%3A64003012~theSitePK%3A4607,00.html

The evolving make-up of the global economy means that some of the most important global cities will be in the global South and East by 2025. According to the McKinsey Global Institute, one in three developed cities will no longer be among the 600 most powerful ones in the world. Concurrently, 136 new cities in the developing world (mostly from China and to a lesser extent India) will be added to this list.[34] The relative importance of cities is also projected to grow over the coming two decades, driving economic growth across the world.[35] A separate study conducted by PWC finds that while the top five cities in 2025 will remain European and North American, South American cities São Paulo, Mexico City, and Buenos Aires will all make it to the top 10 list. Other emerging market cities that will advance significantly by 2025 include Shanghai, Beijing, Mumbai, and Istanbul. Meanwhile, several cities in the West will fall down the list.[36]

---

[34]Dobbs, Richard, et al., "Urban World: The Shifting Global Business Landscape" (McKinsey Global Institute, 2013), p. 1.

[35]Ibid. p.7.

[36]"Which Are the Largest City Economies in the World and How Might This Change by 2025?" UK Economic Outlook November 2009, (Pricewaterhosue Coopers), 2009.

This increased role of cities in the global economy puts additional demands on international governance structures. In many ways, global "alpha cities" such as London and New York are already more inter-linked and interdependent than, for instance, London and Manchester or New York and Denver.[37] This trend of deepening connections among major nodes in the global economy is likely to prevail. The world's "megacities" are already increasingly linked to one another through various financial and commercial flows. Author Parag Khanna argues that megacities will increasingly bypass national governance structures in setting up their own ad hoc city-to-city alliances. Embryos of such networks between global cities already exists, including the World Cities Summits,[38] City Mayors network,[39] or the C40 Cities network. Another type of city cooperation that is going to be more common is direct city-to-city agreements going beyond existing sister city partnerships. One example is the agreement signed between Chicago and Mexico City in 2013 to promote joint initiatives on trade, innovation, education and competitiveness.[40] As we look towards 2030, we are likely to see more of these types of developments as individual cities become major players on the international stage, alongside but occasionally also apart from their own nation-states.

Of course, this is not to say that the world will evolve into some kind of modern version of the medieval city state system—as some scholars have suggested.[41] On the contrary, when it comes to global governance and security issues in particular, the traditional interstate system is still responsible for providing the majority of core public goods that cities depend on. While still a distant possibility, the prospect of rising megacities declaring themselves independent from their nation-state must therefore be considered extremely low, at least during the coming decade. Still, as cities seek to set policies that fit with their local needs—such as on immigration issues—this might increasingly create a discrepancy between cities and the surrounding

---

[37]See, for instance, Loughborough University's "global connectivity ranking." Available at: http://www.lboro.ac.uk/gawc/world2012t.html.

[38]See www.worldcitiessummit.com.

39See http://www.citymayors.com/.

[40]Amy Liu and Ryan Donahue, "Chicago and Mexico City Cut New Kind of Trade Deal," *The Avenue blog* (Brookings Institution, Washington, DC, 2013).

[41]Parag Khanna, *How to Run the World* (Random House, 2011).

nation-state. How cities will interact with national governments will therefore be a key issue in the future in developed and developing states alike. Another related governance issue relates to the growth of metropolitan regions, which can spill over across multiple political jurisdictions. In this case, creating new metro-regions, sometimes even extending between two or more national borders, may become more frequent phenomena.[42] Within the EU, for example, there are already some burgeoning cooperation frameworks between bordering cities in different countries.[43]

Empowerment of Transnational Groups

Increasingly, non-state transnational groups will play a bigger role in shaping both national and international policies. The past few decades have witnessed a proliferation in non-governmental organizations. This process has been driven in part by technology and in part by globalization.[44] The Yearbook of International Organizations estimates that the number of international NGOs have risen from 6,000 in 1990 to more than 65,000 in 2013. More people than ever before are involved individually and collectively to address various societal challenges. This is the case in developed and developing countries alike. As illustrated during the Arab Spring, informal networks of people, enabled by the use of information technology and social media, can play a significant role in their countries. A word of caution, however: recent developments such as the Arab spring but also the 2014 crisis in Ukraine suggest that governments (especially authoritarian ones) are also increasingly becoming anxious about citizens" public opinions facilitated by the internet. Governments from China to Egypt to Turkey have taken active steps to limit popular social media such as Facebook or Twitter.

Within the NGO community, the mission of many groups is also changing. Rather than merely being opponents to the government sector, many non-profit organizations are today involved in a wide

---

[42]According to the NIC *Global Trends 2030* report, there will be at least 40 such mega-regions in 2030.

[43]See http://www.espon.eu/export/sites/default/Documents/Projects/TargetedAnalyses/ METROBORDER/METROBORDER_-_Final_Report_-_29_DEC_2010.pdf.

[44]"The Future Role of Civil Society" (World Economic Forum, Geneva, 2013).

range of different activities ranging from watchdog and advocacy to capacity building and providing services, to mention a few examples. NGOs are increasingly organized as loose networks, while partnerships with governments and the private sector is becoming the norm rather than an exception. Another trend is that NGOs are progressively granted a stronger voice and a seat at the table at major multilateral fora, including the G20 and the UN.[45] This fusion of government, business and civil society is giving rise to new forms of interactions that blur the traditional roles of these diverse actors, creating a shared space in which all can operate. This development could possibly also give rise to hybrid organizations embodying several aspects of different types of organizations.[46] At the same time, it is important to also note that the ability of NGOs to function effectively is also being hampered in many parts of the world, as authoritarian governments seek to impose limits on their freedoms.

Enabling the Dark Forces of Globalization

A global environment that is characterized by a failure of international cooperation and growing regional conflicts will also enable transnational criminal groups to thrive. Terrorism, which was the central focus of security officials in the decade following the September 11 attacks, will continue to pose a threat over the coming decade and beyond. Non-state actors will be able to exploit the opportunities provided by globalization in the forms of easy access to transport and communications as well as the vulnerabilities open societies provide. Moreover, mounting state fragility in some parts of the world may also provide a vital breeding ground for forms of violent extremism.

Weakening state power can also promote "criminal or illegal networks exercising economic and even territorial control."[47] When combined with domestic violence and civil strife, weak governments, particularly in Africa and the Middle East, are a major cause for concern. While terrorism will certainly remain a concern, transnational criminal networks and low-intensity conflicts such as urban violence will increasingly pose serious security challenges. This is particularly the

---

[45]Ibid. p.7.
[46]Ibid. p.10.
[47]EUISS 2011 op. cit., p. 19.

case in countries with weak governance combined with poverty, unemployment and large youth populations. Transnational crime will be a growing priority—one that will often be related to other challenges such as illegal immigration, piracy, and even terrorism. Already, illicit drug trade from West Africa has been documented to benefit terrorist groups operating in the Sahel. These kinds of social vulnerabilities enhance the risk for civil strife "and thus reinforce the 'state fragility-conflict' cycle" and lead to state fragmentation.[48]

Furthermore, arms trafficking and CBRN proliferation—particularly when combined with transnational crime—will pose a worrisome challenge in the coming decades. While the threat from Islamic terrorism is generally predicted to be less severe by 2030, the widespread availability of new lethal and disruptive technologies means that the focus of terrorist attacks might shift from causing mass casualties to inflicting widespread economic and financial disruption. At the same time, the Global Trends 2030 report clearly downplays the risk of nuclear terrorism.

Trend 3: More Human Power—
Will Global Technological Diffusion Create a Level Playing Field?

Increasingly, relationships between individuals, consumers and companies, and between citizens and the state, will be redefined by rising "hyper-connectivity."[49] This development will offer both new opportunities and new challenges, for governments and non-state actors alike.

A Hyper-Connected World

Global internet data flows are growing quickly, and will likely continue to do so over the coming decade.[50] But while the maintenance of

---

[48]Ibid. p. 96

[49]Soumitra Dutta and Beñat Bilbao-Osorio, eds., "The Global Information Technology Report 2012: Living in a Hyperconnected World," Insight Report (World Economic Forum and INSEAD, 2012). http://globaltrends2030.files.wordpress.com/2012/11/global-trends-2030-november2012.pdf

[50]See "Cisco Visual Networking Index: Forecast and Methodology, 2012–2017," White Paper (Cisco, 2013).

free flows of information is a necessity for the global economy to function, an increasingly diffuse set of actors will be responsible for this service. As the World Economic Forum points out, "the hyper-connected world" is one without a central authority. Rising "hyper-connectivity" will have an equalizing effect in the world, but it will not make all countries and actors equal players. While technology can enable weak actors and create a more leveled playing field, emerging economies still have a long way to go to catch up with industrialized nations. In the World Economic Forum's ranking of countries according to their "network readiness"—defined as their ability to profit from rising hyper-connectivity—only a handful of countries score at the top (i.e. Scandinavian countries, Netherlands, UK, and North America). During the coming two decades, technology will become more evenly distributed throughout the world. Technological catch-up will take place, and the fastest growth will occur in those states that have the most catching up to do. Still, technological convergence is by no means automatic and will depend on a country's openness, education system, communication and infrastructure, government and business and investment climate.[51] For example, 75% of the world's population already has access to a mobile phone—in some countries the number of people with mobile phones is even higher than the number of people with access to a bank account, electricity or clean water. By 2030, half of the world's population is projected to have access to the internet, up from 34% in 2012,[52] with the quickest increase expected to take place in many developing countries. In many of these countries, improved access to technology will bring opportunities to improve education, health, and governance and democracy, and will also ease access to the global markets. But the impact of the spread of technology, such as mobile phones in developing countries, is not one-sided. While the distribution of mobile phones in Africa has been proven to go hand in hand with upsurges in violence, it also allows governments and international responders to better track developments on the ground and, thus, to intervene to prevent violence.[53]

---

[51]"The World Order in 2050" (Carnegie Endowment for International Peace, Washington, DC, 2010).

[52]"Information and Communications for Development 2012: Maximizing Mobile (World Bank, Washington, DC, 2012).

[53]Ali Fisher, J.H. Pierskalla and F.M. Hollenbach, "Technology and Collective Action: The Effect of Cell Phone Coverage on Political Violence in Africa," *American Political Science Review* (2013), p. 107.

Still, the distribution of technology will remain skewed, with the poorest population groups in developing states still lacking access to technology such as the internet and cell phones. The discrepancy between cities and rural areas in developing nations in terms of access to technology will also widen. Taken together, the proliferation of technology will thus not always have an equalizing effect, but may in some instances even exacerbate global inequalities within certain societies.

...But an Uncertain Future of Internet Freedom

Though expected to continue being a defining feature, the internet's future is far from certain. Advances in technology such as the advent of big data also give governments an unprecedented ability to monitor and control their own citizens and other countries. At the same time, the digital age is also one of rising worldwide transparency of information. It is increasingly hard for governments to keep secrets from their citizens.

These two trends have already given rise to increased discussion about how to view the trade-off between surveillance, on the one hand, and individual privacy and freedom on the other. The revelations by Edward Snowden of the American NSA surveillance programs have caused a massive stir among governments and citizens alike throughout the world about individual privacy and freedom concerns. The NSA controversy has also expedited the process that some scholars refer to as the "Balkanization of the internet" (or "Splinternet"). This term denotes the process towards a fragmentation of the internet in various ways, including for security and espionage reasons. Proposals to create new closed-off intranets have been suggested by countries such as Brazil and Germany. In fact, Brazil and the EU have recently agreed to lay a new underwater cable from Lisbon to Fortazela in an effort to reduce U.S. eavesdropping on transatlantic communications.[54] Furthermore, attempts to increase state-control and to limit freedom on the Internet have already been put forth by the World Conference on International Telecommunications (WCIT) and the Internet Corporation for Assigned Names and Numbers (ICANN). As advanced surveillance technology becomes more accessible, a growing number of states and non-state actors will use such

---

[54]"Brazil, Europe plan undersea cable to skirt U.S. spying," *Reuters*, February 24, 2014.

tools by 2030. It remains to be seen whether regulation and legislation as well as governance models will keep up pace with technological developments.

Third Industrial Revolution: Driving the Global Economy

The unprecedented technological revolution seen in recent decades will likely continue—or even intensify—in coming years, fundamentally affecting the world in a number of key ways. New technologies will have the ability to create new opportunities for humans and to damage human lives and the planet. Increasingly, technological inventions will serve as the engine of economic growth around the world. However, this also puts additional demands on economies to also respond and adapt to these changes. The McKinsey Global Institute has identified several technologies that will have potentially "disruptive" effects on businesses in 2025, including 3D printing, the automation of knowledge work, cloud technology, advanced oil exploration and recovery.[55] One particular area that is going to make a significant imprint on governments, businesses and ordinary citizens alike is information technology such as "data solutions," "social networking," and "smart city technology." As several reports have pointed out, the advent of data solutions or "big data" will be a defining feature of information technology in the coming decade.[56] The development of process power and data storage will also allow for the provision of new types of global services, especially targeting the social media and cyber security areas.[57] Some authors even go so far as to talk about a "third industrial revolution" (TIR) that will transform not only production but also society at large. According to its proponents, TIR will change production patterns, demand less energy and raw materials, affect social relations, and alter the relationship between people and production.[58] According to *The Economist* magazine, the foundation for TIR is the advent of 3D printing. One potential major effect of 3D print-

---

[55]For the full report, see, James Manyika et al., "Disruptive Technologies: Advances That Will Transform Life, Business, and the Global Economy" (McKinsey Global Institute, 2013).

[56]James Manyika et al., "Big Data: The Next Frontier for Innovation, Competition, and Productivity" (McKinsey Global Institute, 2011).

[57]*Global Trends 2030* (U.S. National Intelligence Council, 2012), p.86.

[58]"Envisioning 2030: US Strategy for the Coming Technology Revolution" (Atlantic Council, Washington, DC, 2013) p.15.

ing in the future is the ability to shift from large-scale assembly lines with a myriad of subcontractors and complex global supply chains[59]— but its true potential use is still highly uncertain.

...But Also Higher Risks for Technological Disruption

As history tells us, technological developments are certainly not always positive. Some technologies will have both direct and indirect disruptive effects. Whether cyber, bioterrorism, precision-strike capabilities or the risk for proliferation of new instruments of war, new technologies will have serious security implications. Non-state criminal actors and terrorists will benefit from the proliferation of new warfare technologies. The proliferation of new technological capabilities such as cyber and bioterrorism can potentially enable non-state actors to wreak havoc. Instruments of cyberwarfare are already available and could be used by non-state actors to conduct an attack on military systems, electricity grids, communication networks or financial systems. Key to addressing many of these new security threats will be effective cooperation between the public and private sectors, as much of the critical infrastructure remains in private hands—and coordination between public and private actors is often poor. The risk for cyber warfare is going to increase during the coming decades. In fact, the effects of sophisticated and coordinated cyberattacks are already starting to be felt throughout the world, giving rise to a tendency to view cyberspace as a new security frontier—in addition to land, sea and air. In response, the United States has declared computer sabotage from another country an "act of war" to which the United States will respond using traditional military force. NATO members declared at their 2014 summit that cyber attacks could trigger the Alliance's Article 5 mutual defense clause. However, many doubts have been raised concerning the use of force as a response to a cyberattack due to the difficulties in identifying and locating an attacker. The consequences could be extremely serious and could even prompt an interstate conflict. Increased cyber espionage targeting governments and corporations alike is also increasingly becoming a serious security threat. The proliferation of global surveillance systems is very likely to a defining feature of the next decade.

---

[59]Ibid. pp.16-17.

Trend 4: Shrinking World—
Growing Population and Resource Scarcity

A defining feature of the next few decades will be growing population, especially in the developing world, along with increases in living standards. Commensurate with this positive development is a more negative one: growing demands for resources will give rise to scarcities, which may in turn give rise to social tension and, in the worst cases, even new conflicts. Managing these prospects should be seen as a key priority for the international community in coming years.

Demographic Trends—A Growing but Aging Global Population

One of the major trends identified in numerous studies concerns the combination of demographic data and predictions of aggravated resource scarcity. In particular, rapid population growth—the world's population is expected to reach 8.3 billion by 2030—will have significant consequences. The bulk of this population growth will take place in developing nations—with the fastest growth appearing in the least developed countries in the world, particularly in Sub-Saharan Africa where the population is projected to rise by 500 million people, and in South-East Asia where we will see an increase of 400 million. India, for example, is expected to surpass China as the world's most populous state by around 2028.[60] In these and other parts of the world, such as the Middle East, young people account for a huge portion of the population. In contrast, the population growth in developed countries is predicted to decrease on average as the population grows older and birth rates decline.[61] As a result, Europe's share of the world population will fall by 2030.

However, it is important to note that global population growth is not predicted to continue at the same rate indefinitely. In fact, demographers expect global population growth to stall around 2030, particularly due to falling fertility rates and rising development levels in many countries. The world's population is also getting older due to longer expected average lifespans. A final demographic trend worth singling out is migration. Although the share of international migrants

---

[60]"World Population Prospects" (United Nations, New York, 2013).
[61]Ibid.

Table 1. Projected Population Growth to 2025 in millions

Region	2013	2025	Change	Percent
World	7,137	8,095	+958	+13
High Income	1,246	1,285	+39	+3
Developing	5,009	5,652	+647	+13
Least developed	876	1,158	+272	+31

Source: Population Reference Bureau. 2013 World Population Data Sheet.

in 2010 only amounted to about 3% of the world's population, a number that has remained relatively steady in recent decades, according to the United Nations Population Division (UNDESA), international migration is likely to rise in the next two decades. One reason for this is to offset shortages in workers that are expected in many developed and developing nations. By 2030, we could also see both internal displacement and cross-border migration due to climate change.[62]

Growing Resource Demands

Global population growth combined with higher standard of living, means that the global demand for resources, including food, water and energy, will increase by 2030.[63] As a result, resource scarcity may be a more common problem, albeit typically on a regional rather scale rather than a global one. Most vulnerable to resource scarcity will be fragile states in Africa and the Middle East (who will face shortages in such things as water and food), along with emerging economies such as China and India who will both have an expanding consumer class. For example, demand for cars in China and India is expected to double to 1.7 billion by 2030.[64]

The NIC *Global Trends 2030* report forecasts that the demand for food will rise by 50% percent by 2030.[65] This will put further pressure on net importers of food to strengthen their food supply security

---

[62]"Resources: Trends and Future Challenges for States and Regions—Towards 2030," Conference report, Wilton Park, January 2013.

[63]However, if population growth (as is expected) flattens out by around 2030, this could cause resource demand to stabilize.

[64]"Reverse the Curse: Maximizing the Potential for Resource-Driven Economies" (McKinsey Global Institute, 2013), p.3.

[65]NIC, op. cit.

through mechanisms such as stronger regulation.[66] This will put an additional need for international cooperation to manage food price and volume shocks and to ensure a steady supply of food. Meanwhile, global demand for water will double by 2035, according to the International Energy Agency (IEA).[67] Estimates by the OECD suggest that nearly half of the world's population will live in areas with high water stress by 2030, including northern Africa, the Middle East, Central and Southern Asia, and northern China.[68] Rapid urbanization, higher standards of living, and climate change may further exacerbate this trend,[69] also posing a serious threat to food supply and food security. The interaction between state fragility and conflict will be especially pronounced in sub-Saharan Africa, where a combination of growing income inequality and a massive increase in urbanization risks paving way for increased social vulnerabilities in coming decades. Such vulnerabilities can give rise to a negative cycle by accentuating state fragility. Efforts to strengthen water security through, for example, better multi-national governance arrangements to address common water resources will therefore become s more pertinent issue for the international community to address.

Similarly, demand for energy will be 35% higher in 2030 compared to 2005;[70] in non-OECD countries rapid economic growth is expected to increase the demand to about 65%. In the BRICS the equivalent number might even be 72%, according to the OECD.[71] Rapid urbanization in many developing nations means that demand for consumption will significantly increase, requiring considerable new investments over the coming decade.[72] Energy demand, for example, is expected to rise by 45% in the developing world over the next two

---

[66]"Future State 2030: The Global Megatrends Shaping Governments" (KPMG International & Motwat Centre, Toronto), p.8.

[67]"Water Demand for Energy to Double by 2025," *National Geographic News*, January 30, 2013.

[68]According to the OECD, the share of the population living under water stress in the BRIC countries will increase from 63% to 80% by 2030, unless better water resource management is introduced.

[69]See "The Security of Cities: Economy and Conflict on an Urbanizing Planet" (Stimson Center, Washington, DC, 2013), pp.31-37.

[70]"World Energy Outlook 2012: Executive Summary" (International Energy Agency, Paris, 2012).

[71]"OECD Environmental Outlook on 2030" (OECD, Paris, 2008), p.6.

[72]According to the McKinsey Global Institute, $11-17 billion will need to be invested in oil and gas and minerals extraction by 2030 to ensure supply remains on par with the souring global demand. See "Reverse the Curse," op. cit., p.4.

decades. While urban areas today comprise about two thirds of global energy consumption, their share will significantly increase (73%) by 2030. The lion's share of this growing energy demand will come from the Asia-Pacific region,[73] making it a major future energy importer. In 2030, the Asia-Pacific region is expected to import some 90% of Middle Eastern oil. China may also increasingly turn elsewhere, such as West Africa, South America and the Arctic for additional energy resources. A potentially important development that may partially help offset the growing gap between global energy demand and supply is the ongoing shale gas revolution. Although several uncertainties remain (including still evolving, regulatory barriers and inadequate infrastructure), the potential for North America to become a net exporter of natural gas to the Asia-Pacific markets could have profound geopolitical and economic effects not the least on global energy prices. But as the technology used for shale gas extraction develops and becomes more affordable, it is feasible that shale gas production will also take place elsewhere in the world, such as South America, which also holds large shale gas deposits.

Finally, it is predicted that the global demand for minerals, metals and biomass will increase by more than 55% by 2030. Another effect of the increased demand for global energy might be that the energy market itself becomes more volatile and unpredictable. Since much of the new demand will come from the evolving global middle class in cities located in emerging and developing countries, efforts to design "sustainable cities" to address ecological challenges will become important. It is clear that cities, in order to have sustainable growth, "must be designed and built in ways that preserve and enhance the virtues of urban life while minimizing the use of land, water, energy, and other resources."[74] A major caveat, however, is technology, which has the ability to improve efficiencies and productivity. For example, the development of agricultural technology such as geonomics, nanotechnology and precision agriculture may increase crop yields while also reducing risks and mitigating the challenges of climate change.[75]

---

[73]"Energy Outlook for Asia and the Pacific" (Asian Development Bank, Manila, 2013).

[74]See "The Security of Cities—Ecology and Conflict on an Urbanizing Planet" (Atlantic Council and Stimson Center, Washington, DC, 2013).

[75]"Resources: Trends and Future Challenges for States and Regions," Conference report, WP1218, Wilton Park, January 2013.

Possibility for Resource Strife and Tension

There is a risk, albeit a fairly small one, that we will see more resource strife in coming decades. Even though historical trends indicate that the number of inter and intrastate conflicts have been in decline since the early 1990s,[76] the combination of demographic trends and resource scarcity suggest that such conflicts may multiply in the future. Growing populations combined with the impact of climate change and environmental degradation also increase the risk for natural disasters which may give rise to massive refugee flows and climate migration which could pose both political and security challenges. Although hard to predict, the International Organization for Migration (IOM) has warned that the number of permanently displaced climate migrants may exceed 200 million by 2050. In particular, humanitarian emergencies triggered by water and food scarcity may combine with failing state situations to generate major humanitarian crises. While the U.S. Intelligence Community Assessment does not view wars over water-related issues as a major risk over the next decade, tensions over shared water resources is likely to grow as access to water becomes more scarce. Challenges associated with water scarcity will likely increase the risk for general instability as well as exacerbate the risk for state failure. The lack of water may also seriously impede food production and economic well-being, particularly in countries in the MENA region and South Asia.[77] Major cities, especially in the developing world, will be key to addressing some of these challenges. Shortage of energy and food and other key resources is known to give rise to social tension[78] and, in some cases, even riots—as was the case during the so-called "world food price crisis" in 2007-2008 in a number of countries in Africa, Central Asia, Asia and Latin America.[79]

Another challenge stems from the potential of rising resource nationalism. The uneven distribution of natural resource deposits in the world means that major resource-producing nations may increasingly opt to alter both market prices and the supply chain reliability

---

[76]See Uppsala Conflict Data Program, available at: http://www.pcr.uu.se/research/UCDP/.

[77]See "Global Water Security," Intelligence Community Assessment, ICA-2012-08, February 2, 2012.

[78]Marc, F. Bellemare, "Rising Food Prices, Food Price Volatility, and Social Unrest." APSA 2012 Annual Meeting Paper, August 3, 2013.

[79]"The Global Food Crisis," chapter in "The Global Social Crisis: Report on the World Social Situation 2011" (United Nations, New York, 2011).

through the use of cartels and export controls. One example of this latter is China's attempts to limit its export of rare earth minerals. Here, the trend towards less privatization and more state-owned enterprises in the extraction sector in many countries gives governments" added capacity to adopt interventionist policies, with detrimental impact on the global trading system as a result.

Challenges But Also Opportunities in the Arctic[80]

The Arctic illustrates the potential challenges but also opportunities brought by climate change and the interaction with geopolitics and resources. As Arctic sea ice continues to melt, the region's waters and hydrocarbon resources will become far more accessible for exploitation and transportation. The United States Geological Survey (USGS) provides the most trustworthy, although still fairly speculative, assessment about Arctic hydrocarbon resources, estimating that the region holds "about 30% of the world's undiscovered gas and 13% of the world's undiscovered oil […], mostly offshore under less than 500 meters of water".[81] Additionally, the Arctic—in particular Greenland but also other regions—holds other mineral resources, e.g. iron ore, copper, zinc or rare earths. Transarctic shipping routes offer both economic and strategic advantages due to shorter distances between Asia, Europe, and North America, a decrease in days at sea and subsequent cost savings in fuel. But both a full-scale exploitation of potentially valuable Arctic hydrocarbon resources as well as the creation of regular transarctic transport lines are still highly speculative due to a number of uncertain variables. Due to several ecological drivers, e.g. the natural climate variability in the Arctic and human-induced impact, reliable predictions on a seasonally ice-free state of Arctic waters will continue to be difficult. Additionally, future economic development in the area will not only depend on favorable regional climatic conditions but also on global economic and geopolitical developments and regional technological innovations and investments.[82] The Arctic area is already today the scene of a flurry of

---

[80]This draws on *The Maritime Dimension of CSDP: Geostrategic Maritime Challenges and their Implications for the European Union*, report for the European Parliament, 2013.

[81]Gautier, et al., "Assessment of Undiscovered Oil and Gas in the Arctic," *Science*, 2009, p. 1175.

[82]For example, oil and gas production potential in other regions, including the price variability of these resources, the likely global exploitation of shale gas and other gas hydrates, the increasing role of renewable energy, lasting shifts in the global trade dynamics and world trade

economic activities, including shipping of raw materials, tourism, and fishing, and the scale is increasing rapidly. But challenges are already evident. These challenges are related to areas such as environmental protection (there is no efficient method for cleaning up oil spills in icy waters), safety (there is very little capacity to assist a cruise ship which has hit an iceberg), or the sustainability of fish stocks. Moreover, Arctic states explicitly emphasize climate change and its consequences for the region's environment, yet often in combination with the benefits of economic development. The highly sensitive Arctic environment and its variety of ecosystems could be significantly damaged by pollution from outside and inside the Arctic, e.g. black carbon, oil spills or nuclear waste.

Trend 5: Global Awakening—
Empowerment of Individuals and Social Vulnerabilities

A combination of several factors, including advances in communication technology, reduction in poverty and middle class growth, will continue to empower individuals over the coming decade. The "global political awakening" of repressed or marginalized peoples in Central and Eastern Europe and—more recently—in the Arab world is a force to be reckoned with for sure in the decades to come.[83]

Rise of the Global Middle Class

Overall, several trends point towards rising individual empowerment across the globe. The emergence of a "global middle class" with better access to education and knowledge, healthcare and access to information and communication are especially salient developments in this regard. This group of individuals will increasingly be found across all continents and will be more influential by 2030. Still, it will remain heavily dependent on continued economic growth in developing and emerging countries. This group of people—defined by the OECD as having a purchasing power between $10-100 per capita per day—is projected to have grown by an astonishing 172% by 2030, at which

---

patterns, the role of the marine insurance industry, logistical and infrastructural developments along the new shipping routes or improvements on new Arctic marine technologies.

[83]Zbigniew Brzezinski, *Strategic Vision: America and the Crisis of Global Power* (Basic Books, 2012).

point this category will constitute roughly half of the world's population. As a result of this growth, overall economic distribution in the world becomes more even. Each of the BRIC countries (i.e. Brazil, Russia, India and China) is expected to have influential middle classes by 2025. The rise of a global middle class, and the advances in health and education that it brings, may also have positive effects on improving gender equality in some countries. The emerging middle class can also lead to more political stability through increasing demand for accountability and good governance in certain countries.

That said, there is also a risk that the gap between the emerging middle class and those left behind will intensify, something that if left unaddressed could trigger societal tensions in some cases. Although absolute poverty is expected to diminish globally, extreme poverty and inequalities will still prevail in some regions in 2030, particularly in low-income countries in Sub-Saharan Africa and in South-East Asia.[84] And even though extreme poverty may diminish overall, nutrition and health poverty will remain a widespread problem in some places.[85] While the bulk of poverty reduction over the past two decades will be accounted for by China, other rising middle-income level countries also hold potential to make sustained progress on reducing poverty.

Moreover, technological advancements are enabling individuals in emerging and developing nations in a variety of ways. While the proliferation of mobile phones and access to the internet generally allows individual citizens and groups to better communicate, the rise in social media also means that social uprisings are aided by better ability to organize protests, shaping different narratives, and putting pressures on policymakers both at home and abroad. Growing populations in combination with massive unemployment levels can also be a destabilizing factor in societies.

Emergence of a "Global Community"

The spread of information and the rise of a global middle class promote (at least in theory) the emergence of a "global community" in

---

[84]In OECD countries, the Gini coefficient measuring the hap between the richest and the poorest has risen by more than 10 percent over the past two decades. In emerging countries such as China and India, the inequalities are widening even faster.

[85]"Developing Co-Operation Report" (OECD, Paris, 2013), p.13.

which ideas and values are exchanged. Particularly values such as human rights, democracy and environmental stewardship are being "universalized" in terms of public opinion support. Data from the Pew Research Center and World Values Survey suggests that growing prosperity in the world tends to foment greater trust among individuals towards democratic institutions and civil liberties—even though this process is rarely linear. In particular, the role of the rising "global middle class" is expected to be a key driver for improving governance and in promoting greater transparency and accountability. At the same time, failures to deliver democratic reforms in many developing states may also cause a growing "governance gap" to occur between citizens' expectations and governments' ability to deliver solutions.

...But Populism and Extremism Will Remain Viable Factors

While the increased demand from civil society for political participation is obviously a positive development, it also risks giving rise to new forms of radical populism. In particular, nationalist populism will be a force to be reckoned with in authoritarian regimes facing rising domestic opposition. While individual empowerment leading to enhanced political awareness can give rise to peaceful democratic transitions, such processes can tend to be turbulent—as seen recently during the Arab Spring. Social media and other technologies that improve communication and organization also aid these types of movements. Moreover, the lure of various forms of radical populism and nationalism has the potential to not only undermine traditional political institutions, but also to "cause societal fragmentation and even conflict."[86] Fragmentation stemming from retrenchment into religious, ethnic, cultural and nationalistic lines is a real possibility in many countries. As the ESPAS report aptly concludes, "wars fuelled by nationalism and extremist identity politics, and the associated dangers of mass murder and genocide, will be the core security challenge of the coming decades."[87]

Of course, lack of societal cohesion is not just a problem in the developing world. Across countries in the "West" we are also witnessing the rise of populist political movements challenging the traditional

---

[86]EUISS op. cit. 2012, p. 14.
[87]Ibid. p. 17.

political elites. Whether the Tea Party movement in the United States or anti-immigration far-right parties in Europe, these types of forces may well become a permanent fixture in the political systems in the West. Europe is experiencing a deep structural crisis that is far more serious than just the eurozone crisis, and is likely to continue to constitute a major political challenge over years to come. Rising euroskepticism and growing populism across the continent have accentuated gaps between European elites and European citizens, challenging the very notion of European integration. This makes achieving cohesion and "solidarity" within the EU all the more difficult. As we look towards 2030, it is not impossible to expect a growing north-south divide and growing domestic tensions (including rising nationalism) within many EU states. Another source of potential societal strains in the developed world is the increased pressure put on pension systems and health care expenditures due to aging populations.

Trend 6: Extreme World—
Climate Change and Environmental Degradation

The Impact of Climate Change

Climate change is increasingly viewed as one of the defining characteristics of the 21st century. While there is no scientific consensus on the exact the scope and scale of climate change, the scientific community shares an overwhelming consensus on the presence of some form of climate change. While climate change is not a new trend but one that has been observed for decades, current research suggests that climate change is increasing in intensity. Case in point: the past three decades where the warmest since modern climate observations started in 1850. This may well have to do with a combination of both human activity and naturally occurring phenomena.

Different climate models show different scenarios for 2030. The International Energy Agency (IEA) estimates that the globe will face a long-term global temperature rise of 3.5°C. Among the International Panel on Climate Change, the effects of climate change includes the melting of snow and ice, rising sea levels, and higher concentrations of greenhouse gases in the atmosphere. If nothing is done, the OECD predicts that greenhouse gases will grow by 37% by 2030 compared to current levels.[88] As a result, in 2030 we may see increased risk for extreme temperatures, diminishing water supply as melting glaciers; increased drought, floods and storms negatively impacting agricultural crop yields; damaging of ecosystems and biodiversity; increased climate migration and risk for conflicts. While some parts of the world such as Africa will but hit harder by climate change, other parts such as Northern Europe will see less extreme effects. Coastal areas will also be affected by rising sea levels and increased risks for floods.

More "Extreme Weather"

As a result of climate change, extreme weather will be more common by 2030, affecting far more people than ever before. When it comes to natural disasters, for instance, we have already seen a growing trend towards more such events in recent decades. This trend is predicted to continue to grow in both scope and scale as we look towards 2030.[89] In accounting for this trend, we must take into account the effects of global climate change and environmental degradation as well as increased population growth and rapid urbanization. Moreover, weak and fragile states, lacking adequate emergency response capacities, infrastructure and health services, are particularly vulnerable to severe natural disasters—with the ones located in the global South predicted to be hurt the most on average. As a result of increased risks for extreme weather and natural disasters linked to climate change, will also contribute to poverty in some developing nations.[90] In particular, food and biofuel production will be affected considerably by these changes. When occurring in weak states, disasters could also easily spill over national boundaries into affecting societal security elsewhere in the world in the forms of massive refugee flows, the spread of infectious diseases, or environmental collapse.[91] In

---

[88]"OECD Environmental Outlook to 2030" (OECD, Paris, 2008), p.4.

[89]EM-DAT, a database maintained by the Centre for Research on the Epidemiology of Disasters, has recorded that the number of natural disasters has risen from 240 disasters in 1988 to 335 in 2009, with an average of 392 during the period 2000-2008 (Vos et al., 2010).

[90]See Andrew Shepard, et al., "The Geography of Poverty, Disasters and Climate Extremes in 2030" (Overseas Development Institute, London, 2013).

[91]Of course, developed states are not immune to severe disasters (e.g. Hurricane Katrina, and recently the tsunami in Japan). Moreover, spillover effects could also occur when a disaster hits a developed country (e.g. the 9/11 attacks also had worldwide economic effects).

poorer states, climate change could also encourage rural-to-urban migration, causing cities to become destinations for climate refugees.[92]

The costs of disasters are also rising. While the full financial costs of climate change are obviously hard to calculate, one estimate suggests that they will amount to $2-4 trillion by 2030.[93] Compounding these trends are the need for disaster preparedness and risk reduction efforts and measures to strengthen resilience—areas that in addition to disaster response will likely be top priorities in the international development and humanitarian communities in coming decades.

Concluding Discussion:
What Relevance for Euro-Atlantic Societal Security?

For the sake of our discussion, global trends, while certainly interesting in and by themselves, are especially relevant given their potential implications for societal security in the Euro-Atlantic area. Protecting the security of societies" critical functions has become a growing policy objective on both sides of the Atlantic, especially following the 9/11 attacks in 2001. Homeland security—or societal security as it is sometimes called—typically refers to a diverse set of policy objectives intended to safeguard territory, citizens and critical societal functions from malicious attacks or man-made and natural disasters. The regional threat perspective has evolved over time. In the immediate aftermath of 9/11 most Western governments understandably placed a strong emphasis on counter-terrorism. While terrorism remains a formidable threat today, other threats to societal security have also received more strategic attention as governments have shifted towards an all-hazards approach. As governments on both sides of the Atlantic prepares to deal with future risks and threats to societal security, understanding the impact of global trends is essential.

Contrasting our discussion about global trends above with the findings of some key government strategic reports makes for an interesting comparison. It allows us to discern whether EU and U.S. authorities are on top of the societal security threats they are likely to face in the

---

[92]See, "The Security of Cities," op. cit., p.39.
[93]"Climate Change Scenarios—Implications for Strategic Asset Allocation," Issue Brief (International Finance Corporation, Washington, DC, 2011).

future. According to the most recent edition of the U.S. Homeland Security Quadrennial Review,[94] the top strategic priorities for homeland security are: security against and the evolving terrorism threat, safeguarding and securing cyberspace, countering biological threats and hazards, preventing nuclear terrorism, managing flows of people and goods, regulating immigration, and strengthening national preparedness and resilience. Although this list only pertains to the United States, a cursory overview reveals that most of these priorities are similar in an EU context as well. Below we explore in more detail how some of the key global trends discussed above may impact some key societal security threats and vulnerabilities in the Euro-Atlantic region in 2030.

Terrorism

In its report, DHS notes that the terrorism threat is evolving in nature, shifting both in terms of geography and tactics. As we look towards 2030, several of the global trends identified above should be expected to have some important effects on the future of terrorism. One such trend is population growth and urbanization, which—particularly when combined with bad governance, economic malaise and high unemployment levels—could lead to more disenfranchised youth becoming radicalized. Another related factor that must also be taken into account is state fragility. Breakdowns of societies and eruptions of civil war are likely to enable extreme militants to go about their business. We have recently seen this phenomenon in places such as Somalia and Iraq. Technology trends can further add to these developments, providing more opportunities for radical groups and ideologies to effectively spread their messages across the world, including in the West. An additional factor is the proliferation of technology and the accompanying "democratization" of warfare. By gaining better access to sophisticated weapons and technology, non-state groups" ability to inflict damage on state targets will doubtlessly expand. Moreover, while detection technology improves, so does violent extremists" ability to bypass them. A particularly worrying prospect is the growth in biotechnology. As this type of technology becomes more readily available, the risk for terrorists" using biological agents also increases.

---

[94]The 2014 Homeland Security Quadrennial Review (Department of Homeland Security, Washington, DC, June 18, 2014).

Cyberspace

The trend towards deeper and more interconnected global digital information and communications infrastructure has considerable implications for societal security. Already today much of modern societies' communication, economies, energy grids and government services depend heavily on information technology. While they bring significant benefits to our societies, they also come with some considerable risks. Major breakdowns or malicious attacks against these critical infrastructures can have catastrophic effects. Moreover, critical infrastructure is increasingly seeing a "cyber-physical convergence" resulting in growing risks across several sectors—ranging from energy to transportation to healthcare. Major disruptions in critical infrastructure thus also runs the risk of giving rise to cascading effects, with serious consequences for societal security as a result.

Furthermore, the global flows of data could become just as important—or in some cases even more important—than physical flows of goods in the future. This is partially due to the emerging revolution of 3D printing. The growing dependence on data flows for ordinary citizens, companies and governments means that societal security may be at growing risk from cybercrime. Developments of new electric payment systems can make illicit trafficking and smuggling easier while investigation and interdiction also becomes more challenging. That said, cyberspace also bring many benefits to societal security. As the Homeland Security Quadrennial Review concludes, "with appropriate protections for individual privacy and civil rights and civil liberties, technology can enhance situational awareness, improve investigative capabilities, and support operational integration."[95]

Natural disasters

As the Homeland Security Quadrennial Review makes clear, climate change will present a "major area of homeland security risk." Already, disasters such as storms, earthquakes, droughts, and floods have affected Europe and North America with unprecedented force. These kinds of disasters are poised to become more common and more severe in the future. The risks they pose are exacerbated by the

---

[95]Ibid. p. 21.

vulnerability of aging infrastructure and rising population density in high risks areas. Moreover, when major natural disasters do take place they have the potential to cause not only severe casualties and economic loss, but also to overwhelm the capacities of a series of critical infrastructure in society. Another aspect of climate change that DHS calls attention to concerns the kinds of "threat multipliers" these events can trigger. By aggravating stresses such as poverty, environmental degradation and social tensions, natural disasters can serve to enable terrorist activity, violence and organized crime. Disasters could also give rise to more frequent migration flows, particularly in vulnerable areas of the southern hemisphere. While DHS points to the particular risks of refugee flows from Central America to the United States, very similar concerns would apply on areas in Europe's vicinity as well. Additionally, climate change would have particular impact on the Arctic. Though melting sea ice can give rise to positive developments in terms of increased resource extraction, shipping and tourism in the Arctic, it could also lead to new routes for illicit trade and illegal resource extraction well as new environmental disasters.

Border Management

Growing flows of people and goods around the world will have profound effects on border security, both in the United States and in Europe. The reliance on global supply chains and travel means that disruptions with potential severe impact for our economies will become a growing risk. The Euro-Atlantic area will also face a growing risk stemming from the increased opportunities for illicit smuggling of goods and humans—particularly organized transnational criminal smuggling. Consequently, it is necessary that Western states invest more in screening and detection capabilities and capacities to meet these future demands. The DHS report also points to the risk for new pandemics as a result of population growth, urbanization and increased levels of global trade and traveling. Another contributing factor is the risk for growing antibacterial resistance. As a result of the growing risks and vulnerabilities associated with disasters, the cost for preparing for, responding to and recovering from such events is anticipated to surge.

Part II

Perspectives on
Global Flow Security 2030

Chapter 3

Flow Security in the Digital Age

Mika Aaltola

> *Everything flows and nothing stays.*
> —Heraclitus

Global and regional orders are increasingly premised on and shaped by global flows. Many of these flows have a hub-and-spoke mobility dynamic. Namely, states distinguish themselves with regard to the mobility of people, goods, and services based on their ability to act as central hubs or relay nodes for such defining global flows as trade, resources, and finance. This means that the local intensity and regularity of such flows is increasingly a crucial indicator of a state's economic viability and its political influence. Securing steady access to such global flows poses a different set of domestic and foreign policy challenges to states in general, and especially to smaller states, than the challenges posed by the traditional Westphalian model, which has been rooted in territorial notions of international order. States are increasingly caught in a cross-current between these two co-existing realities, as the dynamic, flow-centric model emerges and the older territorial state-centric model recedes. Global non-state actors and circulation of activities are challenging traditional state-based geopolitics, rendering old policy solutions—e.g. national self-reliance and related national strategies—increasingly ineffective.

Despite the dynamism of these global forces, nation-based identities will likely continue to provide central and identifying organizing concepts. The central question has to do with finding a way for a country to develop the appropriate conditions to identify and establish access-points to key global flows. How can decision-makers create local conditions that facilitate access for their country to global value chains and the global marketplace of ideas? The policy challenge for states is to make the country fruitful as a riverbed for global flows. How can a state become a "flow-facilitator"? What actors and whose standards are going to have secure or commanding positions in the global maritime, air, and space realms, each of which is increasingly wired into the cyber commons?

For smaller states, the central question is how to influence and adapt to these power conditions. Flows can also have negative influences, of course, and in this respect, decision-makers are also challenged to find ways to ameliorate the impact of the negative entrepreneurship associated with illicit shadow flows.

Emerging Geosecurity, Resilience, and Black Hubs

Political world maps usually point out two types of human artifacts: borders encircling states and land-based logistics networks, i.e. roads, bridges and railways. Much of modern geostrategy has so far been fixed on borders and territories. However, this prevalent imagery can be contrasted with an alternative vision that has historic roots and is again becoming more relevant. This alternative can be exemplified by imperial Rome's territorial imagination.[1] The limits of the empire were not precise in the contemporary sense that modern-day states find it important to demarcate and secure clear borders. To an important degree, Rome's reach was limited by its main roads and various access routes. Most of its legions were based in such a way as to secure and keep open these main arteries of the empire. It may be argued that the increasing transformation of the contemporary world order towards a system of circulatory flows is predisposed to rediscover this old Roman meaning of security.

Today and in the foreseeable future, there is a growing focus on securing the sites, spaces, technologies, and practices of flows.[2] The aim of this "flow security" is to control access to and from the main global flows that connect remote extremities to regional centers or spokes on the one hand, and those regional spokes with the main global hubs on the other hand. Securing access to and ensuring the openness of such flow changes the meaning of security. Traditionally, spatial or territorial entities—e.g. states—were secured. Now, these temporal flow-like processes need to be secured. The regularity of a

---

[1]Andrew Lintott, "What Was the 'Imperium Romanum?'" *Greece and Rome*, 28(1), 1981, p. 65.
[2]E. g., Peter Adey, "Secured and Sorted Mobilities: Examples from the Airport," *Surveillance and Society*, 1(1), 2004, pp. 500-519.

flow's steady rhythm and the regularity of its pulse indicate a high level of security.

This era of global flows may been seen as a golden age of interdependence, but it also poses clear challenges and can cause significant anxieties. The main global arteries guarantee wide access to the most remote regional and global peripheries. This access is often seen as bringing with it many benefits, such as links to production sites, financial centers, knowledge hubs, and security producers. Participation in these flow activities also catalyzes the diffusion of norms, practices, and standards. This fosters learning, shapes governance, and influences how "flow practices"—e.g. interoperabilities, norms, and standards—develop in the future.

On the other hand, growing concerns about cyber-crime, terrorism and human trafficking indicate that there is a much darker side to this emerging age of flows. For instance, unsanctioned or unsecured access to global flows via cybercrime can be a huge vulnerability for a state or a region. Decision-makers are increasingly preoccupied with preventing or mitigating possible disruptions, breakdowns and contagions. These challenges, in turn, are generating more innovative notions of resilience.

Global cyber flows—much like rivers—mold the terrain in which they occur, in terms of both human and physical landscape. They create opportunities for both legitimate and illegitimate activity, and their interaction shapes physical political economies, for instance regional/global flow-hubs such as Silicon Valley.

In addition, cyber flows, much like other flows, are characterized by constant flux. They create confluences of patterns, interact with and disrupt old flow systems, and can facilitate the bypassing of existing interlinkages. In the words of Arjun Appadurai, global flows are disjunctive and chaotic because they "follow increasingly nonisomorphic paths" and the "sheer speed, scale, and volume of […] flows are now so great that the disjunctures have become central to the politics of global culture." In this regard, the term "disjunctive" refers to flows being able to dis-connect or reorient localities from their traditional connections on a territory-oriented geographical map, and to connect or re-connect such localities with other centers that may be more relevant to a region's vitality than localities that may be physically closer.

Figure 1. Global Remoteness Map

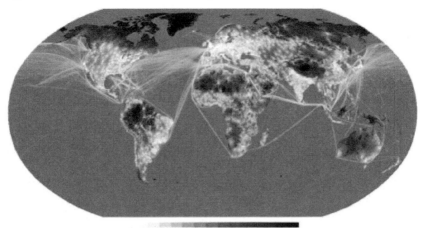

Source: Joint Research Centre of the European Commission

Cyber-enabled social networking, for instance, is reconfiguring the global space. Facebook's world map of its fabric of "friends" show how the social network is unevenly distributed across the globe. Taking the disjunctive effect fully in account, a Facebook-centric map illustrates the geography-shaping power of flows, pinpointing Palo Alto California as the global center of gravity in terms of "friendship" flows. Other places are arranged according to their closeness in terms of "friends."

Akin to this process of "hubbing," other forms of cyber flows recontextualize some hub-sites as parts of the flow(s) rather than as parts of their geographical contexts. They start to live as much or more from the flow than from their physical location. The disjunctive effects of the emerging new maps are plentiful. In Figure 1's global remoteness map, it is possible to see how the speed of physical access—in hours and days—can rearrange the relevance of the global political map to a major city of 50,000 inhabitants or more.

Although the disjunctive effect refers to the power of flows to reshape geopolitics and geoeconomics, it should be noted that—as in the above maps—it is usually directed towards the existing global distribution of power and hierarchies. The map of cyber flows, for instance, highlights existing power hubs in the United States and in western Europe, rather than any radical redistribution of power.

One dramatic effect of such flows, however, has to do with their ability to contest unitary national identities. If publics and elites in a particular region understand that the vibrancy, prosperity and security of their region may be more related to the vibrancy, prosperity and security of other regions beyond their current national borders, as compared to regions within their own country, new political and economic dynamics may emerge.

Another dramatic effect of such flows has to do with their ability to pinpoint emerging types of global exposure and vulnerability. The unwanted effects of flows are clear. Illicit flows of criminal activity disrupt and alter communities. Legitimate global flows may suffer from various interruptions and shocks wherever they occur. Integrated logistics solutions involving sea, air, space, and cyber modalities are in a constant reactive mode, experiencing different types of "shocks."

As digital modality comes to affect most aspects of life, cyber flows are essential for the proper functioning of the overall system of flows that transports goods, people, and information across the globe. The security of the underlying flow system—i.e. flow security[3]—is dependent on the general hub-and-spoke network structure. Although highly directed, such currents can be susceptible to "eddies" that create overflows, by-flows, and side-whirls that can interfere with or disrupt the intended flow of the mainstream. We have all experienced these as unexpected delays, interruptions or cancellations. These disruptions distract and frustrate. They can cost time, energy and money. They take us offline, make us wait, or cause us to try alternative routes. The nature and frequency of such flow problems can highlight the relative power of a particular region, entity, group or individual to connect; their relative remoteness from the main global hubs; and thus their relative resilience. Such disruptions may be measured in milliseconds, but can have outsized social, economic and geopolitical consequences; they have the potential to alter the global political map.

---

[3]E.g., "Without necessarily making territorial security less important, I would argue that 'flow security' is the true challenge for the decades to come." Swedish Foreign Minister Carl Bildt in Mexico City, February 8, 2010; http://www.sweden.gov.se/sb/d/7417/a/139273.

Figure 2. Global Cocaine Flows

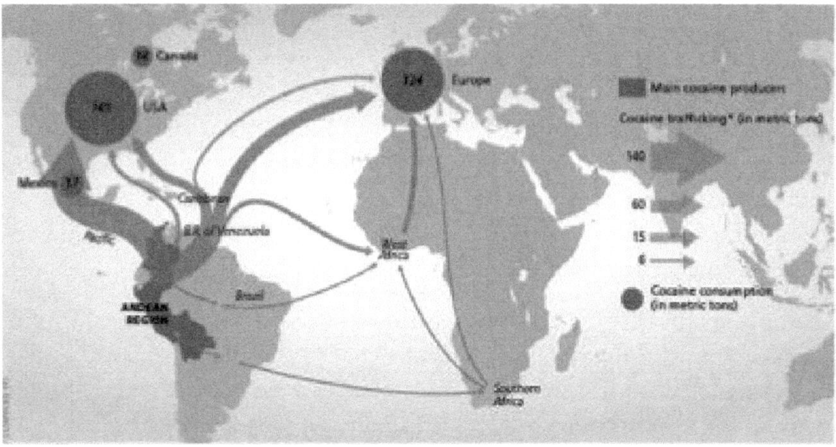

Source: UNODC World Drug Report 2010.

Illegal shadow flows—e.g. of drug smuggling, arms trade, money laundering, human trafficking, and cybercrime—are gaining in importance and can be powerful in shaping local contours of power. For instance, it used to be that criminal organizations had a parasitic relationship with the local polity in which they were based. Today, however, such criminal activity may create symbiotic relationships with regional, national or international reach, and perhaps lower the incentive or ability of local authorities to completely paralyze or kill it off. Central American drug flows are illustrative of this dynamic.

The above map shows the flow of cocaine from production sites in Latin America to markets mainly in the United States, but also in Europe. The disjunctive effect is intense. It shows how networked organizations can live off the flow itself instead of local polities. This gives them immense economic and political power compared to those state and local polities that exist along the flow. These phenomena are generating destructive and crisis-inducing effects in many parts of the world; new approaches are needed to address them.

The speed and scale of flows are important factors determining their overall impact. They are influenced especially by business practices. For example, the cyber-dependent, just-in-time business model relies on regular and planned access to materials and products. Factories need not spend resources on storage since they can count on the logistic flows that deliver in pre-calculated ways. This means that factories are increasingly dependent on the regular flows of materials and resources. The logistics of the flows gain importance at the expense of local resilience and autonomy. Similar to the dependency on the just-in-time business model, actors are increasingly reliant on the existence of cyber flows that allow instantaneous access. From inventory systems and sales sites to information transfers, peoples' lives are intertwined with the regularity of global digital data flows. The scope of cyber space assets—linked to data networks—such as satellites and launching systems even enables navigation by both ships and aircraft. The flows of materials and goods reshape the map by allowing new models of arranging everyday life irrespective of distance.[4] Moreover, the rhythms and tempos of these flows are becoming the main dynamos of life for people who are most directly affected by such flows. The intensification—the pulse—of inter-local processes is becoming regularized. This regular humming of global flows is needed to support contemporary lifestyles, as can be seen in modern consumer societies. Haphazardness or disruptions can be indicative of lesser access or more peripheral location of a person or community in the emerging global hierarchy of power. The degree of regularization—of the flows in and out, and the absence of counter-flows, disruptions, and turbulences—is a key measure of the power to adapt to and harness successfully such global processes.

The system of flows requires secured access points. Harbors, airports, fiber optic cables, cloud servers and satellite launching capabilities are examples of such access points. The range of these access points facilities integration into the flows. Sustained capacity to tap into the flow requires interoperable technologies—e.g. airports able to handle different types of planes and computer systems able to work with extensive cross-border passenger information. Interoperability poses demands also to education systems, as people have to know the standards by which world-class flows take place. The standards created elsewhere have to be understood and applied. In some cases, new standards can be either developed or innovated. However, this norm entrepreneurship is more likely to happen near the global knowledge

---

[4]David Held et al., *Global Transformations: Politics, Economics and Culture* (Stanford, CA: Stanford University Press, 1999). p. 15.

production hubs that have research and development as well as academic research clusters.

The entanglement between localities at distance and the whole system is remaking the geopolitical map. The global map of flows shows considerable unevenness; access to flows is distributed unequally. Access points are clustered around places where there is major economic activity: "The world has long been—and still is—a space where economic and political relations are very uneven; it is filled with lumps, places where power coalesces surrounded by those where it does not, places where social relations become dense amid others that are diffuse. Structures and networks penetrate certain places and do certain things with great intensity, but their effects tail off elsewhere."[5]

The major global harbors, airport hubs, and digital companies, and their associated cloud servers, tend to be located near each other. These regions also have production facilities, financial centers, major universities, and security producers such as effective state armies or private security providers. These regions allow life to be insured by companies that can reduce the risk of adverse events. They also have internet security actors who can facilitate the maintenance of steady cyber connections.

The standardization, interoperability, and access points are based on integrated material technologies and know-how. These technologies, in turn, create structural pressures for new types of political arrangements. Political solidarity has tended to be shaped by the ideologies of nation-states, and after the Cold War by liberal democracy. Now political solidarities can cross state boundaries, as in the case of social media communities such as Facebook and Twitter. People can spend hours of their day online, participating in communities that cross national boundaries. The corporations that maintain these cyber connections do not exist in a political vacuum, even though their independent power to determine such things as people's privacy is widening. The judicial and regulatory frameworks within which they operate, however, are provided by states or supra- and international organizations. The power of such entities to construct and enforce

---

[5]Frederick Cooper, *Colonialism in Question: Theory, Knowledge, History* (Berkeley: University of California Press, 2005), pp. 91–92.

such frameworks, in turn, is quite differentially distributed. The states with major access hubs and standards power create rules for other. In this sense, the United States remains in a predominant position, although its ability to act as a single unitary actor is made harder by the increasingly predominant influence of actors and lobbyists who that represent these emerging dynamic global processes. For smaller states, the power of international organizations, and coalitions with more powerful states, have become increasingly vital.

The emergence of the flow world—in which a person may be more engaged with such flows than with their local surroundings—contains also dystopian characteristics. Besides the global hubs and spokes, there are "black holes" that may form a system of anti-hubs.[6] In these politically or regulatory failing or failed anti-hubs, access to mainstream flows may be minimal, while access to illicit or illegal shadow flows may be open and unregulated. These black hubs, in turn can have their own satellite system of "black spokes" that facilitate flows of drugs and human trafficking and are catalysts for instability. Spokes are composed of places where cyber security is not maintained and computer systems are vulnerable to acting as relay stations for broader attacks.

The Democratic Republic of Congo, for example, has been in a state of failure for 20 years. However, its vast mineral deposits have been flowing out of the country and ending up in such high-added value products as mobile phones. These shadow flows have supported local criminal, terror, and rebel groups and sustained high levels of corruption among state officials.

In a related way, Nigeria is an important point of origin for many cyber scams; it may be considered to be a black hub of cyber because its authorities lack the will and ability to tackle cybercrime.[7] Nigeria is often used as identifiable source of the email scams because the country has a reputation for being corrupt, which "makes the strange tales

---

[6]Michel-Rolph Trouillot, "The Anthropology of the State in the Age of Globalization: Close Encounters of the Deceptive Kind," *Current Anthoropology*, Vol 42(1), 2001, p. 129; James Ferguson, *Global Shadows: Africa in the Neoliberal World Order* (Duke University Press Books, 2006).

[7]The scams related to Nigeria come either from inside the country or from adjoining countries. Cormac Harley, "Why do Nigerian Scammers Say They are from Nigeria?" http://research.microsoft.com/pubs/167719/WhyFromNigeria.pdf.

of dodgy lawyers, sudden death and orphaned fortunes seem plausible in the first place."[8] Nigeria's perceived corruptness makes the country and its IP-addresses useful as a hub for cyber-scammers.

These examples offer simplified accounts of the "dark web." Besides scammers, there is a growing online trade in stolen identity and credit information. This trade in credit data—and in goods such as drugs and medicines—is conducted by internet crime networks that can be located anywhere on the globe. Although the servers are usually out-side of the United States and money is laundered through tax havens, the individuals or groups running them can be in or near legitimate cyber-hubs, where the necessary technical and financial know-how exists. From this perspective, the black hub-and-spoke system can hide the perpetrators, who can go to great lengths to disguise their real location, and thus creates a serious attribution problem. In addition, most shadow networks operate along the same routes and means as sanctioned systems, making it hard to separate geographically illicit networks from licit flows. Such black flows such as drugs or human trafficking can even operate in reverse, i.e. instead of transporting people and goods from peripheries to hubs, they often are in the business of moving people and products from hubs to the peripheries of world hierarchy.

The overlap among different legitimate and shadow flows can generate powerful and often contradictory gravitational forces in the localities where these flows connect. Such flows rely on a secure environment, yet may bring with them immense vulnerabilities. They can empower and disempower, create opportunities or disadvantages for particular entities, groups or individuals in a given location, and thus can be transformative for geopolitics.

Flow Security and Power

The key to understanding the political ramifications of global flows is to examine their intimate relationship with power. Flows characterize the crosscutting feature of the interconnected global domain. The rela-

---

[8]*The Economist*, "Blatancy and latency- Why internet scams seem so obvious," available at http://www.economist.com/node/21557726.

tive ability to command such flows, control their paths and practices, and find ways to adapt to them can signify power or lack of it. Arguably, the global dynamic of interconnection is increasingly the basis of modern life, irrespective of state boundaries. However, this mobile fabric is not evenly spread throughout the global sphere. Its corridors are highly differentiated and structured in ways that mirror the world order and its distribution of power. Based on material technologies and on socially shared practices of interoperability, they follow a hub and spoke pattern akin to that of international air travel.[9] However, one should not forget that the emergence of the flows does not take place in a historical or conceptual vacuum. In several ways, the developments in Western geostrategy and geopolitics have long contained scenarios where power has been seen in terms of flows and mobilities.

Power and mobility can be seen as highly interchangeable concepts in the canon of Western modernity. The most influential manifestations of the "flow and power nexus" are U.S. geostrategic imageries. For instance, the mythical notion of "frontier" provides a case of how United States has seen itself as a power on the move.[10] Power, in this sense, is moving power, i.e. power to produce, maintain, and secure continuous mobility. This "mobility as power" theme fits well what Daileda concludes under the heading "America on the move": "transportation in all its modes embodies the uniquely American ideal of Manifest Destiny".[11] Daileda continues to make a point about exceptionality of air-mobility as the new "final" frontier: "...air travel made distance a completely manageable obstacle." Nearly instantaneous cyber flows can be placed along this continuum of managing distance. Technologies for the management of crossing distance have generated

---

[9]The tight conceptual bridge between imperial governance structures and hub and spoke political architecture is often made in the research literature (e.g. Alexander Motryl, "Why empires re-emerge: imperial collapse and imperial revival in comparative perspective," *Comparative Politics*, 31 (2), 1999; Hafner-Burton et al., "Network Analysis for International Relations," *International Organization*, 63(3), 2009. For example, Nicola Phillips in *U.S. Power and the Politics of Economic Governance in the Americas* (2005, p. 3) sees a distinctly "hub and spoke" set of regionalist arrangements in the Americas that has allowed the U.S. to "capture control of the governance agenda and to ensure that the regional economic regime takes a form consistent with U.S. interest and preferences."

[10]E.g. John R. Eperjesi, *The Imperialist Imaginary: Visions of Asia and Pacific in American Culture* (Dartmouth: Dartmouth College Press, 2004), p. 59.

[11]D. A. Daileda, "America on the Move," in N. Solomon and R. Ivey, eds., *Architecture: Celebrating the Past, Designing the Future* (New York: Visual Reference Publications, 2008), p. 225.

not only highly regulated but also regular form of power and governance, and thus become tools in the process of controlling, ordering, and managing the consequences of human interaction. Moreover, such tools can be both material and ideational.

In other words, flow security and power are closely related to mobility management practices and embedded technologies. Sustained, effective governance—both national and global—derives from and is dependent on the engineering of various technologies of mobility. This governance mentality of mobile power has been developing towards a relatively de-territorial and de-centralized global system of asymmetric interdependence.[12] From this mobility-centered paradigm, scenarios of interdependence are developing beyond the static spatiality inherent in the term "network" towards conceptualizing global processes in terms of flows and circulations. Visions for evolving global structures of power are less and less static. The imagery is more dynamic and fluid, focused on flows—regular and unstable—that are becoming increasingly significant, and suggest that in such systems even the nodal points may move.[13] This imagery's fluidity and flexibility is accordingly far from the geopolitical maps of Cold War times.

Emerging flows have a logic that is hard to control by territorial entities such as states, unless those entities are prepared and able to transform themselves, at least partially, into flow-like entities. Moreover, global flows are generating their own expressive language, which is becoming increasingly central to how actors" power and security are benchmarked and evaluated. How smooth is a particular state's or region's access to the global flow-dynamic? How well are the access points secured? How resilient are they and how well is their continuity guaranteed? How they can secure a more stable hold on these often

---

[12]E.g. M. Hardt and A. Negri, *Empire* (Cambridge, MA: Harvard University Press, 2001), pp. xi-xiii, 160; J. Urry, "Aeromobilities and the Global," in Saulo Cwerner, Sven Kesselring and John Urry, eds., *Aeromobilities* (London and New York: Routledge, 2009), p. 34.

[13]Robert D. Kaplan, in "How We Would Fight China" (2005, p. 53) calls aircraft carriers "the supreme icon of American wealth and power, the aircraft carrier" and Michael Horowitz, in *The Diffusion of Military Power: Causes and Consequences for International Politics* (2010, p. 65) declares that "short of the atomic bomb, nothing signifies the power of a great nation like ... a fleet of aircraft carriers". See also Norman Friedman, *British Carrier Aviation: The Evolution of the Ships and Their Aircraft*, (London: Naval Institute Press, 1988), p. 384.

moving hubs? Are they willing and able to attract the building of further access points (harbors, airports, data cables, cloud servers, etc.)?

Flow specificities are becoming increasingly expressive. Various actors and publics are trying to make sense of their regional and global surroundings through the increasingly nuanced and sophisticated language of flow movements—e.g. regularity, resilience, disturbances, disruptions, and counter-flows. More and more, actors are exploring their wider political identities and connections in a world of flows. The answers to the question "Who am I," "you," "we" and "they" are increasingly related to the sense and feel of being part of things, people and ideas coursing through global flow systems. Citizens are sensing their global position and the health of their region or country through the ease at which they can travel, find information, do business, maintain social relationships, use the banking system, or order goods online. And as technological systems and flow practices become ever more deeply integrated into modern life support systems, tolerance of disruption is shrinking.

The tendency of individuals or communities to use flows as indicators of their relative position in the global hierarchy of power explains one focal point of the nexus between mobility and political power. The global position of a state—and actors within it—is increasingly dependent on (ir)regularities of its access points to key global flows.

Global flows themselves can also create new contexts for crisis. Problems with underwater digital cables have caused widespread disruptions in banking systems. Ongoing piracy off the coast of West Africa or in the waters of Indonesia demonstrates the potential ramifications of a flow disruption and, on the other hand, the growing importance of good resilience practices by the maritime shipping industry. Local, regional, or even global crises can be sparked by flow-related problems. From this perspective, the root causes of a particular crisis may not be local, but they can have dramatic local impact.

Besides bringing new types of "flow crises," the flows paradigm offers a new perspective to more traditional forms of crises, as the flow dimension is increasingly present in such crises. This dimension can manifest itself in a number of ways. First, there is increasing recognition that flow-related dynamics can contribute to local crisis by creating particular political economies reliant on transnational circulation of, for instance, soldiers, funds, weapons, blood resources (minerals, drugs, etc.), and refugees, and that both licit and illicit or shadow flows can and often do take place in the same flow corridors. Second, there is a growing awareness of the various ways in which a territorial political crisis may spill over to disrupt the steadiness of global flows. State failure in Somalia, for instance, manifested itself as piracy disrupting the southern maritime corridor of the global economy that runs through the Gulf of Aden, resulting in several multinational counter-piracy military efforts. The piracy problem, and the nature of the response, may be seen as possible portents of future *flow crisis management* mechanisms. Third, as access to global flows becomes increasingly imperative to states, different sanction regimes are becoming part of emerging flow politics. Sanctions on Iran, for instance, are forcing the country out of global flow dynamics and, therefore, denying it important sources of financial and political capital. Just as the "carrot" of enabling access to global flows is important, so is the "stick" of denying or disrupting access to such flows, in terms of conditioning state or group behavior.

In addition to crises in flows themselves, circulatory and flexible flows can become a constitutive feature of local violent crisis. Greater attention is being paid to the notion that global flows are often connected with local security and order. These flows, in turn, are also significant mechanisms supporting the prevailing world order and most visible articulations of power.[14] The overall mobility system is a beacon of modern, liberal, and cosmopolitan ideals of diffused power.[15] Nonetheless, in many cases such liberal, cosmopolitan spaces can be enabled by, or themselves enable, illiberal structures of security and power.[16]

---

[14]Urry, op. cit., p. 32; Adey, Peter et al., "Flying Lessons: Exploring the Social and Cultural Geographies of Global Air Travel," *Progress in Human Geography*, 31(2), 2007, p. 780.

[15]Gillian Fuller and Ross Harley, *Aviopolis: A Book About Airports* (London: Blackdog Publications, 2005); S. Kesselring, "Global Transfer Points: The Making of Airports in the Mobile Risk Society," in S.B. Cwerner, S. Kesselring and J. Urry, eds., *Aeromobilities* (London: Routledge, 2008), p. 86.

[16]E.g. Giorgio Agamben, 1998, *Homo sacer: Sovereign power and bare life.* (Stanford, CA: Stanford University Press), p. 123; Michael Dillon and Julian Reid, "Global Governance, Liberal Peace and Complex Emergency," *Alternatives*, 25(1), 2000, p. 117.

Flows as Contexts for Geopolitical Innovation and Transformation

Global critical infrastructure may be seen as dynamic contexts of cognition and ideas as well as people, goods, and information. They move physically, yet also cognitively, culturally, and politically. Knox et al., citing Castells,[17] calls them "spaces of flows" that emphasize temporal qualities such as process, speed, fluidity, improvisation, and flexibility over more static notions of space and networks.[18] On the other hand, flows are particularly susceptible to mutual resonances and dissonances. Mobility systems are perpetually in constant reactive mode of experiencing different types of disruptions. This condition has been referred to as "constant-shock syndrome:" "There is no doubt that the public has become highly sensitized to risk, both real and perceived."[19] The flows themselves are in a continual state of reflexivity, self-monitoring, and self-repair. The flow's underlying mechanisms fails here and there, even as it interacts with other currents.

The tempos and pulses of the flow are such that, besides producing a sense of sequential monotony, they can bring forth consonant contrivances within a broader temporal context of social interaction.[20] Adey highlights the endless possibilities inherent in the process of flow-related emergence: "...speed and slowness means that is difficult to know"[21] what will end up happening, what combination of events will take place. Experimentation with different positions at the flow-

---

[17]Manuel Castells, *The Information Age: Economy, Society and Culture, Vol. I: The Rise of the Network Society* (Oxford: Blackwell, 1996).

[18]Knox et al., "Rites of Passage: Organization As an Excess of Flows," *Scandinavian Journal of Management*, 2007, pp. 23, 266.

[19]Ibid., p. 266.

[20]International air traffic flows provide well-experienced examples of the constant interferences across a wide spectrum of possibilities: "The accumulation of factors—9/11, the bombings in Bali and the Philippines, the Iraq war—meant that the arrival of the "killer mystery virus [SARS]" hit a nerve that was well and truly exposed" (Thomas 2003, 30). Airlines are vulnerable to world economic (e.g. 2008 recession) and geo-political (e.g. 9/11) events as well as to pandemics (e.g. SARS), natural catastrophes (e.g. the ash cloud episode), and accidents (e.g. the crash of the plane carrying the Polish political elite). Besides these types of accented eddies, the aero-mobility dynamic mediates and reflects other more explicitly political dynamics. Some of these are quite situational/random, yet others are by now relatively well established.

[21]Peter Adey, "Airports, Mobility, and the Calculative Architecture of Affective Control," *Geoforum*, 39(2), 2008. p. 447.

hubs produces predictable yet not determined results; hubs become *avant garde* playpens of both technological and geopolitical experimentation. From the perspective of designers and users, the overall flow systems provide a very different playing field than that offered by traditional nation-states. The overall combinatorial play is constant. It is about experimenting and innovating. However, it is also about random processes such as shutdowns, disruptions, and accidents. On the whole it is about designing and gauging how the "Legos" of the mobility "playpens" can be arranged and combined and how they cannot, even if we experiment and try very hard.

Case Study: The Emergence of Millisecond Geopolitics

Although the revolution in information technologies poses major challenges to big and small states, the basics of cyber-geopolitics are becoming clearer. The United States is the central node through which most digital information flows. Major U.S. digital companies, from Amazon and Apple to Microsoft and Google, have created popular services via efficient digital routes. The likelihood of an email from London to Manchester or from Stockholm to Moscow passing through a U.S.-affiliated actor is high. This creates pressures for smaller states to collaborate in cyber surveillance matters with more capable private and public actors. At the same time, the tools that can be used by other government authorities from other states may collide with certain principles, such as privacy protection, important to those smaller states. The business interests of companies from third countries—e.g. from Russia or China—can also weigh in the calculation of different government authorities as they plan their national cyber strategies.

The geopolitical practice in cyber has been seen as replicating the existing state of affairs since the end of the Cold War: states, especially the bigger ones, are establishing their parallel structures in cyberspace. However, the cyber aspect highlights a new vision of world order based as much on the geopolitics of milliseconds as on strategy based on geographies. These two tendencies are relatively reinforcing, since the ability of communicate more instantaneously is not distributed evenly. It reflects the existing hierarchical world order that places the United States and the West at the center of the map, even as some other countries or regions are making significant gains in comparison with older geopolitical actors.

Trading in financial products needs increasingly speedy connections across global financial hubs, and is driving the development of the geopolitics of milliseconds. This practice drives global technological innovation, but it will also have local or regional effects, for instance in the Baltic Sea region, as its practices seep into broader political and security discourse.

Contrary to often-repeated slogans, the global digital information network is not instantaneous. Einstein's theory of relativity gave the universe a finite speed. The speed of light was determined to be the ceiling. 300 km per millisecond is also the maximum speed at which information flows in the global arteries of the digital realm. This limit on the transmission of information might seem trivial. Yet, every millisecond counts in the cyber commons. A few milliseconds can be as important to transactions of global exchanges in London (banking), New York (stocks) and Chicago (financial futures) as the week that could be saved for maritime shipping by opening up the Northern Sea Route. The speed of information flows is becoming increasingly imperative as a factor influencing the location and profitability of the connections to major financial systems.[22]

The complexities of the intertwined financial system are affected by underlying digital networks. For example, the Chicago-based futures exchanges influence how stock markets move in New York. Any upgrades in one place resonate across the entire global trading system. This complexity opens more room for taking advantage of almost infinitesimal differences in time and discrepancies in setting prices. The better temporally-enabled servers and situationally-aware algorithms are able to detect these anomalies, the better they can exploit them. The cyber-based financial arms race is based on these underlying factors. The practice of high-frequency trading is seen as a cause for market volatility, and was implicated at least one major incident. The so-called flash crash in May 2010 shaved about 10% off of the trade market value in matter of a few moments. Besides leading to

---

[22]In 2007, it was estimated that, for a New York major brokerage firm, one millisecond advantage translates into profits worth $100 million a year ("Wall Street's Quest to Process Data at the Speed of Light," Richard Martin, April 21, 2007. www.informationweek.com/news).

lightning-fast and sometimes significant market reactions, the practice is seen as conductive to unfair market practices. Some firms get more privileged positions in the markets because they can buy into speedier access. The risks of market manipulation grow. The feeding of wrong information can echo across the markets in highly damaging ways when the system is calibrated to react automatically, in a split second, when new information becomes available. Regulators are considering new guidelines and restrictions, yet the challenges of real-time responses are apparent.

As a general rule of thumb, one's gains from financial trading via data flows decrease the weaker one's processing power and the further one's distance from major trading hubs. The connections between Stockholm and London or Helsinki and New York do not take place through a straight path that would have been optimized for Swedish or Finnish users. Furthermore, even such optimization would not be able to eradicate the actual geographical distance between Sweden or Finland and the major financial hubs. Geography still matters to the geopolitics of milliseconds. More remote locations are in a disadvantageous position; it is hard for them to match the gravitational pull of the financial hubs on those interested in the fastest and most powerful connections. Advantages have to be gleaned from other aspects of cyber-related economies.

The logic of milliseconds is an increasingly influential driver in the building of transatlantic fiber optic cables. Transmission speeds between London—a traditional relay station of financial transactions—and New York—the most diverse financial hub—are especially vital. Having privileged access to these cables is expensive. However, any new cable that can shave off milliseconds from the average transatlantic transmission speed of about 64 milliseconds is financially viable, despite the initial investments required, which are in the hundreds of millions of euros. Lucrative trading opportunities can be opened up with speedier connections, better processing power, and optimized algorithms. Benefits outweigh expenses.

The race to build new cables or upgrade existing ones is based on the principle that shorter is faster. Latency time is measured by the temporal difference between starting a transaction and completing it. This means that one key factor is the length of the cable, since the speed of time is finite. Every kilometer of cable counts. The logic of shortness is vital in calculating routes for future cables. However, this logic also carries some risks. Cables that run through shallow waters may be more exposed to human or natural disruption, whether from fishing or from whales and sharks, and may be more susceptible to espionage and surreptitious tapping. Deeper lines are more costly, since they need protective layers—e.g. steel covers—or need to be dug into the sea floor.

Another driver of the race for milliseconds is the need to respond to the changing habits of people, whose demand for more rapid and thicker bandwidth transfer of data and video is crowding existing networks.

In response to these demands, innovations in technology continue, since information transfer speed is influenced not only by distance but by processing power and efficiency of algorithms in encoding and decoding. Even as high-frequency trading continues to develop via fiber-optic cables, other technologies are emerging. A chain of microwave dishes, for instance, can replace or complement an infrastructure of fiber-optic cables, especially where the costs of building new land-based cables can be very high, for instance in urban environments. Wireless technologies are becoming the new norm in digital communication outside the special but highly profitable field of high-frequency trading. The technology based on microwaves is well-known, as it was used by telephone operators already in the 1970s. The idea is simple. Whereas land-based cables have to take into account the specific topography of a terrain, a microwave tower is better able to approach the ideal of straight line. There are some additional risks, for instance bad weather or poor data capacity, that limit the possible uses of such new networks. The building of the land-based microwave route also requires significant investment, and takes time as permits are needed to place the dishes on tall structures in different jurisdictions. The straight-line logic does not give much room for make it easy to obtain building and other permits. Moreover, fiber optic networks can carry thousand times more information than a system based on microwaves. Nonetheless, a microwave system at the margin can make a difference, and despite all these hurdles, the race is on to build a transatlantic microwave network that would enable superfast trading. It would be supported by a system of barges, drones,

Figure 3. Map of Global Submarine Cable Networks

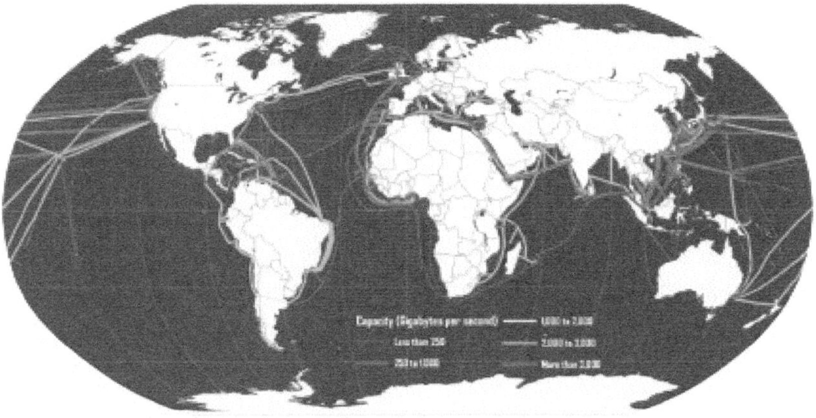

Source: https://people.hofstra.edu/geotrans/eng/media_maps.html

balloons, and/or satellites. Many such plans are secret and proprietary, and even when such projects may be realized they might remain known only to their investors and users.

A second alternative or complement to high-fiber optic cables is also being developed. Laser technology, first developed by the U.S. military for the communication among aircraft, offers advantages over microwave connections because laser beams are less affected by weather. Its reliability is close to that of fiber optic networks.

These new technologies and practices are spreading from the United States to Europe and to Asian financial centers. Microwave connections, for instance, have recently been built between strategic hubs such as Frankfurt and London. Along this route, laser technology is also likely to become established practice in a matter of months. This has almost halved the latency time associated with fiber optic cables. The distance between these two major financial hubs has been halved; whereas the distance used to be about 4 milliseconds, it is now just a bit more than 2 milliseconds. In this sense, the two cities are closer than ever and their communities of traders intimately inter-twined. The route has now more than one competing network owned by U.S. and Europe-based companies.

These innovations means that high-frequency trading practices that prevail in the United States are likely to spread also in Europe as newer technologies are introduced. In the United States such practices constitute the majority of all trade, and now account for a large plurality of transactions in London and Frankfurt. High-frequency trading is still small scale in the Nordic exchanges based in Stockholm. However, its rapid growth is a driver for the building of new connections between Stockholm and London/Frankfurt and between Stockholm and Moscow. The planned cable connection across the Arctic sea to Asia can be also seen as opening one more opportunity for high-frequency trading.

Another important element of the race to win milliseconds is to move servers closer to the exchanges" data centers. This logic of co-location seems to increase the hubbing-effect in the cyber-dependent financial system: servers are attracted to servers. The closer they are to each other, the greater their potential advantage over microwave and laser technologies. High-frequency trading companies are directly wiring their connections and servers into the heart of the exchanges.

The advantage of a single millisecond can generate significant profit. This is a high stake game of relative gains. Not only do you need a fast connection, you need a connection faster than that of your competitors. This means that for a company based in the Nordic area, latency times are much longer than for competitors in London and Frankfurt-based companies. They are at an inherent disadvantage, which means that some business and trading models are not available to actors located in more peripheral regions.

There are other practices, however, that can be sustained in more remote locations. For example, Finland has a relative advantageous location as a relay point between East Asia and Europe, as is borne out by the country's air-traffic infrastructure. Finland can also gain from business models for fiber optic networks that are not built around high-frequency trading, for instance those based more on connecting cloud-servers and serving users who need bandwidth- heavy formats.

Moreover, the ability to exploit asynchronous stock values financially is not limited to places with speedier connections, such as London and Frankfurt. On a smaller scale, the potential for exploitation exists between any exchanges. In this sense, the logic of milliseconds should also drive Stockholm-based trading actors. The connections between Moscow and Stockholm, which have improved, offer opportunities for beneficial value proposals.[23] This also drives the need for better connections to Germany and the UK along a straighter line across the seas. Such connections also offer alternatives to Moscow-based traders since they would shave milliseconds off of a connection between Moscow and London or between Moscow and Frankfurt.[24] The exploitation of emerging and developing markets is a key driver for the building of Northern-European fiber optic networks. The emerging of new trading practices in Europe is changing perceptions that northern Europe is disadvantaged with regard to cyber market access. Much depends on how well Nordic capitals and other business centers are connected to as many as possible hubs as possible.

Cyberflows as Geopolitical Drivers in the 21st Century

The cyber commons is an important driver of current and emerging flow connectedness. Cyber-attacks and the vulnerabilities that enable them have been steadily increasing. According to Cisco's annual report on cyber security, the attacks are at unprecedented levels.[25] However, despite growing risks related to cybercrime, the overall infrastructure development is driven more by such factors as technological innovation and new business potential inherent in the cyber commons.

To truly understand the background factors, the key developing communities of practice needs to be mapped. For example, the state system is under heavy pressure from the cyber dimensions of peoples" interaction. It is adapting by trying to devise access strategies at the national level. States are connected political entities that have

---

[23]The London Stock Exchange trades Russian securities in its IOB market. These securities are also traded in Moscow, thereby opening possibilities for arbitrage. For example, the stocks of Gazprom are listed in both, leading to small differences in the value of the same security that can be exploited if you have a faster connection than others.

[24]Indirectly, Helsinki benefits from the new Swedish connection to Moscow built by TMX Atrium (owned by Canadian company TMX), and the recent faster connections between Stockholm and London. Moscow traders—based on Micex-RTS exchange—can connect much more directly with London—about 40 milliseconds faster.

[25]Cisco, *Annual Report on Cyber Security*, 2013, http://www.cisco.com/web/offer/gist_ty2_asset/Cisco_2014_ASR.pdf.

resources at their disposal to assist in building infrastructure. They can be instrumental in shaping societal agendas through their research and development strategies. Some are reformulating their national security strategies towards emerging security conceptualizations such as resilience, agility, adaptation, and preparedness. These newer national security practices are constitutive elements of "cyber-ization." If the hardware is detached from this community of state practice, the underlying trends become much harder to discern. Similarly, without greater understanding of the motivations and methods of different hacker communities—i.e. criminals, terrorists, or states—risk mapping and horizon scanning are relatively meaningless.

The geography of cyberspace includes countless companies operating cloud-servers, social networking sites and banking systems that are accessible to actors of all shapes and sizes. Distance is relatively inconsequential in the near-instantaneous cyber context, yet the politics of power and the race to gain financial advantage still matter. These are not evenly distributed in the map. Historically-embedded national contexts and belief system, state capabilities and wealth, and ethnic and religious patterns are examples of older geopolitical notions that still matter in at the age of global internet. Actors new and old are located on the political map, which also sheds insight also into the structures and hierarchies of cyberspace. On the other hand, state boundaries are not easily replicated in cyberspace. While there are some attempts, such as the Chinese national firewall and internal cyber censorship, to do so, on the whole such efforts are rather feeble and futile, as they are easily bypassed by people with knowledge.

This complexity can be reduced if the various activities in the cyber context are seen as embedded in communities of practice. These communities establish, maintain, develop, and innovate intertwined practices where such activities as social networking, cyber defense, or global logistics take place. Without understanding the transnational communities of practice, any insights into cyber are context-less and overall technological. Any risk analysis that does not take into account the communities of digital information flows is bound to lead into paralyzing complexity of hundreds of thousands of possible vulnerabilities. Only by understanding cyber as a part of overall human activities and motivation it is possible to evaluate the actual likelihood of disruptive behavior caused e.g. by credit card fraud or power struggles between states. Purely passive, self-contained and self-focused, internet security is difficult to achieve if the nature and range of possible exploiters is not known. The maxim "know thy enemy" is very relevant in the world of cyber geopolitics.

Chapter 4

The Future of the Global Energy Flow Map and its Strategic Implications

Paul Isbell

The Global Flow Map

Our contemporary world is increasingly dependent on global flows of merchandise, services, money, people and innumerable other material and immaterial "flows." This is particularly true of merchandise trade, which makes up the bulk of global material flows.[1] Such international merchandise trade flows—including both high valued-added manufactured and technology goods, along with large-scale international energy and resources trade—have tripled over the past ten years and are expected to continue increasing into the future.[2]

Indeed, in recent years a "global flow map" has taken shape both in real human-geographic terms and as a conceptual tool for calibrating the contours of the strategic horizon. For at least 200 years, the central driving force behind the coalescing emergence of today's global flow map has been the continued growth of international trade, measured as a share of global economic output.[3]

Although there is a broader "ecological flow map" beyond the boundaries of what is strictly human geography and political economy, what can be called the "human global flow map" finds its dynamic roots in a millenary evolutionary interplay between technology, the economic division of labor, and human politics—i.e., what could be considered the key historical determinants of the depth and extension

---

[1]This paper considers only "legitimate trade," and excludes "illicit flows." Nor does it consider immaterial (i.e., informational), biological or ecological flows.

[2]See UNCTAD, *Key Trends in International Merchandise Trade* (UN: New York and Geneva), 2013.

[3]See Hendrik Van Den Berg and Joshua J. Lewer, *International Trade and Economic Growth* (M.E. Sharpe, Inc.), 2007.

of "the market." However, this "flow map" has only recently emerged into clear global consciousness as a result of the international dynamics of post-Cold War "globalization,'" which effectively brought the "First," "Second," and "Third" worlds into a single global "market economy" at the end of the 20th century. Nevertheless, while "globalization" brought about the wide-spread perception of the most completely globalized political economy ever experienced in history, it also generated the mirage of "flatness" in global affairs and "the end of history" in political thought, thus obscuring the contours of the actually emerging global flow map.[4]

After at least a decade of recurrent "globalization crises," however, and nearly another of tightening impasse across nearly all realms of Cold War-era global governance, the mirage has finally faded. In its place a sense of strategic unmooring now pervades the global community as most global governance structures have failed to arbitrate disputes successfully among varying international interest groups; facilitate global economic growth and sustainable development; or maintain the peace during the turn-of-the-century generation of post-Cold War "globalization."

A conscious mapping of the "seascapes" of the current global flow map at least restores a physical, geographical grounding to any of our preferred strategic abstractions. The fresh framing of a such a global flow map, and an emphasis on its "seascapes," might also begin to challenge the "Eurasian-focused," "world-island-centered" abstractions that still influence much of our strategic thinking. Dominated by seaborne flows, the global flow map actually fleshes out—due to the rising strategic significance of the oceans themselves, some three-quarters of the planet's surface and accommodating the shipping of over four-fifths of global trade—into a new, multidimensional and dynamic "geopolitical *flow globe*," which is marine-centered and ocean basin-based.

Our world has long been dependent on the shifting dynamics of this multidimensional, geography-bound global flow map—at least to some degree since the 16th century. However, the strategic value of the

---

[4]Thomas L. Friedman, *The World Is Flat* (New York: Farrar, Straus and Giroux, 2005); Francis Fukuyama, *The End of History and the Last Man* (New York: Free Press, 1992).

security of such flows has continued to accumulate with the deepening of the global market and the on-going penetration of international trade, and has never been greater than at present. The relevance and value-added of such a strategic focus on the global flows of the "geopolitical flow globe"—both in terms of geo-economic "volumes" and geopolitical "physical-logistical routes"—comes into even sharper relief when cast against a number of currently unfolding megatrends and macro-realities—both independent and interlocking—which are reshaping the contours of 21st century geopolitics.

Such megatrends include:

- the growing share of the developing world (the "South") in both global GDP and seaborne merchandise trade (particularly in container traffic, but also in energy);[5]

- broad technological change across the global energy landscape (including the sometimes competing revolutions in "unconventional fossil fuels" and low carbon technology);[6]

- the re-emergence of the broad Atlantic Basin (as opposed to simply the "northern Atlantic') as an increasingly coherent and potentially influential geopolitical space;[7]

- on-going climate change, driven principally by fossil fuel use, which has taken global temperatures to around 0.9 degrees Celsius above pre-industrial levels (with a 2 degree rise virtually built-in to our current global business-as-usual trajectory, and with a 4 degree rise increasingly likely);[8]

- the incipient birth of the Arctic as a truly functioning ocean basin[9]—paradoxically, the result of human-induced climate

---

[5]UNCTAD, op cit.

[6]See Paul Isbell, *Energy and the Atlantic: The Shifting Energy Landscapes of the Atlantic Basin* (GMF, Brussels and Washington, DC, 2012).

[7]See Daniel S. Hamilton, "Towards a Governance Agenda for the Emerging Atlantic Hemisphere," *Revista CIDOB d'Afers Internacionals*, n. 102-103, (CIDOB, Barcelona, September 2013), pp. 51-71.

[8]See, for example, Vergara et al, *The Climate and Development Challenge for Latin America and the Caribbean: Options for Climate-Resilient, Low-Carbon Development* (Washington, DC:ECLAC-IDB-WWF, 2013).

[9]See Daniel S. Hamilton, ed., *A New Atlantic Community: Generating Growth, Human Development and Security in the Atlantic Hemisphere* (Washington, DC: Center for Transatlantic Relations, 2014).

change stemming from our energy, agriculture and land-use practices;[10] and

• the rapidly growing significance of the oceans relative to land, in
terms of economy, geopolitics and ecological balance.[11]

The intensifying centrality of the oceans, in particular, as a key variable within the equations of global geopolitics—and as an increasingly
critical aspect (ie, the global "seascape") of the global flow map—is
underpinned and strengthened by a number of other dynamic trends
working simultaneously across many sectors. Perhaps the most important global macro reality in this regard—at least with respect to global
material flows—is the fact that nearly 90% of global merchandise trade
(by volume, and nearly three-quarters by value) is transported by ship at
sea. Total global seaborne trade has increased since 1970 at an average
annual rate of 3.1% and is expected to double yet again by 2030.[12] Furthermore, just the *seaborne oil trade* in 2010 (2700 mn tons) was approximately 30% of total seaborne merchandise trade (8400 mn tons).[13] In
fact, total international energy trade (including oil, but also liquefied
natural gas, coal, biofuels and synthetic fuels) could account for as much
as a third, or more, of all current seaborne merchandise trade.[14]

There are many other expanding flows, legitimate and illicit, private and public, economic, scientific, ecological, military-strategic, etc,
which add to the growing and changing significance of both the global
flow map—or "geopolitical flow globe"—and the primary space—the
global "seascape" of interlocking "ocean basins"—through which the
fastest-growing volumes now pass. There are also fast-growing
resource reserves within the oceans themselves (energy, minerals, fisheries[15] and aquaculture, bio-genetic resources, etc), further augment-

---

[10]See G.S. Eskeland L. S. Flottorp, 2006, "Climate Change in the Arctic: A Discussion of
the Impact on Economic Activity," in S. Glomsrød and I. Aslaksen, eds., *The Economy of the
North* (Oslo: Statistics Norway, 2006).

[11]See, among other innumerable sources, John Richardson, et al., *The Fractured Ocean* (Brus-
sels/Washington, DC: German Marshall Fund of the United States, 2012).

[12]UNCTAD, *World Economic Situation and Prospects* (New York: UN, 2012).

[13]*International Shipping Facts and Figures—Information Resources on Trade, Safety, Security and the
Environment*, International Maritime Organization (2012).

[14]BP *Statistical Review of World Energy* (2013), IMO (2012), Ibid., and own elaboration.

[15]Global fisheries, and other "biological flows" are actually on the decline. See Richardson et
al., op. cit.

ing the weighting of the oceans as a variable within the geopolitical equations of international conflict and transnational cooperation.

Nevertheless, global energy trade—always a key geopolitical variable—remains the single most important global flow on the seas, both in terms of size and centrality to economic and geopolitical interests. Even though container traffic (mainly consumer goods) has grown faster since the 1980s than seaborne oil trade (driven mainly by rising Asian consumption), the seaborne energy trade remains the most strategic flow, from the most perspectives (economic, environmental, geopolitical, and military). In the same way, the "global energy seascape" remains the most strategic dimension of the "global flow map" (i.e., the "geopolitical flow globe").

The sections to follow will examine, in turn: (1) global energy trade flows, (2) their underlying drivers and dynamics, and (3) their geopolitical and strategic significance within the context of the evolving megatrends and macro-realities outlined above.

Global Energy Flows

Globally traded energy flows include, in the main: oil, gas, coal, biofuels, synthetic fuels and electricity.[16] Such energy trade occurs in liquid, gaseous, solid, and electric form. Liquid energies are typically transported by ship, but some also move by international pipeline. These *liquids* include: oil (both crude and derivatives, like gasoline); liquefied natural gas (LNG); biofuels; and synthetic fuels (or "synfuels"). Gases include, mainly, natural gas—most of which moves in gaseous form though pipelines (although about 30% is LNG, mentioned above, and moves internationally as a liquid by ship).[17] Solids include, mainly, coal—which is traded internationally by both sea and land (railroad and truck). Finally, electricity—the smallest flow of the internationally traded energies—is mainly moved just domestically although, in some limited cases, it does flow internationally, and typically by transmission cable through international interconnections.

---

[16]Globally traded energy is a subset of total global energy flows; the other subset is domestic energy flows that do not cross international borders.

[17]BP (2013), op. cit.

In terms of relative volumes, as we will examine further below, the largest flows of internationally traded energy come from oil (and its derivatives), then coal (most by ship, but some by land) and gas (some by LNG, a liquid, but most still by international pipeline), and finally in a minor way other liquids like biofuels and finally synthetic fuels, still in virtually residual quantities. In 2010, oil accounted for 90% of all international energy trade (measured in terms of total exa-joules).[18] However, although oil currently dominates global energy flows as well as the global material flow map, by 2050 internationally trade in energy will nearly double (under a business-as-usual scenario) and around 80% of the total by then will be gas (much of it LNG). So while liquid energies will continue to be the single most central global material flow, the dominant globally traded energy will shift from oil to gas over the course of the coming decades.[19]

Oil Flows

In 2012, global oil production hit an all-time high of 86.15 million barrels a day (mbd). Global oil consumption was also at an all-time high of nearly 90 mbd. Of this quantity of globally produced oil (including relatives and derivatives), 64.2% is internationally traded oil (55.3 mbd). Furthermore, over 55% of global oil production—and nearly 88% of total traded oil—is shipped by sea (some 48.5 mbd). Less than 13% of internationally traded oil (6.7 mbd) travels by land (mainly pipeline but also rail and road), although more than an additional 30mbd (or 35% of total oil production) also travels by land, but only domestically, without crossing national borders.[20]

LNG Flows

Total global gas trade reached 1 trillion cubic meters (1 tcm) in 2012, or 50% of total world gas production (2 tcm). The global LNG trade—the liquid, ship-transported portion of the gas trade—came to 328 billion cubic meters (bcm), or 5.93 mbdoe[21] (just over 30% of total

---

[18]IIASA GEA Model Projections Database (2013) and own elaboration.

[19]Ibid.

[20]BP (2013), op. cit., and own elaboration.

[21]For conversion from bcm of gas to million barrels a day of oil equivalent (1bcm x 6.6 divided by 365), see BP op. cit.

global gas trade) and 16.4% of total global gas production. Global pipeline-traded gas—the portion of the international gas trade that moves by land—came to 705.5 bcm last year, some 70% of total global gas trade, and 35% of total gas production. Of course, almost all of the 1 tcm of gas that is produced—but not traded internationally—travels by pipeline domestically, without crossing national borders (50% of the global total).[22]

Moreover, far more oil, as a percentage (64%) is traded internationally than is the case with gas (50%). In addition, more oil (55% of the total) than gas (16.4%) travels by ship. Furthermore, oil still accounts for a higher share of total global energy (33%) than gas (25%).[23] All of these parameters make oil the most significant flow on the "global energy seascape."

Biofuels Flows

Total global production of biofuels reached 1.2 mbd of oil equivalent (oe) in 2012, or around 3% of the global transportation fuel market.[24] Of this, approximately 2 billion liters,[25] or 4.5 Mtoe[26] (around 350,000bdoe or 0.35mbdoe) is traded internationally, basically all by ship. Compared to oil and LNG, however, this liquid flow (together with that of synfuels) is still marginal. Nevertheless, over 80% of this international trade takes place within the Atlantic Basin.

Coal Flows

Coal currently accounts for 30% of the global primary energy mix. Total global coal production in 2011 came to 7 billion tons; about one-seventh of this total (1 billion tons) was internationally traded (a tripling since 1999). Some 94% of all globally traded coal (978 million tons) is transported by sea, while only 6% moves by land (mainly rail). In comparable terms with oil (measured in million barrels per day of oil equivalent, or mbdoe), the global seaborne coal trade comes to

---

[22]Natural gas and LNG data from BP (2013), op. cit., and own elaboration.

[23]Ibid.

[24]Ibid.

[25]Greenfacts (http://www.greenfacts.org/en/biofuels/figtableboxes/figure-18.htm).

[26]IFP, "Panorama 2012: Biofuels Update: Growth in National and International Markets," 2011 (www.ifpenergiesnouvelles.com).

9.35 mbdoe. Of this total global seaborne coal trade, some 75% is hard/steam coal (7.5 mbdoe), while the remaining 25% of seaborne trade is in coking coal. The seaborne hard coal trade has declined recently in the Atlantic Basin (-8% between 2008 and 2011) but expanded significantly (+30%) in Asia (or in the Pacific and Indian Basins).[27]

Electricity Flows

Total world electricity imports (596bnkWh, or *1mbdoe*) come to 3.1% of total world electricity production (19,038 billion kilowatt hours, or 32mbdoe) and 3.4% of total world electricity consumption (17,445 billion kilowatt hours, or 29mbdoe).[28] However, nearly all of this international electricity trade takes place by land-based transmission cable, while only a tiny fraction occurs through sea-based transmission cable.

"Landscapes" versus "Seascapes" on the "Geopolitical Flow Globe"

The world produces some 222 mbdoe of "tradable energy" (including oil, gas, biofuels, coal and electricity).[29] About 38% of this "tradable energy" production is *actually traded* internationally, across borders (or about 84 mbdoe). Nearly 77% of this globally traded energy is moved by sea (or some 64 mbdoe), the equivalent of 29% of total

---

[27]Global coal data comes from: Lars Schernikau, "Economics of the International Coal Trade: The Renaissance of Steam Coal," (Springer), 2010; HMS, Bergbau AG (http://hms-ag.com/en/energy-coal-market/world-coal-trade.html); and Arne K. Bayer and Maggi Rademacher, "Seaborne steam coal market dynamics and future production costs," EON, Resources Workshop "Long-Term Costs and Reserves of Coal, Oil, & Natural Gas," March 22, 2012. Note: Divide million metric tons of coal (mn tons) by 2.1 to get "million tons of oil equivalent'; then divide million tons of oil equivalent (mtoe) by 49.8 to get million barrels a day of oil equivalent (mbdoe).

[28]Electricity data is from the Energy Information Agency (EIA) of the US Department of Energy. See the EIA "International Energy Statistics," (http://www.eia.gov/cfapps/ipdbproject/IEDIndex3.cfm?tid=2&pid=2&aid=12), 2013. For electricity to oil conversion factors (1 kilowatt hour = 3412 BTUs divided by one trillion x 0.18 for million barrel oil equivalent) see BP, op. cit.

[29]The world actually produces/consumes around 250mbdoe of energy, although a significant share of it is energy which cannot be traded internationally, like most traditional (and even some modern) biomass.

Table 1. Global Energy Production, Trade and Seaborne Energy Trade, mbdoe, 2012[30]

Tradable Energy Source	Total Tradable Energy Production	Total Energy Traded	Seaborne Energy Trade	Seaborne Energy Trade (mbdoe)	% Seaborne Energy Trade (mbdoe)
Oil (2012)	86.15mbd	55mbd	48.5mbd	48.5	75.6%
Gas (2012)	2 trillion cm (36mbdoe)	1 trillion cm (18mbdoe)	328bcm	5.93	9.2%
Biofuels (2012)	1.2mbd	0.35mbd	0.35mbd	0.35	0.54%
Coal (2011)	7bn tons (66.6mbdoe)	1bn tons (9.5mbdoe)	978mn tons	9.35	14.6%
Electricity (2010)	19 PWh (32mbdoe)	596 TWh (1mbdoe)	--	--	--
Total mbdoe	222mbdoe	83.85mbdoe*		64.13mbdoe**	100%

* 38% of total tradable energy production.
**29% of total tradable energy production; 76.5% of total energy traded.

global "tradable energy" production. Less than 20 mbdoe of globally traded energy travels by land (some 23.5% of globally traded energy, or 8.9% of total global produced "tradable energy"). Table 1 lays out these global energy "land" and "seascapes.'

The large majority of energy flowing "globally" moves in liquid form by ship (49mbdoe). This "liquid flow" is complemented to some degree by solids, like coal, much of it also transported by sea (another 9.35mbdoe). However, much oil, gas, biofuel and coal (59mbdoe) is not physically traded across national borders. Piped gas and electricity, in particularly, are generally still limited to regional markets; even then, the densest flows tend to be domestic. Of total "tradable energy" produced, some 62% is consumed domestically, without crossing bor-

[30]*Oil and Gas: BP Statistical Review of World Energy* (2013); Biofuels: IFP, "Panorama 2012: Biofuels Update: Growth in National and International Markets," 2011 (www.ifpenergies-nouvelles.com); Coal: Lars Schernikau, "Economics of the International Coal Trade: The Renaissance of Steam Coal" (Springer, 2010); HMS, Bergbau AG (http://hms-ag.com/en/energy-coal-market/world-coal-trade.html); and Arne K. Bayer and Maggi Rademacher, "Seaborne steam coal market dynamics and future production costs," EON, Resources Workshop "Long-Term Costs and Reserves of Coal, Oil, & Natural Gas," March 22, 2012; Electricity: Energy Information Agency (EIA) of the US Department of Energy. See the EIA "International Energy Statistics" (http://www.eia.gov/cfapps/ipdbproject/IED Index3.cfm?tid=2&pid=2&aid=12); and own elaboration.

Table 2. Global Energy Land and Seascapes: Total Global Tradable Energy Consumed Domestically and Traded by Land and Sea, 2012

Total Global "Tradable Energy" Produced	Consumed Domestically	Traded Internationally by Land	Traded Internationally by Sea
222 mbdoe	137.64mbdoe	19.75mbdoe	64.13mbdoe
% of total	62%	8.9%	29%

ders; meanwhile of this total global "tradable energy" produced, only 38% is actually traded globally, and 29% of this total "tradable energy production" is traded by sea.

From one angle, then, the global energy flow map reveals an international energy "seascape" in which energy is globally traded (38% of the total tradable energy produced), and transported principally by ship via the world's sea lanes (76.5% of total traded energy, or 29% of total tradable energy produced). From another angle, however, the global energy flow map is an essentially domestic "landscape" (62% of total tradable energy produced), with energy transport almost exclusively terrestrial (either by transmission cable, pipeline, rail or road).

This latter, more domestic and land-based version of the global energy flow map reflects the energy landscape of the interior of the Eurasian landmass, while the former expression of the global flow map—the one expanding the most rapidly—reflects the energy "seascapes" of the "ocean basins" (ie, the Atlantic Basin, the Indian Basin, the Pacific Basin and, possibly someday, even the Arctic Basin), which now command nearly one-third of the global total of tradable energy produced. This means that the "global energy seascape" constitutes nearly a third of the "global energy flow map"—including all domestic energy flows that do not constitute international energy trade—and for three-quarters of globally traded energy. Yet the strategic significance of the "global energy seascape" is heightened further by the fact that it provides the critical binding spaces between global loci of production and consumption, across ocean basins.

Oil, however, is by far the dominant flow, accounting for three-quarters of this "globally traded energy seascape." Nevertheless, by 2050 80% of globally traded energy flows will be accounted for by gas, as mentioned above, as oil is progressively squeezed out of the global energy mix, even under a business-as-usual scenario.[31] To the extent that the gas market becomes global, based on LNG, the globally-traded energy seascape will be increasingly dominated by liquid movements of gas.

Drivers and Dynamics of the Global Energy Flow Map

To begin to foresee the shape and rhythms of the future global energy flow map, one must analyze the drivers—and underlying dynamics—of the past and present versions of this map. Historically, and perhaps systemically, the principal driver, dominating the directions of the flows, has been the interplay and relationship between the centers of global energy production and the centers of consumption.

A Century of Shifting Oil Production and Consumption Loci

The world's oil production locus was first located in the United States, a product of the original Pennsylvania-Texas Wildcat booms. Within decades the production locus began to be shared with the Caspian, as the old Eurasian "heartland"—that transfixing strategic mirage of the 19th and 20th century—became overlaid in a thick layer of oil. By the end of the Second World War, however, both the Americas (Mexico and Venezuela were on the scene by now) and Central Asia and the Caspian were gradually being displaced by the rising Middle East. Meanwhile, the United States had surpassed Europe as the world's principal locus of consumption (which eventually balanced out during the post war years to include, more or less, all of the OECD economies).[32]

As a result of the oil price shocks of the 1970s, the Northern Atlantic (particularly Europe) began to experience a secular shift in energy demand, as efficiency rose and as certain material demands became mature or saturated. At the same time, Asia began to emerge as an increasingly central locus of consumption, as its economies

---

[31]IIASA GEA Model Projections Database (2013) and own elaboration.

[32]For a history of the evolution of world oil production and consumption from the mid-19th century to the end of the 20th, see Daniel Yergin, *The Prize: The Epic Quest for Oil, Money and Power* (Simon & Schuster, New York, 1991).

Figure 1. Seaborne Crude Oil Trade in the late 20th Century Global Oil Flow Map, mn metric tons, 1994

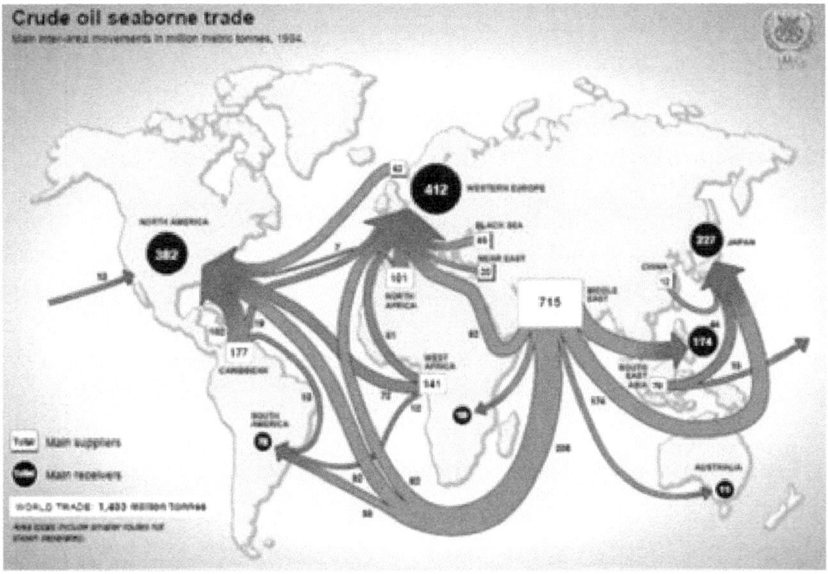

Source: International Maritime Organization.

began to grow—and as consumption in OECD economies began to level or even peak.

For several decades after the Second World War, then, global flows of oil were increasingly dominated by crude oil coming from the Middle East and then shipped by sea: first into the Atlantic Basin—where the United States and Europe remained more or less highly dependent on imports of Mideast oil (making Suez and Hormuz crucial chokepoints)—and then to the Indian Basin and, with time, even more so to the East Asian rim of the Pacific Basin (lending the Straits of Malacca their strategic significance). During the classic age of the Seven Sisters, the global oil market functioned smoothly with its heart beating the oil out of the Persian Gulf in increasingly voluminous flows, with a largest share shipped westward. Then, after the Sisters' loss of control and the oil shocks of the 1970s, another increasingly large flow shipped eastward, to emerging Asia (see Figure 1). The Middle East—in particular, Saudi Arabia, Iran, Iraq, Kuwait and the

Figure 2. Global Oil Trade Flows Shifting Eastward, 2012-2020

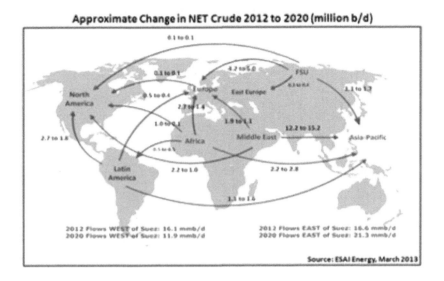

Source: ESAJ Energy, March 2011.

Emirates—was the strategic exporter of a barrel at the margin (to all ocean basins) on the previous global energy flow map.

From the late Cold War of the 1980s—when prices precipitously fell from oil shock levels—to the time of the Great Recession, which plunged global oil prices from shock-levels again in 2008, such patterns of dependency began to unravel, and the flow map, in turn, has changed. A number of factors have contributed to this slow series of interlocking shifts in the dominant sources, destinations, and transport patterns of the global energy flow map. Figure 2 reveals the emerging land/seascape of global oil flows, with the global center of gravity of consumption (or global consumption locus) shifting eastward from the Atlantic Basin to Eurasia—and East Asia, in particular.

As can be seen in Figure 2 above, global oil trade flowing west of Suez reached 16.1mbd in 2012, while global oil trade flowing east of Suez came to 16.6 mbd. By 2020, however, the westward flow will have fallen by more than 4 mbd (to 11.9), as the eastward flows are expected to rise by 4.7 mbd (to 21.3). A number of trend shifts affecting the global loci of production and consumption underlie these changes in the global energy flow map, reversing the previous East-to-West nature of the preponderant flows.

On the demand side, the shift from East-to-West to West-to-East flows has been driven by:

- slowed consumption growth in the Northern Atlantic (first in Europe, and then in the United States);
- increased demand in "Eurasia," a trend set to continue: including among both the major exporters (Russia, Central Asia, the Middle East) and importers (South and East Asia) of the region.

On the supply side, the reversal in the East-to-West flow has been underpinned by:

- expanded conventional hydrocarbon reserves and increased oil and gas production from all corners of the Atlantic Basin: North America, South America, Africa and even (at least for a while) North Sea Europe;
- increased U.S. production in unconventional hydrocarbons (shale gas and "light tight oil"), reversing a heightening dependency trend and reducing U.S. imports of oil and gas for first time in generations;
- the related "unconventional revolutions" of the broader Atlantic Basin: including shale, LTO and tar sands in Northern Atlantic, and the deep offshore and shale resources in the Southern Atlantic.

While similar supply side developments may be occurring in other ocean basins or other terrestrial regions, on all counts they are being outstripped by their manifestations in the Atlantic Basin. Figure 3 reveals the impact of such factors shifting the global loci of production and consumption upon the global energy flow map (and in particular upon global flows of oil). As the global consumption locus shifts east to Asia, the global production locus continues to shift in a westward direction, leaving the global center of gravity (or global equalization point) in the Atlantic Basin, from where the marginal barrel of oil will be exported to the world market in the future and, increasingly, to Eurasia—East Asia, South Asia and the "Great Crescent" (including the Middle East, Russia and Central Asia), and in that order.

Figure 3. Oil's Global Center of Gravity Shifting into the Atlantic Basin

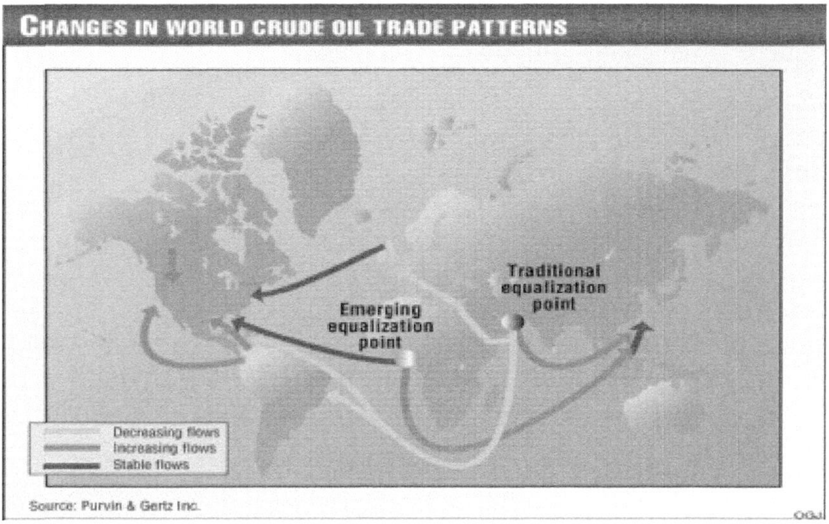

Source: Oil and Gas Journal (from Purvin & Gertz Inc.)

Already, nearly 80% of U.S. imports comes from the Atlantic Basin.[33] Furthermore, the IEA has recently called attention to the increased segmentation of the global oil market, noting that the "Western Hemisphere" is increasingly autonomous in terms of oil.[34] More than 60% of all new oil production to 2035 will come from the Atlantic Basin; even now, no more of the world's import quota for oil is filled by the Middle East (35%) than by the Atlantic Basin (the same).[35] Given that U.S. oil production is now rising, while consumption levels off and imports fall; and given that oil production in the Southern Atlantic (in both Africa and Latin America) is also rising, the "Atlantic Basin," too, is increasingly autonomous in terms of globally traded oil.

This new, but still oil-dominated, global energy flow map is rounded out by an Atlantic Basin preeminence in a number of other

---

[33] Own elaboration, based on data from BP op. cit.

[34] International Energy Agency (IEA), *World Energy Outlook 2013*.

[35] See Isbell 2013; BP op. cit. and own elaboration.

marginal, but increasingly significant, energy flow categories. These include LNG (which is following a dynamic similar to that of oil, with increasing Atlantic gas reserves and LNG production lending the Basin a growing autonomy and much future export potential to Asia, at least at the margin), biofuels (with the Atlantic possessing 85% of the global biofuels economy and incorporating global leaders like Brazil and the United States), and synthetic fuels (where South Africa and the US have the lead). Much the same could be said about coal: increasingly European coal demand is being met by the United States and to some extent Colombia, while South African coal is more and more bound for India, and farther east. There exists a growing trend toward greater Atlantic Basin autonomy across a range of energy sectors and the global energy flows that typically came into the Atlantic Basin from the Indian Ocean Basin are now reversing their flow, moving from the West to the East, toward the Pacific. And the trend has only begun.

Chokepoints and Key Sea Lanes: East-West Limitations and "High-Latitude" Spill-overs in the Global Energy Flow Map

The most visible, major thrusts and contours of the global energy flow map are explained by the production-consumption loci layout and its evolution. However the physical geography of the oceans' shipping chokepoints and key sea lanes also interacts with technological evolution affecting transportation to contribute some unique dynamics to the global energy flow map.

Shipping flows shift when canals are opened, shut, widened, technically disabled, potentially threatened or even actually sabotaged. Some of these factors affecting canal traffic can be planned for; others cannot and imply certain amounts of technical and political risk. The world's sea straits—similar to canals, but subtly different—are also vulnerable to these latter forms of risk. However, while such factors can affect the energy flows of the global "seascape," and even indirectly of the "landscape," they do so only in dialectical relation with the dynamics of transportation, particularly shipping (ie, technology/ size of shipping vessel, weather constraints, etc). Therefore, the shifting political and technical dynamics of the world's strategic straits and other chokepoints and strategic sea lanes impact upon the flows as they interact with the broader dynamics of transportation.

In fact, the world's two most important chokepoints are straits, not canals. More than 17mbd of oil pass through the Straits of Hormuz, at the mouth of the Persian Gulf—meaning 17 million barrels every day.[36] This is equivalent to 35% of all seaborne oil trade, and nearly 20% of globally produced oil.[37] More than 85% of it is going to Asia (India, China, Japan and South Korea), and by 2035 nearly all of it will be Asia-bound. Well over 75% of the oil moving through Hormuz daily also passes through Malacca in Southeast Asia, through which passes some 15mbd—including the bulk of the Hormuz oil and some flows coming from West Africa through the Cape Passage on their way to the Far East.

For as long as the new global energy flow map has been emerging (since the late 1970s) this crucial sea lane—from the Persian Gulf to East Asia—has been gaining in global importance. First, an increasing share of global oil has continued to pass through these straits. While such oil contributes to global supply and to the world oil price, increasingly the Hormuz oil, at least, is directly providing for consumption in the East, not the West, linking with Malacca in an increasingly strategic energy supply chain of fast growing Asia. Nevertheless, even as the currently emerging global energy flow map changes with time, this strategic chain of chokepoints will only increase in its significance. The shut-down of either of these straits—or both—would take more oil off the market than is produced by Saudi Arabia. Furthermore the only potential swing producer with excess capacity to replace such lost oil from the market would be Saudi Arabia itself (if not, increasingly in the future, some countries of the Atlantic Basin). But in the case of a shutdown of Hormuz, in particular, it would be precisely Saudi Arabia which would have no way to bring its potentially heightened production to world market. The pipeline links between the Gulf countries and the Mediterranean or Red Sea are minimal, and would take years and untold billions to build

---

[36]"In addition, Qatar exports about 2 trillion cubic feet per year of liquefied natural gas (LNG) through the Strait of Hormuz, accounting for almost 20 percent of global LNG trade. Furthermore, Kuwait imports LNG volumes that travel northward through the Strait of Hormuz. These flows totaled about 100 billion cubic feet per year in 2010." EIA, "World Oil Transit Chokepoints," August 22, 2012 (http://www.eia.gov/countries/regions-topics.cfm? fips=wotc&trk=p3)

[37]EIA, op. cit.

new sufficient capacity capable of backing up the Strait of Hormuz. Regardless of the nature of the strategic maps preferred by the Indians or the Chinese, they have clearly captured this.

Indeed, for China and its East Asian neighbors, the Straits of Malacca (together with Lombok and Sunda) are existential. Some 80% of China's energy imports and some 40% of its consumption is dependent on oil passing through these straits. Japan and South Korea are even more dependent on this energy flow. Within the frame of obsolete geopolitical thinking, it is no wonder that there exists a strong narrative—and perhaps even a partial reality—that China is building up its "blue water" navy to be able to protect the Hormuz-Malacca flows: an international public good that from World War II to the present has been provided by the United States.

While they are important as crucial gateways for the energy flows of the global "seascape," the Suez and Panama canals remain marginal to the potential overall evolution of the global energy flow map in the future. Together they account for around 4mbd of oil traffic, and will unlikely every surpass 5mbd. Even though the Panama Canal is set to inaugurate its new expansion, already the largest ships in both tanker and container shipping are too large to be accommodated by even the enlarged Panama Canal.[38]

At the margin of future shipping growth, size and technological capacity will dictate that the increasing flows at the margin will use the Cape Passage in the south linking the Atlantic Basin with the Indian Basin (or in the mapping of some, with the Indo-Pacific continuum). The other possible seaborne flow to grow (as a result of the size and technologically-induced "spill over" flows from the ultimately restricted canal passages), is the Arctic passage, particularly the "Northern Route," from the entrance of the Atlantic into the Arctic Basin, around the top of the Nordic countries and then all along the Russian northern coast to the Bering Strait.

Although it is true that notable Arctic traffic will still be long in coming, and ultimately also capped by technological and political-economic circumstances, much like the canals, it is nevertheless also true that, after the Cape Passage—the strategic passage to gain the most

---

[38]See "New Challenges for Panama Canal at 100," *The New York Times*, August 21, 2014.

traffic on the future global energy flow map—the other potential chokepoint, or strategic passage, to see its significance rise, at least notably—would be the Northern Russian coastal passage and in particular the Bering Strait. This is because the most likely scenario is that some Arctic oil and gas will in the end be produced, at least by Russia, even if the Arctic is left relatively unexploited, for whatever reason. However, such new energy flows, perhaps potentially notable—again, at least for Russia—will flow east and south through the Bering Strait to East Asia. This means that the Bering Strait, already traditionally significant in military and geo-strategic terms, now also becomes so with respect to the global energy flow map for the very first time.

By contrast the canals will be increasingly saturated and, in Panama's case, handling a relatively small amount (when compared to the projected growth in future global demand) of increased energy and other flows to the Pacific Basin (particularly to East Asia) from the Atlantic Basin (like some Venezuelan oil to China). In the case of Suez (and the companion SUMED pipeline), the growing flows will increasingly be container traffic to Europe from Asia through the canal, as energy flows through this route, at least flowing East to West, dry up.

A secondary consequence of the ultimate limitations faced by the strategic canals—even while they remain vital links for certain global trade flows between the world's ocean basins—is that such flow limitations reinforce an already notable new trend of rising energy flows *within* the Atlantic Basin. Other chokepoints, like the Danish Straits and the Turkish Straits, serve to further constrain the capacity of energy to move from East to West. As the global energy flow map continues to evolve to lend an even greater role for the Cape Passage, the crucial point is that the growing energy flows will be both intra-Atlantic and, in the longer run, moving from West to East, as they begin to serve as the oil and gas exports at the margin to Asia.

The Atlantic Basin energy "seascape" will become much denser on the future global energy flow map. At the same time, the deepening energy links between the exporters of the "Great Crescent" and the importers of South and East Asia will logically demand a denser network of land-based pipeline, rail and electricity connections—a development which would correspondingly intensify the Eurasian energy "landscape." Nevertheless, the Eurasian energy "seascapes," including the Hormuz-Malacca flow and the potentially new eastward and southward flows through the Bering Strait, will remain crucial for Eurasian logistical feasibility, and therefore key flows on the future global energy flow map.

The Emergence of an Ocean-Basin World: The Ocean-Basin Thesis

Provoked by shifts in the energy land- and seascapes, changes in the global material flow map are now interacting with changes in the relative importance of—or the relationships between—the oceans and the land. Marine technologies are opening up the sea in numerous ways, revealing its potential, its difficulties and its hazards. The new trends already embrace energy in particular—from offshore hydrocarbon and wind power production to other forms of marine energy and coastal energy interfaces for maritime uses—but economic activities are set to span from seabed mineral, fishing and aquaculture production to the exploitation of sea-based resources by the pharmaceutical and biotech industries. The role of the oceans in the maintenance in species diversity and of coastal ecosystem services, and in the absorption of carbon dioxide, is also critical, and—given the deplorable state of oceans in general and their rapid rate of deterioration—it will demand more and more intensive transnational collaboration. Such collaboration should logically be based on new "ocean basin communities," much like that already forming around the Rovaniemi Process and the Arctic Council in the Arctic Basin, and like that envisioned in the proposal for a new Atlantic Basin Community developed by the Eminent Persons Group of the Atlantic Basin Initiative in the Atlantic.[39]

Oceans are increasingly significant in strategic terms if for no other reason than that they are at once (1) the next great "economic," "scientific," and "geopolitical" frontiers, and (2) the collapsing foundation of the broader global environment. The great game over the future of global stability will be played out increasingly on and around the seas, and the four ocean basins in particular will shape its physical evolution in geopolitical space. Indeed, this shift in the realities of physical and human geographies will also demand a recasting of our land-locked,

---

[39]See Daniel S. Hamilton, ed., *A New Atlantic Community*, op. cit.

"world-island-based," Eurasian-centric strategic thinking to allow for our mental maps to actually see the potential of an "ocean basin world."

Ocean basins—with their new and evolving interfaces between ocean and "maritime rimlands"—are becoming the new nexus of geo-economics, geopolitics and transnational environmental collaboration. The result is a reconfiguration of the international landscape—to use what is now, for us, a less than useful metaphor, given the specificity of the increasingly important global seascape. Certainly, however, a new "geopolitical globe" is taking shape faster than most of us can alter the structure of our mental maps to perceive, and—like the strictly physical planet—it is an "ocean-basin world."

On the most obvious levels, such ocean emergence trends are manifest in the currently-unfolding and multifaceted reconfiguration of the Atlantic Basin and in the climate change-induced emergence of the Arctic. Such manifestations unfold within the contexts of other existing trends: the emergence of previously "developing" economies in Asia, which has provoked a great cleavage in the international division of labor, with the global center of gravity of manufacturing moving East, along with the center of gravity of energy demand. For the first time in modern history, the growing source of energy supply could be located beyond the Eurasian landmass (the "world-island") and providing energy to the growing source of global energy demand on the Asian side of the Eurasian landmass. Because energy from beyond Eurasia must pass through the world's ocean basins to reach it, oceans register an increase in the strategic import while ocean basins become key governance frames for responding to any related strategic challenges.

Climate Change and the Opening of the Arctic

Some future global material flows could shift, if melting ice allows the Arctic basin to become more feasible for economic exploitation (mainly hydrocarbons production and mining, both on- and offshore), other forms of scientific, social, political and military engagement, and for transportation shipping.

Although there is now much economic over-hype and geopolitical hyperbole concerning the "imminent opening" of the Arctic, it is nearly inevitable, on the other hand, that at least some more human activity will take place in the Arctic zone in the decades to mid-century (under almost any scenario). The Arctic countries have already been involved in increasing transnational collaboration, particularly through the so-called Rovaniemi Process. According to most interpretations, this process of collaboration, inspired by the famed "Murmansk Speech" of former Soviet Premier Mikhail Gorbachev in 1987 and launched by two Arctic meetings in Rovaniemi, Finland (in 1989 and 1991), led to intensive environment monitoring and protection collaboration in the form of the Arctic Mapping and Assessment Program (or AMAP), and eventually to the creation of the Arctic Council.

Any of the potential Arctic passages could substantially cut the journey time—by as much as one-third of the distance and time—between the Pacific and the Atlantic Basins. Economics will therefore dictate that much future Pacific-Atlantic seaborne trade will "spillover" from the ultimate bottleneck limitations of the "low-latitude" canals (even if enlarged) to move in and out of the Atlantic both northward through the Arctic routes and southward through the Cape Passage. As a result, in the future at least some additional shipping traffic will move through the Arctic.

But the most likely flows will be bulk traffic and some manufactured goods trade, between the Northern Atlantic and East Asia, most likely along the Northern Route passing along Russia's northern coast. Nevertheless, even with warmer temperatures and melting ice, a range of additional costs and risks associated with the still extreme conditions of the region—including special ice and weatherization shipping technologies, accompanying ice-breaker and related escorts, and related issues affecting insurance costs—will ultimate impose limitations on the potential shipping traffic volume that can be absorbed by the Arctic route. More importantly, in the end, the Arctic's ultimate impact on global *energy* flows is likely to even more marginal than its probable limited impact upon global shipping flows in general.

We have already mentioned the more-than-likely production of at least some Arctic hydrocarbons (probably most from Russia) and their likely passage through the Bering Strait to East Asia. But all the same extra costs and risks affecting shipping will also limit the amount of oil and gas that ultimately will be extracted from the Arctic. While the region is estimated to possess some 30% of all "undiscovered" gas in the world and some 15% of all "undiscovered" global oil, these estimates do not take into account "unconventional" hydrocarbons. Including "unconventional" resources in the analysis only renders Arctic oil and gas—almost all of which is not yet considered "proven reserves"—to the insignificant margin of the global energy picture. But because the shale and offshore revolutions have left the Atlantic Basin increasingly awash in oil and gas, most of the potential but ultimately limited hydrocarbon flows out of the Arctic will move east through the Bering Strait to the Pacific—not south and west into the Atlantic. While Europe still provides the exception to the new profile of Atlantic Basin hydrocarbon abundance, LNG imports from the US, Latin America and Africa are more likely to provide for future European gas demand than are any such hydrocarbons from the Arctic.

Therefore, while some early increases of Atlantic-Pacific trade will be absorbed by the enlarged Panama Canal, over the coming two decades more excess incremental West-East traffic will be diverted to the Arctic and the Cape Passage. But given the relatively modest level of ultimate Arctic traffic as a result of the volume limitations of the Northern Route, most of the future growth in this inter-basin trade will be diverted to the Cape Passage—the only potential major sea lane, capable of linking the Pacific to the Atlantic for seaborne trade, that has no traffic limitations physically inherent to the passage. Indeed, while the unfolding story of the contemporary Arctic is very compelling, it will only marginally affect global flows.

The vision of an "Arctic Renaissance"—to say nothing of a new "northern polar center of global geopolitical gravity"—could only ever be realized if the associated and underlying climate change— paradoxically responsible for any such opening the Arctic—does not completely disrupt the rest of the global system upon which almost all new Arctic economic activity, along with the political-social cohesion of the region, would ultimately depend. There is still much of interest that is now at stake in the Arctic, and in the on-going collaborative discussions of Arctic concerns. This is particularly true in the area of scientific collaboration, environmental protection and local sustainable development, especially with respect to Greenland and the Arctic's numerous indigenous nations. But the current trend to "securitize" the Arctic and to cast the opening of the region as a "new great game" overstates the Arctic's ultimate potential and exaggerates even the current rate of change.

Renewable Energies and Low Carbon Energy:
Driver and Shock-Absorber of the Global Energy Flow Map

The penetration of renewable energies into national energy mixes generally reduces both energy imports (and international energy trade in general) and the volumes of flows on the global "energy seascape." However, given the current lack of international interconnection infrastructure, either in physical or regulatory terms, land-based electricity trade will not initially take off, even as renewable energies expand. This means that, during the immediate decade or two to come, "external energy dependence" will continue to mean external dependence upon the global energy seascape as well as upon the original geographic source of the energy.

However, over the longer-run, renewable energy expansion and low carbon development in general will catalyze momentum toward electrification of the transportation sector and a deeper level of efficiency and technological sophistication in the electricity sector in general. Such trends will be particularly pronounced in the Northern Atlantic, but they could later unfold in the Southern Atlantic (and they could also easily involve—and bind—Eurasia). Renewable energy has a clear electricity bias, which primarily offers the potential of a land-based alternative to the entire global energy transportation network currently configuring the global energy flow map: including the dominant energy seascape and the minor, but important, road-rail-pipeline segment of the global energy landscape. At a certain point the movement toward electrification would catalyze a profusion of international electricity interconnections, which in turn would provoke demand for new structures of transnational energy collaboration around them.

There is no contradiction between (1) a low carbon roll-out (which reinforces the significance of electricity in general, vis-a-vis the other globally "tradable" energies, and progressively displaces international energy trade from the global energy seascape), and (2) the necessary collective Atlantic Basin effort to successfully (and simultaneously) exploit and protect an already rapidly deteriorating Atlantic Ocean. The business-as-usual global shipping trends have total seaborne cargoes rising by around 3% a year for decades. Any trend which could blunt the effect of that future increase in sea traffic would be a significant boon for the overall ecological health of the Atlantic Ocean, and make

Atlantic Basin transnational collaboration on ocean and other related issues all the more feasible in geo-economic and geopolitical terms.

Conclusions: Past Map versus New Map versus Future Map

Energy flows will nearly double by 2050, powered by a significant increase in the international trade in gas, particularly LNG, which will account for nearly 80% of with energy trade flow by then.[40] This projection is based on status quo and other already foreseen dynamics in which gas displaces oil through market forces operating within our fragmented but still largely global energy market. Given that much of this gas will be liquefied, a majority of global energy trade will continue to depend on the global "energy seascape." Nearly all of this global energy trade will be moving from West to East.

West-East (Energy) Flow Dynamics and Marginal
Traffic Spillover to "High Latitude" Inter-Basin Passages

In the short-run, the canals may gain marginally in absolute significance, with their various current enlargements (or "dry canal" or pipeline supplementary transport capacity additions); but they will continue to decline over time in relative strategic terms compared with other key maritime passages between the Atlantic and the Pacific (where the Panama Canal, in theory, competes with the Drake Passage and the still unfeasible Northwest Passage), and between the Atlantic and the Indian Ocean (where Suez competes with the Cape Passage and the now opening Arctic Northern Route). These dynamics—in which the "low-latitude canals" ultimately face growing limitations on their capacity to absorb growing east-west flows—rebound in favor of the "high-altitude" Arctic (Northwest Passage and Northern Route) and Southern Ocean (ie, the Drake and Cape) passages.

The potential opening of the Arctic passages, in particular, highlights the possibility that some of these growing East-West flows will spill over from the "low-latitude canals" to the "high-latitude passages" like the Northern Route and the Bering Strait. However, more future East-West flows will spill into the Indian Ocean, via the Cape

---

[40]IIASA GEA Model.

Figure 4. Current Global Maritime Shipping Routes

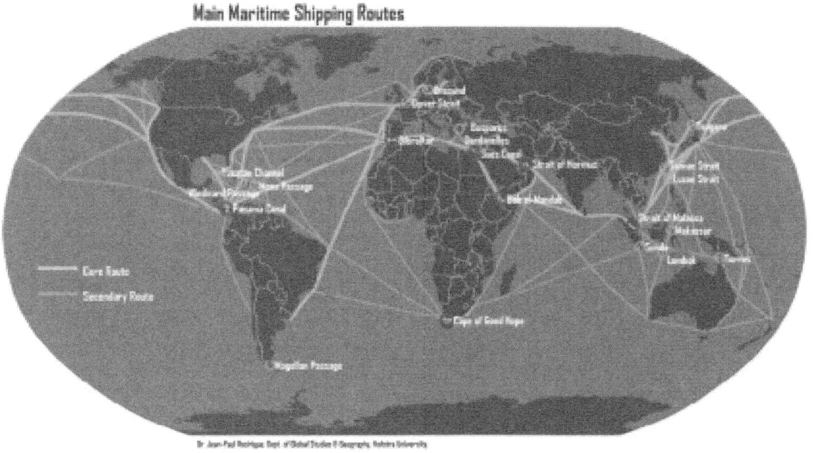

Source: https://people.hofstra.edu/geotrans/eng/media_maps.html

of Good Hope passage, and much of the very same traffic will continue through Malacca to East Asia in the Pacific Basin. This is because weather conditions, even with climate change, will still impose capacity limitations on the ultimate East-West traffic capacity through most of the "high-latitude" passages. Weather limitations are currently the most restrictive for—in descending order—the Northwest Passage, the Northern Route, the Drake Passage, and the Cape Passage. Nevertheless, the Northern Route is poised to gain more than the Drake Passage—despite the fact that the latter faces less restrictive weather circumstances than the Arctic passages—due to the extraordinary width of the Pacific Ocean. The passage from the Northern Atlantic to East Asia around the northern coast of Norway and Russia will remain significantly shorter and faster than that of the Drake Passage and the long Pacific crossing, although the more significant weather constraints of the Arctic will eventually impose a limit on flows, causing all spillover, at the margin, of future growth in East-West flows to pass through the "high-latitude" passage that benefits from the most benevolent weather conditions and from the relatively small Indian Ocean—that is to say, the Cape Passage.

Therefore, the big winner among sea lanes on the future global flow map, in terms of strategic traffic, will be the Cape Passage. Nevertheless, the transpacific transit route across the northern Pacific Basin will likely also gain in significance, although this will be driven mainly by general intra-basin trade between North America and East Asia (with some North American hydrocarbons eventually finding their way to China). In terms, specifically, of global *inter-basin energy flows*, the Bering Strait will emerge in a secondary way as a key choke-point and inter-basin passage, as Arctic energy flows to East Asia augment the Bering Strait's traditional strategic significance in military terms. However, at the margin of future changes in the global energy flow map, the most strategic inter-basin sea lane passage on the global energy seascape will increasingly be the Cape Passage, through which energy will pass to the east, even as container traffic passes to the west into the Atlantic Basin.

Four Interlocking Global Theses

The conclusions of the previous analysis could be called the "high-latitude sea lane thesis," the working hypothesis of which is that growing future East-West flows (particularly West-to-East energy flows) will outstrip the capacity of the "low-latitude canals" and "spill over" to the most feasible alternative "high-latitude passages." Although this hypothesis assumes that the "low-latitude straits" (Hormuz and Malacca) will remain the key critical chokepoints of the global energy system, it also implies that the sea lanes to gain the most in strategic significance, at least at the margin, will be, primarily, the Cape Passage and, in a secondary sense, the Northern Route and the Bering Strait.

The "high-latitude sea lane thesis" interacts with three other theses impacting on the global energy flow map to generate a range of potential implications for foreign, defense and security policies and for global strategic postures over the 2035-50 time horizon. Each of these working hypotheses have already been presented, at least in skeletal form, earlier in our analysis of the dynamics of global energy flows:

1. *The Atlantic thesis*,[41] with its two corollaries:

---

[41]Of these four thesis, the Atlantic thesis has been explicitly addressed the least in the body of this analysis. For incipient expressions of the thesis, see Paul Isbell, *Energy and the Atlantic: The Shifting Energy Landscapes of the Atlantic Basin*, 2012, op. cit., and "Atlantic Energy and the Strategic Horizon," 2013, op. cit.

- an increasing share of global flows in general—in contrast to the universally accepted thesis of increasing predominance of the Pacific Basin—are becoming purely (intra-basin), or partially (inter-basin), Atlantic flows. While we have highlighted energy flows here, opportunities are presented, and challenges range, across a number of traditional disciplinary and policy areas—and in particular at the multidisciplinary borders between them—for Atlantic Basin transnational collaboration.

- an increasing share of *global energy demand at the margin* will come from Eurasia and be met by seaborne flows of Atlantic Basin energy into the Indian Ocean Basin via the Cape Passage. Already the Atlantic Basin supplies some 35% of total world petroleum imports—the same percentage of world imports coming from the Middle East. To 2030, over nearly 60% of the increase in oil production will come from the Atlantic Basin.[42]

2. *The Arctic thesis*: the opening of the Arctic—the result of the progressive melting of arctic ice—will present opportunities and challenges for local autonomous governance and Arctic transnational collaboration, particularly in the realm of local sustainable economies, scientific research and environmental protection. However, while the global public goods of the Arctic commons will likely be increasingly threatened by a lack of sufficient transnational governance, and by the incentives perceived by certain private interests (energy, minerals, etc.), it remains unlikely that much of the Arctic Basin's resources will ever be exploited, given the harsh realities of even a moderating climate, together with a number of other unfolding economic dynamics, like the recent widespread appearance of shale gas and unconventional oil. However, the Northern Route will also eventually attain a minor role in the global sea lane network, and the Bering Strait will achieve a significance rivaling that of the Panama Canal on the global energy flow map.

3. *The ocean basin thesis*: the increasing economic and strategic importance of the oceans relative to landmasses will generate an increasingly coherent argument for a new style of transnational collaboration based on the new regional geopolitical unit of the "ocean basin." The rise of an ocean-basin world will reveal the partiality of our long-held Eurasian-centric thinking. Our strategic focus—shifting over the course of the 20th century from the

---

[42]BP *Global Energy Outlook 2030* (2013), and own elaboration.

Eurasian "heartland" to the "continental rimlands" of Eurasia—will now view the same geographic coastlines of Eurasia (and elsewhere) as "maritime rimlands." This coming "marine-centered" transformation of our mental maps will place the oceans themselves at the center of a ring of "maritime rimlands"—flipping the perspective of the "continental rimland" of the land-locked "heartland" for that of the "maritime rimland" perceived from the unifying and increasingly strategic "seascape." Such a technology and market driven focus on the oceans in the coming decades will also lay the foundation for new ocean basin-based regionalisms—or new "lake communities" composed of the societies of their "maritime rimlands" and integrated by the ocean itself and the imperative for its effective transnational governance. In these new perceptual spaces of the geographic ocean basins, new "epistemic" transnational communities will overlap with both "geographically and physically-based transnational associations" and new "imagined transnational communities."

Implications of the Future Global Energy Flow Map and the Shifting Global Energy Seascape

The dynamics behind the shifting global flow map will have a number of strategic implications over the coming decades. The heightened strategic import of the seas, continued increasing international seaborne traffic, the emerging westward shift of energy reserves and production, an ongoing eastward shift of manufacturing production, along with the growing spill-over from the capacity-limited "low-latitude" canals benefitting the Cape Passage and the Northern Route: all these dynamics, and others, will interact to transform the strategic horizon.

Implications for the U.S. foreign policy "pivot" debate. According to the "Atlantic thesis," the geopolitical autonomy of the West will be increasingly heightened over the years to 2035 as a result of reduced "extra Atlantic energy dependency" stemming from flattening energy demand in the Northern Atlantic, greatly enhanced hydrocarbons reserves and rebounding production, and the relatively faster roll-out of renewable energies in the Atlantic than in the Indian or the Pacific—at least for some time. Moreover, the Atlantic Basin could become the world's swing source of each new barrel of oil consumed at the margin in Asia, once Eurasian demand begins to outstrip Eurasian Supply.

Whether expressed explicitly or not, this underlying change in the tectonics of the geopolitical globe is ultimately what lies behind a desire in the United States to reduce its strategic footprint in Middle East. Traditionally, however, the geographic center of gravity of our strategic focus has coincided with the major geographic areas of energy supply (i.e., the ex-Soviet Union, or Russia and Central Asia, along with the Middle East)—at least since the Bolshevik Revolution. With the currently unfolding pivot to Asia, on the other hand, for the first time since the rise of oil the center of our strategic attention is being focused on an area of the world that is not a major source of resource supply—but rather one of a competitive energy consumer. That China, for example, represents a major part of an increasingly critical Eurasia rimland, with more possibilities than any other Eurasian power to influence the "heartland" (through a strategic alliance with Russia, for example, with the latter as the "junior part-ner'), and the capacity to be "contained" through an alliance of various "offshore" island allies, and subtle diplomacy with other rimlands (like India), only reveals our continued unconscious enslavement to an incomplete and obsolete mental map of the geopolitical globe first conceived by Halford Mackinder, the British geographer and geopo-litical theorist, around the turn of the 19th to the 20th century, and our incapacity, at least so far, to come to grips with the actual geopolitical flow globe as it is now emerging.

The well-known "pivot to Asia" has been motivated by war fatigue, deepening fiscal restrictions, and over-blown but real competition with—and fear of—China. The pivot is also backed and enveloped by a near global consensus that the 21st century will be the "Pacific cen-tury" and unconsciously reinforced by the above-mentioned lingering subservience to Mackinder's many continentally-obsessed mantras (and the many mantra-like modifications introduced into this "realist" tradition of geopolitics by the Americans Mahan and Spykman).[43] But today's geopolitical globe resembles far more a set of interlocking major seas—which, together with their surrounding "rimlands," make up four natural ocean basin regions linked together in geographically

---

[43]See, for instance, http://www.foreignpolicy.com/articles/2011/10/11/americas_pacific_century

specific ways—than it does the geopolitical map of the Mackinder-Spykman tradition—one of many islands ranged in concentrate circles around the "world-island," the Eurasian megacontinent—which many of our leading geopolitical thinkers still employ as their implicit point of departure.

The first strategic alternative to "the pivot" as currently conceived would be for the United States (and to some extent its Northern Atlantic allies) to remain anchored geopolitically in the Middle East and Central Asia. To pursue such an option would be tantamount to attempting to maintain the Eurasian-centric, status quo vision of the strategic horizon. A range of U.S. and global critics across the political spectrum argue passionately that a number of geopolitical realities—including the vulnerability of Israel, the danger of Iranian nuclear proliferation, and the ongoing challenge of Wahabi/Sunni-inspired radical Islamic political violence—are simply too critical for existential security to allow for the broader Middle East to be relegated to anything other than US global strategic priority number one.[44]

The second alternative to "the pivot to Asia" would be to also "pivot back" to the Atlantic. The "forward pivot to Asia," according to this thesis, should be accompanied by this dual "return pivot to the Atlantic Basin" within the equation of our strategic priorities. Indeed, a growing share of the security threats to Atlantic nations are to be identified, traced and challenged solely within the Atlantic Basin.

Implications for Human Security in the Atlantic Basin. A conventional, or "hard," security focus tends to reinforce our "continentally-biased," "world-island based," Eurasian-centered strategic visions of the great "heartland" and its encircling "rimlands" which together form the "world-island"—or the supercontinent of Eurasia. To "epistemologically break" from the incomplete yet anchoring frame of Eurasia within our strategic thought is to shed light upon the relevance of both what is beyond the supercontinent—i.e., the ocean basins, meaning the oceans themselves and their other extra-Eurasian rimlands—and beneath the realm of "hard" security concerns—ie, proliferating illicit flows (drugs, money, humans, arms) and spreading threats (piracy, organized crime) to legitimate flows. Indeed, a restructuring of

----

[44]See, for example, Kenneth, M. Pollack and Ray Takeyh, "Near Eastern Promises: Why Washington Should Focus on the Middle East," *Foreign Affairs*, May/June 2014.

our mental map of the geopolitical globe which focuses upon the Atlantic Basin as a single unit of analysis, reveals a density of intensifying transnational human security problems within the broader Atlantic that demonstrates the need for an "intra-basin focus" in our attempts to augment "human security." This means a new transnational collaborative human security process within the Atlantic Basin itself.

A deeper and more threatening web of security threats than those posed in the Indian Ocean and Pacific Basins—stemming from lingering poverty and state weakness in certain parts of the basin, along with technological evolution—now threaten the stability of the Atlantic Basin. The Southern Atlantic in particular—despite its record as a relatively peaceful zone, free of conventional "hard" security threats, is particularly vulnerable. The confluence of state weakness, poverty, corrupted oil and drug money, piracy, national secessionist struggles and violent Islamic fundamentalisms is now threatening what is becoming an increasingly important global oil hub in the broader Gulf of Guinea and the security of the sea lanes along which oil and gas flow north to Europe, and south to the Cape Passage. Atlantic Basin transnational security cooperation would logically address this threat. It would also be more likely to achieve success than a global, bilateral or ad hoc approach because none of these frameworks are geographically-specific, nor are they capable of filling the relevant voids in the Southern Atlantic that is currently being pursued by the powers of Eurasia (China, Russia, India, Iran) under the rhetorical banner of the Global South.

Implications for sea lane security and management of chokepoints. Requiring still further strategic attention is the question of the security of sea lanes critical to global trade. From the 19th century onward, our tendency has been to view the security of the seas (but particularly of critical sea lanes) as a global public good entrusted to the global hegemon for its provision. The status quo arrangement has the security of the seas and their critical passages—including the global energy chokepoints—under the "benign stewardship" of the United States, the global hegemon since the Second World War. But following the above analysis—and assuming the ultimate inevitability of at least some kind of reconsideration of the global strategic posture of the United States—the shifting tectonics of the emerging "geopolitical flow globe" call for a US priority focus on the Pacific and Atlantic Basins. The question now arises as to future evolution of the Indian Ocean Basin and the form of security management that will stabilize the Persia Gulf- East Asia flow of oil and gas through the Indo-Asian chain of chokepoints (Hormuz and Malacca) and key controversial sea lanes (South China Sea, Taiwan Strait, East China Sea).

Should the status quo of informal and formal U.S. protection be maintained globally? In any particular basins? Should a global multilateral approach to sea lane security be pursued—perhaps through the context of the UNCLOS or under the aegis of the IMO? Or should regional approaches to transnational collaboration in this arena be encouraged? If so, what regions are ripe for such collaboration?

Some are willing to consider such sea lane security a "global public good." However, while it may qualify as a public good, sea lane security is perhaps, in at least some cases, more "regional" than "global" in its most immediate nature and implications. For example, the security of the energy flows through the Strait of Hormuz and the Straits of Malacca has a much more direct and immediate energy security relevance for the regional Asian neighborhoods than for the global community, or global market, as a whole. Given that nearly all Persian Gulf oil already passes through Hormuz and Malacca to various destinations in Asia, a disruption along one or more of the critical passages of the Indo-Pacific seaborne energy flows has greater negative implications in Asia than in the Atlantic Basin (particularly if the disruption occurs at Hormuz, cutting off Saudi capacity to respond by bringing into production idle capacity in response to the price shock), even though eventually the supply shortfall will be filled through an upward adjustment in the global oil price. While the upward price adjustment negatively affects all consumers in the global market, many (particular those in net exporting regions) bear only a portion of the total price increase and with some inelasticity-produced delay, and none of the direct negative output effects of the actual supply shortfall.

Independent of the price effect of any such supply shock, the direct economic impact on output of supply shortages falls only on the particular importing countries in question. This observation suggests that oil is only "imperfectly fungible" and that the global oil market is highly segmented, and in part according to the geographic realities of the "geopolitical flow globe." The implication is that the logic to deal with critical sea lane security at the global, "multilateral" level breaks down if the security of certain maritime passages are more critical in energy (or any other) terms for some consumers than for others.

Given that in the 21st century Middle East oil and its transport security is basically an Eurasian affair, some might be tempted to take a laissez faire approach of benign neglect. While this might force the Eurasians to work out among themselves the security of the Indo-Pacific sea lanes and chokepoints of the South and East Asian rim-lands, others will no doubt view laissez faire as a dangerously precipitous and isolationist lurch in U.S. foreign policy, particularly in light of the already pronounced "pivot to Asia." However, there are more balanced options available which are consistent with both a double pivot out of the Middle East and Eurasian "heartland" to the Pacific and Atlantic Basins and an increasingly coalescing "ocean basin world." While as a Pacific Basin power the United States could logically continue its current role—or change or even intensify it—in the key sea lanes of the Pacific Basin, it might consider some kind of interim partnership between the United States and the principal Indian Ocean and Pacific Basin naval powers to collaborate on the collective security of the Persian Gulf-East Asia energy supply lines. In an ocean basin world of regional governance processes, the United States might still remain constructively present in the Indian Ocean, for example, as a secondary participant. In any event, the option and capacity to continue the current de facto U.S. protection of all global sea lanes, and these Indo-Pacific lanes in particular, should not be construed as a strategic imperative to be maintained at all costs.

Could regional transnational collaborative or governance structures to guarantee the security of key sea lanes and critical chokepoints replace the current regime in which the global hegemon guarantees the security of the global sea lanes as a global public good? Might not future transnational collaboration over sea lane security devolve to new ocean basin-based arrangements, like an Atlantic Community (or some other Atlantic Basin-based collaborative approach to particular issues like sea lane or energy security) or an equivalent Indo-Pacific Basin initiative?

Chapter 5

Beauty and the Beast: Opportunities and Threats Arising from Distorted Global Flows of Materials

Raimund Bleischwitz

Commodity Markets under Stress

Critical access to natural resources has led to a number of different strategies. A few countries, such as the United States, are strengthening or re-inventing national extraction policies. Other regions, such as the EU, are embarking more strongly on resource efficiency strategies to lower dependencies on natural resources.

This chapter stresses three threats that challenge both strategies—managing functional threats of price volatility and peaks; managing political threats from new players and fragile countries; and managing ecological threats resulting from environmental pressures.

Managing the functional threats of price volatility and peaks. It is highly unlikely that a country or a company would be able to lower all dependencies on major commodities. For instance, the United States is becoming less energy dependent. But it will continue to depend on international markets for metals and critical materials, and is likely to become more vulnerable in its water consumption. All commodity markets have shown signals of increasing price volatilities and erratic peaks since the 2000s.

Managing the political threats of new major players and of fragile countries. Major suppliers such as Russia and Brazil look at their resources as strategic assets; major commodity platforms such as China and India impose all kind of policies to maintain their development interests. They all have established state-owned enterprises with tremendous power in international markets and do not adhere to principles of open markets and open access. Smaller but relevant suppliers such as South Sudan and the Democratic Republic of the Congo are fragile and often act to maximize the short-term profits of an elite rather than long-term yields. In more than forty countries extraction brings in more than two-thirds of total government revenues.

Managing the ecological threats of environmental pressures. The use of *all* natural resources is increasingly identified as a source of environmental pressures along their life-cycles. Extraction, processing and each phase in a product's life entail substantial harm to the environment, aggravated by the subsequent processes of recycling and waste. Rapid urbanization generates additional effects on the use of natural resources. Today's issue is how to manage such *material flows* in a sustainable manner.

The concept of global flow security, as outlined by Tomas Ries in this book, is thus appealing to scholars and for strategic intelligence. From the perspective of commodity markets and material flows it needs to be understood as a dynamic concept of global interdependencies, not just among political actors but also at the interface between economy and ecology.[1] Research increasingly realizes that global drivers can overshadow local drivers in the management of common pool resources such as river basins management and agriculture. On top of this, increasing connectivity allows local turbulence to spread rapidly, with unintended side-effects on other resources and regions.

At the heart of any such global flow security is what is now called the "global resource nexus," i.e. the increasing interlinkages across the use of a number of resources.[2] No natural resource can be utilized without using another one. No energy service reaches a final consumer without water and materials being used during earlier production stages, which in turn require energy for their production and distribution. To give an example of related risks and threats: the struggle for land and water in the Andes can put the copper production in Chile—the biggest producer worldwide—at risk with supply chain security issues for subsequent electronics production.

---

[1] S. Bringezu and R. Bleischwitz, *Sustainable Resource Management: Global Trends, Visions and Policies* (Sheffield: Greenleaf Publishing, 2009).

[2] H. Hoff, "Understanding the Nexus. Background Paper for the Bonn 2011 Conference: The Water, Energy and Food Security Nexus" (Stockholm: Stockholm Environment Institute, 2011); T. Graedel and E. v.d. Voet, eds., *Linkages of Sustainability* (Cambridge: MIT Press, 2010); Philip Andrews-Speed, et al., "The Global Resource Nexus—The Struggles for Land, Energy, Food, Water, and Minerals" (Washington, DC: Transatlantic Academy, 2012).

Response Strategies Fragmented at an Early Stage

Business and policy makers have recognized some challenges and cautiously started to formulate response strategies. Quite often, however, those strategies focus on one dimension. They tend to be either predominantly supply-oriented ("raw materials strategy," "unconventional fuels") *or* demand oriented ("resource efficiency," "sustainable consumption and production"). A comprehensive international strategy defining some early consensus while approaching critical issues step-by-step is at stake. Interests and aims tend to differ: while manufacturing companies have an interest in cutting material purchasing costs and managing volatility, their interest in long-term sustainability strategies tends to be lower. Countries with rich endowments evidently have other interests compared to countries depending on the imports of commodities. The United States and Canada appear enthusiastic about their new markets for unconventional gas and oil supply. Potentially, resource-rich developing countries could use revenues from oil, gas, and minerals for sustainable investments into well-being of their people. Others start to formulate and implement resource efficiency strategies, most notably in the EU as one flagship project of its 2020 strategy.

International oil markets illustrate these challenges: unconventional oil sources have led to a price gap of as much as $10/barrel between Texas and Europe (North Sea Brent). Unconventional oil, however, needs considerably more water and chemicals for extraction; new technologies such as horizontal drilling need more critical materials than previous technologies. Oil-based combustion engines for cars and trucks contribute significantly to climate change, while the production of alternative sources such as biofuels competes with food and drives up its price, and thus faces a trade-off with the overarching political aim of eradicating poverty in a number of regions. There are no easy solutions. The challenge for oil markets is to coordinate a secure supply and support innovation towards carbon reduction, food security and international security alike.

What research needs to understand are the unwanted side-effects of stove-piped management approaches that treat commodities separately, and the dynamics of impacts across multiple scales. Yet, there is no political economy analysis that captures the global material flow security along with the resource nexus. Our contribution seeks to move this objective forward.

Global Trends:
More and More Demand, Slow and Uneven Decoupling

The global commodity markets have expanded both in terms of physical volume and monetary value. International trade is one of the key drivers for global connectivity. The physical volume of traded goods increased by a factor of 2.5 over the past 30 years, with more than 10 billion tons of goods now being traded around the globe.[3] Non-renewable materials account for more than three quarters of commodity trade in physical terms, dominated by oil, while renewable materials that include forests products and agricultural goods account for less than one quarter. It is worth noting with regard to global flows that international trade of water and construction minerals is almost negligible because of a good regional distribution and relatively high transportation prices. In contrast, the share of metals has increased over the years due to development needs and an uneven distribution. Extraction rates have been rising even faster than international trade, reflecting the high amount of used and unused resources that remain in the countries of origin.

The demand for almost all natural resources is widely expected to increase and tighten markets over the next years and decades:

- **Energy:** all "business as usual" scenarios forecast an increase in energy demand. The World Energy Outlook of the International Energy Agency expects an increase by 33% by 2035 compared to 2010, with over-proportionally growth for natural gas, and maintained pressure on oil prices. The shale gas revolution and the ensuing downturn of U.S. energy prices gives incentives for

---

[3]Surprisingly little data and evidence exist on the physical dimension of international trade; with bustling prices it is usually difficult to realize what amounts of commodities have exactly been traded. See e.g. M. Dittrich, "The physical dimension of international trade, 1962-2005," in R. Bleischwitz, P.J.J. Welfens, AND Z.X. Zhang, eds., *Sustainable Growth and Resource Productivity. Economic and Global Policy Issues* (Sheffield: Greenleaf Publishing, 2009), pp. 85-98; M. Dittrich and S. Bringezu, "The Physical Dimension of International Trade: Part 1: Direct Global Flows Between 1962 and 2005," in *Ecological Economics* 69 (9), 2010, pp. 1838–1847; see also: www.materialflows.net.

energy-intensive industries to relocate to the United States; gas prices in Asia are eight times and those in Europe five times the U.S. level. Solar energy producers are under enormous pressure to cut costs too, resulting in many crashes and insolvencies of previous shooting stars such as SunTech, SolarWorld, Solyndra, SpectraWatt, Q-Cells, FirstSolar and SunPower.

- **Minerals:** there are no well-established future scenarios for minerals yet. McKinsey Global Institute expects an increase in steel demand by 80% by 2030 compared to 2000.[4] Chatham House forecasts supply gaps for a number of materials in the next few years (e.g. for copper a 30—50% supply gap, but also for iron and steel).[5] Many critical materials are expected to experience two-digit growth in demand. Five rare earth metals (dysprosium, neodymium, terbium, europium, and yttrium) face serious supply challenges.[6] Several clean energy technologies (wind turbines, PV, electric vehicles, lighting) use such materials at risk of supply disruptions in the short term, or others that are environmentally intensive (concrete, steel, copper).

- **Food:** To eradicate hunger along with population growth, more food needs to be provided to people, particularly in Asia and Africa. For sure, food waste needs to be minimized along the supply chain. But supply and the resource nexus with land, water, energy, and mineral nutrients is also at stake. The FAO estimates that agricultural production needs to grow by about 70% by 2050 at a time when agricultural productivity is lower than in previous years, access to land has become difficult, and climate change comes on top of that;[7]

- **Water:** future demand is very difficult to estimate; at least 20% increase by 2050 can be expected to follow demand for food, and

---

[4]B. Lee, F. Preston, J. Kooroshy, R, Bailey, and G. Lahn, "Resources Futures" (A Chatham House Report, London, 2012), p. 35.

[5]Ibid.

[6]U.S. Department of Energy, *Critical Materials Strategy* (2011); JRC (2011), R. L. Moss, E. Tzimas, H. Kara, P. Willis, J. Kooroshy, "Critical Metals in Strategic Energy Technologies: Assessing Rare Metals as Supply-Chain Bottlenecks in Low-Carbon Energy Technologies, JRC Scientific and Technical Reports," European Commission Joint Research Centre, Institute for Energy and Transport, 2011.

[7]Frank Rijsberman, head of the world's 15 international CGIAR crop research centers, estimates an additional 60% will be needed by 2050, according to *The Observer*, April 13, 2013.

much more if water-intensive food patterns, biofuel strategies, non-conventional energy sources are pushed;[8] McKinsey expects an increase by 41% by 2030 compared to 2000.[9] Scenarios done by the Water Resources Group (a public-private platform) estimate demand for water could be as much as 40% higher than supply by 2030. Especially Asian rivers are subject to a number of expected conflicts. The energy sector's water needs are expecting to grow, making water an important criterion for assessing the viability of future pathways.

These demand trends and the perspective of a tripling of global annual resource extraction by 2050 as suggested by the International Resource Panel[10] will very likely lead to intensified competition for resources. The prospect is for high volatility.[11] While some new supply will come on stream shortly (oil, gas, iron ore, copper, etc.), the mid-term perspective after 2020 is less bright due to a number of restrictions: new mining sites tend to be of lower ore concentration, in remote areas, offshore and in landlocked countries. In addition, price volatility will make all prospects much more uncertain and lowers the incentives for investments. The Chatham House report thus predicts a looming investment gap in agriculture and food, energy supply infrastructures, natural gas, and metals.[12]

A New Market Geography

Analyzing global trends for material flows is not an easy task. The geography of different scales of drivers and impacts matters. Over the past fifteen years, a new geography of commodity trade has clearly emerged. The obvious changes relate to the end of the socialist system in the 1990s and the shift from a G8 to a G20 world in the 2000s. The

[8]H. Hoff, "Understanding the Nexus. Background Paper for the Bonn 2011 Conference: The Water, Energy and Food Security Nexus" (Stockholm:Stockholm Environment Institute, 2011), p.10.

[9]Richard Dobbs et al., "Resource Revolution—Meeting the World's Energy, Materials, Food, and Water Needs" (McKinsey Global Institute, 2011), p.35.

[10]UNEP, Decoupling Natural Resource Use and Environmental Impacts from Economic Growth, A Report of the Working Group on Decoupling to the International Resource Panel," 2011, p. 10.

[11]"Commodity Market Review" (Washington, DC: IMF, 2013).

[12]B. Lee, et al., op. cit., p. 56f.

weight of the developing world has become more obvious, with exports and imports of commodities connecting major emerging economies.[13] A good indicator is the role of China in markets for metals, energy and forestry products, but it is also striking to note a number of other features.

North America hails the shale gas revolution and other unconventional fuels on its way to energy security and independence. However the interest in "bringing our jobs back home" by strengthening the domestic manufacturing base suggests analysis of remaining import dependencies for metals and the vulnerability towards water stress, weather extremes and climate change. Along with it, the global repercussions of ramping up the production of Liquefied Natural Gas (LNG) with potentially new global distribution systems beyond pipelines make future shifts in global gas markets very likely.

As the EU has been the largest consumer of fuels and imports a very large share of natural resources it is well aware of international dependencies; this is likely to be expanded to agriculture because the EU uses more land in foreign countries than it offers. Its emphasis on bilateral partnerships in combination with resource efficiency thus is a rational response to all those dependencies.

Strong suppliers are likely to remain strong: the major position of Russia as commodity exporter of energy and minerals, Central Asia in gas and oil, Brazil in minerals and agricultural goods are all obvious; so is the Middle East for oil, with a likely comeback of Iraq and Libya in the next few years. However those countries underperform in terms of general economic, social and political indicators compared to other emerging economies with a more diversified portfolio and more open structures.

In addition, "new kids on the block" are likely to be of growing importance: exporting countries of Africa (oil, minerals), Central Asia (oil and gas, minerals), and Southeast Asia (biofuels, minerals). The conundrum is that these resource-dependent countries usually rank low in the Human Development Index. The "Africa Mining Vision"

---

[13]R. Muradian, M. Walter, J. Martinez-Alier, "Hegemonic Transitions and Global Shifts in Social Metabolism: Implications for Resource-Rich Countries," *Global Environmental Change*, 2012, pp. 22, 559–567.

Figure 1. Patterns and New Geography of Commodity Trade

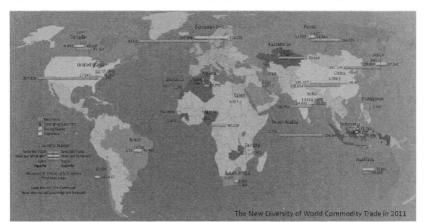

and the "Africa Progress Report" express the hopes that those endowments can be turned into development opportunities for the people if managed properly.

A number of emerging economies (e.g. China, India) are increasing their production capacities for refined materials and key products such as steel and cement. India is a good case for a country with rich endowments (e.g. coal) but a challenging mining environment due to a land use conflict with forestry, local and indigenous people, and a lack of transportation infrastructure. China and India can be characterized as "swing states" for global material flows because their strategies towards either more imports or more exports will have significant impacts on international markets and politics.

The global geography of water and food is more diverse than ever before. While countries such as Brazil, China, Canada, and Turkey are water hegemons, downstream countries in Asia, Middle East and elsewhere depend on proper water supply. Food import dependencies in countries such as The Philippines, Egypt, Mexico are high and put them at risk of social unrest when food prices start soaring. It is here where the resource nexus becomes strategically important as any social unrest may jeopardize their ability to export other commodities.

Identifying winners and losers is thus a task for research in an agenda about material flow security. Certainly big mining companies, their state-owned counterparts, and elites in resource-rich countries have benefited a lot from previous booming years. But it is far from being clear that those golden years are going to last. The emergence of a global middle class with some three billion consumers will alter the patterns of resource use globally. While the current estimation is that high consumption patterns occur in the industrialized countries, the average of the developing world is still well below, with India and many African countries at the lower end. The aspirations of market newcomers may clash with restrictions on the supply side, whether for fuels, food, or other resources.

There is neither a North-South divide nor any preoccupation favoring either OECD countries or resource-rich countries. The security angle suggests that all countries and industries should be aware of challenges resulting from unexpected shortages in areas that might have been overlooked in the past. Local and regional stress factors are likely to hit critical nerves of global supply chains, and might transform strong systems into fragile ones or even into secessionism of shattered pieces. The strategic conclusion, however, is that some thirty countries from all over the globe matter most with regard to resource supply, while no country can claim a full independence from resource risks.

International trade policy will be decisive for the nature of future competition. The dawn of a new age of resource nationalism can be observed, be it in the form of supporting large national corporations, trade restrictions of any kind, or a neo-mercantilism of favoring exports. The United States, the EU and Japan have taken China to the WTO in the case of rare earth export restrictions. According to the Global Subsidies Initiative, subsidies for fossil fuels increased almost 30% in 2011, up to $523 billion, led by the Middle East and North Africa. In comparison, subsidies for renewable energies were $88 billion in 2011.[14] Biofuels are believed to receive $20 billion in subsidies for production and consumption.[15] Countries such as India and Spain spend millions of dollars on irrigation.

---

[14]D. Jones and R. Steenblik, "Subsidy Estimation: A Survey of Current Practice,"Global Subsidies Initiative (GSI) of the International Institute for Sustainable Development (IISD), Geneva, 2010.

[15]Ibid.

Figure 2. Institutions and Actors of Resource Markets: Polycentric and Multilevel Governanace

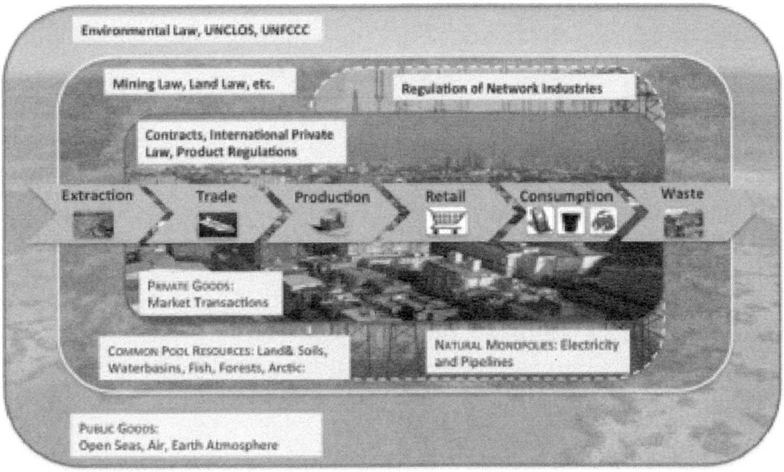

Environmental Law, UNCLOS, UNFCCC

Mining Law, Land Law, etc.   Regulation of Network Industries

Contracts, International Private Law, Product Regulations

Extraction   Trade   Production   Retail   Consumption   Waste

Private Goods: Market Transactions

Common Pool Resources: Land & Soils, Waterbasins, Fish, Forests, Arctic   Natural Monopolies: Electricity and Pipelines

Public Goods: Open Seas, Air, Earth Atmosphere

In the future, a further global shift in agricultural production can be expected: the capacity to increase agricultural production in Latin America and Sub-Saharan Africa is huge, while large parts of Asia (in particular India and China) will probably have huge difficulties to increase food production along with their domestic demand and difficulties with irrigated agriculture coming under water stress.[16] The changing climate is likely leading to enhance geographical disparities. The 2012 World Bank report on the likelihood of a 4° C world warns that such change would significantly exacerbate existing water scarcity in many regions, particularly northern and eastern Africa, the Middle East, and South Asia.[17] In such world, food security could be substantially undermined. Compounding these risks is the adverse effect of projected sea-level rise on agriculture in important low-lying delta areas, such as in Bangladesh, Egypt, Vietnam, and parts of the African coast.

The new geography of bustling commodity markets requires more stringent efforts to coordinate private and public actors at a global scale

---

[16]FAO (2011), "Anticipated Trends in the Use of Global Land and Water Resources," SOLAW Background Thematic Report, Nachtergaele, F., Bruinsma, J., Valbo-Jorgensen, J., Bartley, D.

[17]"Turn Down the Heat: Why a 4°C Warmer World Must Be Avoided" (Washington, DC: World Bank, 2012).

while today's and tomorrow's needs ought to be fulfilled and environmental concerns should be taken into account. One may put forward the argument that the market stress ahead can only be coped with from a governance perspective that covers the levels of value chains, states, and actors on the ground—a polycentric and multilevel governance perspective comprising business, other stakeholders, governments, international organizations and the respective institutions.[18] At the same time, the paradigm of "more is better" should be put in question.

The Temptation of Resource Efficiency: Decoupling Resource Use from Economic Growth?

Expectations for volatile and high prices will help to curb demand. Therefore the general trend of using lesser resources to produce one unit of real GDP is likely to be continued. The discussion is about "decoupling," referring to reducing the rate of resources per unit of economic activity and—partly as a side effect, partly as deliberate attempts—reducing their environmental impacts. If countries or the world economy manage an increasing rate of resource productivity the result is called "relative decoupling"; if an increasing resource productivity even exceeds the growth rate of an economy and, consequently, the resource use declines in absolute terms, the result is called an "absolute decoupling.[19] The empirical evidence is good because dur-

---

[18]Defined by Ostrom, Tiebout, and Warren, "The Organization of Government in Metropolitan Areas: A Theoretical Inquiry," *American Political Science Review*, 55(4), 1961, pp. 831–842. Following their analysis of water management systems in California as "Polycentric" connotes many centers of decision- making that are formally independent of each other. Whether they actually function independently, or instead constitute an interdependent system of relations, is an empirical question in particular cases. To the extent that they take each other into account in competitive relationships, enter into various contractual and cooperative undertakings or have recourse to central mechanisms to resolve conflicts, the various political jurisdictions in a metropolitan area may function in a coherent manner with consistent and predictable patterns of interacting behavior. To the extent that this is so, they may be said to function as a "system'." See also the work of e.g. Philipp C. Schmitter on polycentric governance.

[19]There is a related literature about the "Environmental Kuznets Curve," a hypothesized relationship between environmental degradation and income per capita that may take the form of an inverted U-shaped function, i.e. environmental degradation rises in early stages of development and might fall during later stages. The EKC concept emerged in the early nineties with a number of papers (e.g. by the World Bank) and is now more critically examined along with indicators such as CO_2 and biodiversity that do not appear to decline. Thus "decoupling"

ing the 20th century global GDP rose faster than the use of resources: e.g. about 25% less material input was required in 2002 compared to 1980 to produce one unit of real GDP.[20]

The question, however, is whether this trend is likely to be continued at a rate, at a speed, and across different scales in line with the challenges ahead. If, for instance, half of future demand could be met by increasing efficiency of using resources, how could such efficiency increase be realized, and how could the remaining gap be filled? For a number of reasons, decoupling should become an issue for international policy-makers, rather than viewed as an automatic development.

Countries are not on track. While most developed and industrializing countries manage a relative decoupling, absolute decoupling is very rare yet, and some countries actually increase their resource use faster than GDP. Among those with relative decoupling, significant differences can be observed between efficiently performing countries such as the UK, Japan and Germany, and less efficiently performing countries such as the United States, Australia, Turkey, and Canada.[21]

The resource nexus is not yet accounted for. Resource categories give rise to concerns. The World Bank points to the trend that the metal intensity of global development, which should fall according to decoupling trends, has actually been increasing since the late 1990s and is now back at the levels of the early 1970s.[22]

Problems are shifted to weaker countries. A number of studies and indicators demonstrate the bias favoring industrialized countries with huge imports stemming from resource-intensive processes taking place in other regions of the world; the territorial resource use of consuming countries appears lower than life-cycle based assessments of

expresses the more recent discussion about a wider range of indicators and economic activities. UNEP, op. cit., p.8; R. Bleischwitz, "International Economics of Resource Productivity: Relevance, Measurement, Empirical Trends, Innovation, Resource Policies," *International Economics and Economic Policy* (7), 2–3, 2010, pp. 227–244.

[20]Fridolin Krausmann, Simone Gingrich, Nina Eisenmenger, Karl-Heinz Erb, Helmut Haberl and Marina Fischer-Kowalski, "Growth in Global Materials Use, GDP and Population During the 20th Century," *Ecological Economics* 68(10),2009, pp. 2696–2705.

[21]Dittrich and Bringezu, op. cit., pp. 1838–1847.

[22]World Bank, "China, Global Metal Demand, and Super-Cycle Hypothesis" in *Global Economic Prospects 2011, Commodity Outlook Annex*, p. 57. Available at http://go.worldbank.org/DA78QLAEI0.

resource use reveal. Thus the spatial dimension of more comprehensive indicators of resource use such as "ecological rucksacks", material footprints, carbon footprints, water footprints, etc. is crucial to any decoupling analysis.

Resource Efficiency as a Challenge for Business...

A key insight is to address the business dimension of using materials, energy, water and processing food. Given that resources have a price (even if negative externalities are not properly accounted for) and price expectations are generally upwards business does have incentives to perform manufacturing at lowest possible material costs. A closer look reveals that the material costs to business actually outweigh the prices of raw materials. German manufacturing firms report shares of materials in their gross production value of 40–45%: European companies have reported similar shares lately.[23] Accordingly, the potential for cutting those costs through process innovation is high. The German program DEMEA reports average savings per company in the order of some €200,000, with increases of marginal returns to sales of 2.4%. Similar experiences have been made in the UK and other EU member states.

It can be assumed that a majority of manufacturing companies have strong incentives to get engaged in efforts to save material purchasing costs. They will consider making resource efficiency a core element of their strategy and business models. Early barriers are the lack of attention and information deficits, followed by availability of financing and uncertainties about future demand.[24] Many of those early improvements will be on-site at the level of individual companies and incremental process innovation rather than addressing the whole life cycle of products or material flow systems.

Given that most business operations are value-chain oriented and on an international scale, it could become good management to monitor the flow of materials along value chains and to establish material stewardship where by-products could be re-used and recycling offers tangible benefits.[25] Our suggested approach offers potential benefits

---

[23]EIO (2011): The Eco-Innovation Challenge; Pathways to a resource efficient Europe, Funded by the European Commission, DG Environment, Brussels. www.eco-innovation.eu
[24]Ibid.; Dobbs et al., op. cit. pp. 118ff.

of reducing operating costs through improved internal management of water, waste, energy, materials, carbon and hazardous materials in an integrated manner. Indeed this can and should be combined with efforts to reduce environmental impacts. While these strategies will improve the return on capital, other strategies can improve growth and contribute to better risk management:[26]

- Guide investment decisions at portfolio level based on resource trends and risk analysis
- Develop new products and services with resource-efficient features able to attract customers
- Manage risk of operation disruptions (be it from scarcities, climate change, regulatory changes, etc.).

A life-cycle approach helps to identify more tangible benefits and prioritize key initiatives such as the resource efficiency of buildings, increasing yields on large-scale farms, reducing food waste, reducing municipal water leakages and higher overall efficiency rates in end-use products such as vehicles. As the World Economic Forum points out, ambitious business will seek to transform demand through interactions with the consumer and transform value chains through new business models.[27] Value creation with less use of resources may become a strategic management profile. Worth to note: emerging economies are on the verge of entering the market for such eco-innovation; Walz points to catching up competences of countries such as South Korea, Singapore providing favorable conditions and high absorptive capacities for eco-innovation technologies, while countries such as Brazil and Malaysia show promising specialization for renewable materials and recycling.[28]

...and for Policy Makers

Public policies and international organizations can be influential in helping to overcome barriers and to stimulate market development in

---

[25]International Council on Mining and Metals (ICMM), "Materials Stewardship, Eco-efficiency and Product Policy" (London, 2007).

[26]McKinsey 2011 op cit; World Economic Forum, "More with Less: Scaling Sustainable Consumption and Resource Efficiency, Geneva, 2012.

[27]Ibid.

[28]R. Walz, "Competences for Green Development and Leapfrogging," *International Economics and Economic Policy*, 2010.

favor of developing new resource-light products and systems.[29] Hybrid forms of governance, such as agencies with partners from the private sector and public-private alliances, can certainly help to promote best practices and disseminate knowledge as well as to improve qualification and training. Nevertheless, promoting resource efficiency is also a task for policies. Without an explicit international dimension, resource efficiency strategies face an uphill battle against existing distortions and unfair competition. Volatile prices and lack of transparency about unfair production processes abroad undermine efforts undertaken by industry.

The strategy of resource efficiency is high on the European policy agenda[30] and is well-rooted in Japan, China and elsewhere, while it is still almost invisible in the United States. This is in line with a roughly 30% better performance in the EU compared to the United States or other countries. What is missing in all countries, however, is an explicit international policy dimension of resource efficiency or decoupling strategies.

More transparency of payments in the extractive industries and downstream is an important step toward properly functioning markets and good governance.[31] Combating corruption in mining countries via disclosure of payments strengthens democratic institutions and increases participation. Additionally, fair contracts can stabilize the income of producer countries. With resource revenues dwarfing development aid, it is by no means unrealistic to assume that a robust extractive industry and investment in sustainable development can offer promising economic prospects for the 100 or so resource-rich developing countries and their 3.5 billion people. The case of Ghana, where mining revenues for the state could quadruple from 2010 to 2011, demonstrates potential achievements if all partners agree.

---

[29]M. Jaenicke and K. Rennings, "Ecosystem Dynamics: The Principle of Co-Evolution and Success Stories from Climate Policies," *International Journal of Technology, Policy and Management*, Vol. 11, No.3-4, 2011, pp. 198–218; EIO 2011 op cit.; Bleischwitz, Welfens and Zhang, op. cit.

[30]See e.g. www.eco-innovation.eu; http://ec.europa.eu/environment/enveco/resource_efficiency/.

[31]RevenueWatch Institute, "Resource Governance Index. A Measure of Transparency and Accountability in the Oil, Gas and Mining Sector," New York, 2013, available at http://www.revenuewatch.org/rgi

Resource-rich developing countries may establish a prosperous financial order with extraction taxes and green sovereign wealth funds from resource revenues that potentially leverage investments in clean energy, resource efficiency, and inclusive wealth. With assets estimated worth round $3 trillion in 2011—twice as high as global hedge fund assets—such market development may enable those countries to eradicate poverty by the year 2025. But as expressed, this requires international efforts and should be done in light of the threats that may arise if nothing is done.

Accumulating Threats if Material Flows are Not Managed

A comprehensive assessment of global material flows and the resource nexus should also contain a number of stress multipliers and cumulative risks. Recent evidence of the dangerous conjunction of high prices for food and water and social tensions could be witnessed during the Arab uprisings in 2011. Sternberg points to the drought that occurred in Northern China as a global trigger mechanism for higher food prices;[32] the International Food Policy Research Institute underlines additional domestic factors such as malnutrition, the phasing out of food support programs and a high share of angry young men caring for their families. Future impacts of climate change as stress multiplier are obvious.[33]

It may also be worth noting that in historical perspective the impact of food prices on the great revolutions in France (1789), Russia (1917), and other civil wars helps to explain the security dilemmas of the population and contingent political outcomes.

All these factors and more are likely to increase in many regions of the world. Two risks are inherent to commodity markets: illicit trade and supply breakdowns.

---

[32]T. Sternberg, "Chinese Drought, Bread and the Arab Spring," *Applied Geography* 34, 2012, pp. 519-524.
[33]Bleischwitz, Welfens and Zhang, op. cit.

Figure 3. Main Global Transnational Organized Crime

Illicit Trade and Transnational Crime

Illicit trade of so-called conflict minerals may cover some 20% of the world market, perhaps even more. But the issue goes much further. The United Nations Office on Drugs and Crime (UNODC) reports on how markets for these activities are intertwined, with markets for heroin, cocaine, firearms, smuggling of migrants, female trafficking victims, counterfeit consumer goods, counterfeit medicines, and illicit trade with wildlife, timber, gold and other minerals. Since the world's biggest trading partners are also the world's biggest markets for illicit goods and services, this is certainly a huge risk that requires tough action.

Any certification of single materials will not be sufficient, since global material flows along complex value chains can hardly be monitored[34] and organized crime will be able to switch to more profitable

---

[34]R. Bleischwitz, M. Dittrich, C. Pierdicca, "Coltan from Central Africa, international trade and implications for any certification," *Resources Policy*, 2012; V. Haufler, "Disclosure As Governance: The Extractive Industries Transparency Initiative and Resource Management in the Developing World," *Global Environmental Politics* 10(3), 2012, pp. 53–73.

Figure 4. The Wheels of Fire:
How Stress Multipliers Exceed Institutional Resilience

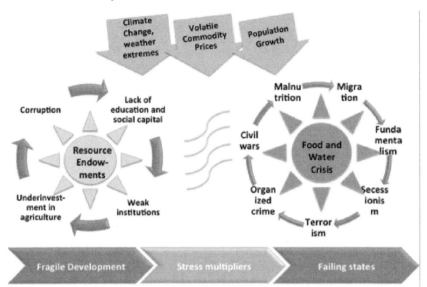

activities. The accumulated risks and threats can be described as follows. First, citizen attempts for smart consumption, fair trade, etc. are likely to fall short; lack of consumer confidence is likely to become an issue. Second, international markets are severely distorted, with many side effects in global business operations. Third, whole countries may be captured by organized crime, and efforts to establish resilient institutions towards sustainable development are likely to fail. At the same time, organized crime and money laundering are unlikely to be contained if no further action is taken.

Breakdown of Fragile Suppliers and a Resource Curse Redux

Many commodity suppliers can be considered fragile; in particular new suppliers are at risk of suffering from the "*resource curse,*" the institutional inability to transform natural endowments into prosperity for the poor.[35] Sure, the price rally may offer opportunities to escape the

---

[35]P. Collier, "Laws and Codes for the 'Resource Curse,'" Oxford University; D. Lederman and W.F. Maloney, eds., *Natural Resources: Neither Curse Nor Destiny*. (Palo Alto:Stanford, 2007).

various traps of underdevelopment.[36] But fragile states cannot yet comply with international social or environmental standards. Their institutions are not yet inclusive and still too weak.[37] According to Paul Collier, a domestic institutional capacity comparable to Portugal in the 1980s deems it necessary to embark on a path for inclusive and sustainable growth.[38] With stress multipliers such as climate change, volatile commodity prices and pressure from population growth—factors that are very difficult to be influenced by those states—they more probably stuck at the bottom, risks of violent conflicts increase, and many of these countries may actually fail. This is especially likely in those countries that are in a post-war period such as Afghanistan, Iraq, Libya, and others.

The combination of these factors could translate into cumulative risks of what we call a redux of the resource curse:[39] triggered by the emergence of a food and/or water crisis—whatever the causes may be—local and national governance mechanisms are vulnerable and may not be able to cope with such a shock. If people start rioting for access to water and food and if the existing institutional resilience is low, fragile states and regions will be put at risk of further instability, where the above-mentioned mechanisms might escalate. Any such escalation may then lead to interruptions of supply chains for essential materials and have international repercussions.

Our mapping analysis based on (a) assessing the future likelihood of food and water stress, (b) political fragility and (c) importance for resource supply has revealed a number of countries that may potentially break down.[40]

---

[36]P. J. Luong and E. Weinthal, E., "Oil is not a curse. Ownership structure and institutions in Soviet successor states," Cambridge 2010.

[37]D. Acemoglu and J.A. Robinson, *Why Nations Fail: The Origins of Power, Prosperity and Poverty* (New York: Crown Publishers, 2012).

[38]Collier, op cit.

[39]R. Bleischwitz, C. Johnson, M. Dozler, "Re-Assessing Resource Dependency and Criticality. Linking Future Food and Water Stress with Global Resource Supply Vulnerabilities for Foresight Analysis," *European Journal for Futures Research*, Special Issue on Futures Research As Instrument for Policy Development and Strategic Reasoning, 2013, http://dx.doi.org/10.1007/s40309-013-0034-1

[40]Bleischwitz, Johnson and Dozler, op cit.

Table 1. Countries at High Risk and their Relevance

Country	Relevance
Afghanistan	Major resource endowments (e.g. lithium) estimated to be near $1 trillion; long-lasting war and civil war; large drug producer
Algeria	Major producer of natural gas
Democratic Republic of the Congo	Major endowments of copper, diamonds, and critical minerals; long-lasting civil war In eastern portions of the state
Guinea	Major endowments in bauxite (aluminum) and iron ore
Indonesia	Major producer of forest products and agricultural goods (e.g. bio-fuels) as well as fuels (natural gas), nickel, copper and aluminum ores; vulnerable to sea level rise and climate change; secessionist conflicts; strategic position at the Strait of Malacca
Iran	Major producer of natural gas and oil; regional de-stabilizer
Iraq	Major producer of natural gas and oil; long-lasting war and civil war
Libya	Major producer of gas and oil; recent civil war
Nigeria	Major producer of oil, including major offshore oil reserves; recent political changes towards democracy
Sierra Leone	Major reserves of bauxite (aluminum)
Somalia*	Holds strategic position near the Strait of Hormuz
Sudan, South Sudan**	Major producer of oil; currently in armed conflict about disputed areas, including oil fields; plans to erect dams for agricultural use along parts of the Nile River that may put downstream countries at risk of water shortages
Yemen	Severe water shortages; home of terrorists; strategic position at the Strait of Hormuz

*In this paper Somaliland is considered to be a legal part of Somalia, since Somaliland does not have internationally recognized independence. Furthermore, the data for political stability, agricultural stressors, and resource reserves does not consider the two entities separately. Therefore, on the map, the designation between Somalia and Somaliland is shown with a dotted line, but the data and evaluation does not distinguish between the two.

**The data for this chapter comes from before South Sudan's separation from Sudan proper in July 2011. Therefore, for the purposes of this chapter, assessments of Sudan and South Sudan's political stability, agricultural stressors, and resource reserves were considered as a unified Sudan. When new data for the two separate countries becomes available, new risk assessments should be made in which case both countries may not necessarily be at high risk.

Reconsidering Criticality

Altogether, these threats underline a need to reconsider the criticality of resources. The standard measures emphasize the availability of individual resources in the future, as extrapolated from reserves, production capacities and future demand, and supply bottle necks resulting from quasi-monopoly situations. Our approach however brings in a criticality of inter-linkages—the local water demand for extraction, food demand during the construction period of mining sites, etc., as well as of the security repercussions if whole regions fail. This requires a more strategic approach to any criticality assessment, environmental or social impact assessment: a need to include foresight exercises that assess ex ante potential changes in local and regional availability of water and food, intersections with global material flows, and resulting risks. The realms of material flows, inter-state and regional security thus have to be strengthened in criticality assessments..

Conclusions

Our analysis has direct implications for the two main strategies that emerge in parallel in the United States and the European Union: pushing the resource supply frontier forward through more domestic extraction has its limitations as countries and companies can only partially withdraw from global material flows. The resource efficiency strategy may look smart, but faces an uphill battle as long as international market distortions prevail. Both regions are likely to be affected if other major world regions face stress resulting from food, water and material flow security. Thus the direct implications are risks and threats for supply chain security for manufacturing companies and economies in the transatlantic space and elsewhere.

With a view towards 2030, the way forward may start along the following policy pillars:

Integrate supply and demand strategies. Good governance of commodity markets will comprise more transparency with better information in the extractive industries and downstream, stringent resource efficiency efforts, and empowerment and measures to turn natural endowments into opportunities for the world's poor.

Improve knowledge for managing global material flows and the resource nexus. The establishment of an international data hub would be an important step forward, along with expert groups on foresight and disseminating best practices for principles of stewardship and metals recycling.

Better transatlantic cooperation is crucial in both regards. Despite current tensions resulting from the energy price gap and competitiveness concerns as well as from a number of political difficulties, there is a rationale for a coordinated management of material flows. Further steps could include the establishment of a transatlantic multi-stakeholder forum on material flows security that actively promotes the inclusion of G20 and other countries.

Research is needed to understand better the interlinkages across the political, economic, technical, and environmental dimensions of both the opportunities and threats arising along global material flows. Comparative assessments of case studies as well as integrated modeling appear to be important for any future research agenda for international scholars. No doubt that this agenda will be in demand.

Chapter 6

The Global Financial Order in 2030: Moving—Glacially—Towards a Multi-Polar Financial World

Joseph P. Quinlan

The aftershocks of the U.S.-led financial crisis of 2008 and the ensuing financial crisis in the eurozone have produced cracks in the global financial architecture and triggered multiple calls for a re-examination of the post-war, Western-led global financial system. Adding urgency to this narrative: the U.S. government shutdown and the bitter debt ceiling debate in 2013, which damaged the global brand of the United States and raised doubts in the minds of many foreign investors about the credit worthiness of the United States, the world's largest debtor nation.

Trust in the standard bearers of the postwar financial system—the United States and Europe, along with Western-backed multilateral financial institutions like the International Monetary Fund and World Bank—has been diminished. Meanwhile, China in particular and developing nations in general are flush with capital and agitating for a greater say on how the global financial system is run and governed. The massive capital accumulation of the developing nations gives this cohort more power when it comes to shaping the financial order of the future. On a grand scale, however, change will be more evolution-ary than revolutionary, gradual rather than sudden.

More than five years after the collapse of Lehman Brothers, Wall Street and the United States remain at the center of the global finan-cial universe, backed by one of the largest and most resilient economies in the world. The global appeal of the U.S. dollar remains relatively strong, while the eurozone crisis has diminished investor appetite for the euro. Meanwhile, developing nations—despite having over $10 trillion at their disposal in the form of international reserves—have failed to use their financial firepower effectively to stave off a cyclical economic slowdown, let alone marshal their massive savings to fundamentally remake the global financial order in their image. Fears of "tapering" by the U.S. Federal Reserve, or the removal of excess liquidity from the U.S. capital markets, sparked a firestorm in the emerging markets in 2013, prompting massive capital outflows in many developing nations and attendant macroeconomic problems for nations like South Africa, Brazil, Russia, Turkey and many others. These trends were a strong reminder that the developed nations still largely dictate and influence global capital flows and remain at the center of the global financial universe.

That said, the global financial architecture is being reconfigured. A more multi-polar financial world will evolve between now and 2030, with the United States and the U.S. dollar likely to remain first among equals. Below, we examine the various metrics supporting the status quo—or a dollar-anchored world—as well as the key underlying trends pointing towards the beginning of a more multi-currency world. Various crosscurrents are at work.

The Present Baseline:
It's a U.S. Dollar-Based World (For Now)

Any discussion of the global financial system has to start with the U.S. dollar, since the greenback has been the long-time anchor of the world financial order. Ever since representatives from the United States, the United Kingdom and 42 other nations met at Bretton Woods, New Hampshire, to hammer out a new international monetary agreement in 1944, the U.S. dollar has dominated global trade and finance—the currency of choice whether in world oil trade, global mergers and acquisitions, and daily transactions in the foreign exchange markets.

Reflecting the latter, according to the latest figures from the Bank of International Settlements, trading in the world's foreign exchange markets now averages a staggering $5.3 trillion a day, a rise of 331% from the levels of 2001 (see first exhibit).

The dollar was the leading currency behind all this activity, involved in 87% of all trades in April 2013, the last available data. That was up from 2010, when the dollar was used nearly 85% of the time. The euro was the second most traded currency, although its

Figure 1. Global Foreign Exchange Market Turnover
(Net-Net basis*, Daily averages in April)

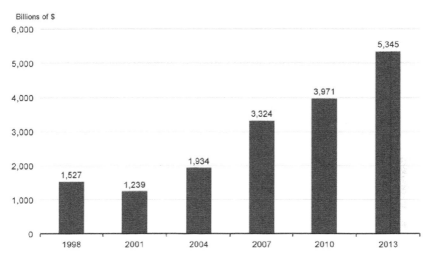

*Adjusted for local and cross-border inter-dealer double-counting.
Source: Bank for International Settlements.
Data as of September 2013.

share fell to 33% in April 2013 from 39% in April 2010. The turnover of the yen rose from 19% in 2010 to 23% in 2013.

After the U.S. dollar, euro and yen, the most popular currencies are the British pound, Australian dollar, Swiss franc, and Canadian dollar. While the shares of Australian and New Zealand dollars rose in the latest survey, the British pound, the Canadian dollar, the Swedish krona and Swiss franc all lost ground in global FX trading.

It is clear from all of the above that the currencies of the developed nations are at the forefront driving global foreign exchange trading, and at the top of this monetary hierarchy—unequivocally—is the U.S. dollar. That is another way saying that is far too early to write the dollar's obituary—a favorite and common narrative of some. Granted, the world financial order is in flux. The West—namely the United States, developed Europe, and Japan is severely in debt and in the midst of a multiyear period of deleveraging and austerity. The developing nations, meanwhile, are flush with capital and in a very strong position to demand a new global monetary order. But the anchor of the global monetary order remains the U.S. dollar.

Figure 2. Global Foreign Exchange Market Turnover
(Net-Net basis*, Daily averages in April)

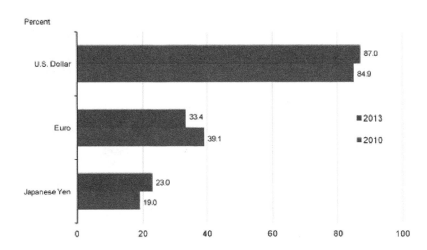

*Adjusted for local and cross-border inter-dealer double-counting.
Source: Bank for International Settlements.
Data as of September 2013.

The Staying Power of the Buck

A number of factors undergird the dollar's world reserve currency status. One such underpinning is America's capital markets, among the deepest, largest and most innovative in the world. This gives the dollar a built-in competitive advantage relative to other currencies—or, as some say, the power of incumbency. Notwithstanding the "Made in America" financial crisis and the staggering growth of the financial assets of the emerging markets, the U.S. remains at the core of the global capital markets. America is not only a global titan when it comes to total bank deposits, government debt securities, corporate debt, and equities but is also at the forefront of financial innovation and expanding financial services.

Underpinning support for the dollar is that global trade remains predominantly denominated in U.S. dollars, with more than 80% of world trade estimated to be invoiced in U.S. dollars. This is despite America's declining share of global trade over the past half-century. More than 80% of trade exports of South Korea and Thailand are

Figure 3. Total Foreign Holdings of Developing Countries

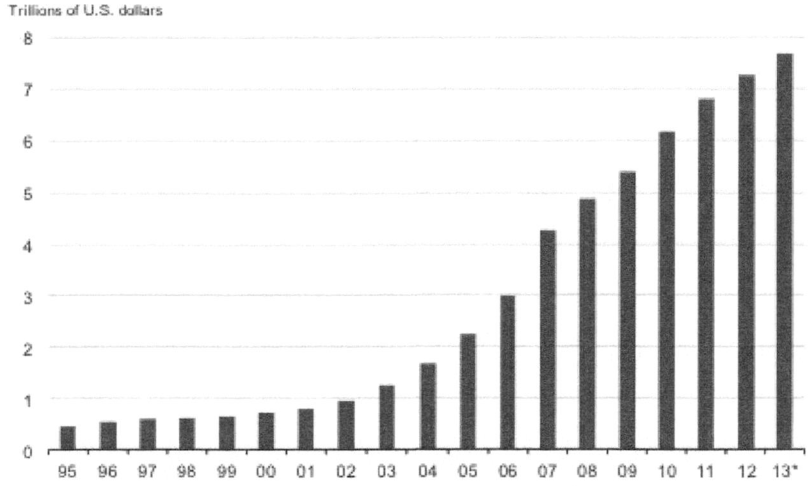

Trillions of U.S. dollars

Source: International Monetary Fund.
*Data through Q3 2013.
Data as of December 2013.

priced in dollars, notwithstanding the fact that only 20% of their exports are destined for the United States. Similarly, more than 70% of Australia's exports are invoiced in U.S. dollars, although the U.S. accounts for just a fraction of Australia's total exports. In the aggregate, the U.S. dollar is used in 85% of all foreign exchange transactions.

The widespread global use of the dollar gives the greenback more staying power than most observers recognize. To this point, key commodities like petroleum continue to be invoiced in dollars despite grumblings from some Middle East states over the steady decline in the value of their petrodollars. There has been increasing talk of creating petroeuros. But the talk has been just that—talk. The status quo in the Middle East pivots around oil being priced in dollars and dollar-pegged currencies—this decades-old arrangement in the Middle East will continue in exchange for U.S. military services and protection. America's massive military commitment to the region suggests that the dollar-oil nexus will remain quite strong over the medium term.

In addition to the above, there are a host of other variables that continue to underwrite the global supremacy of the U.S. dollar.

Figure 4. The Wealth Gap: China vs. the U.S.
(GDP per capita, nominal $)

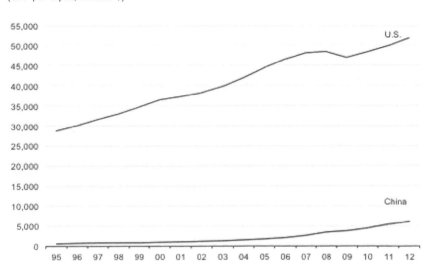

Source: World Bank.
Data as of December 2013.

Notably, the dollar's dominance reflects the fact that the U.S. economy is the largest, most productive and resilient economy in the world. While much has been made of the rise of China in recent years, the usual ominous narrative about China's budding strengths rarely mentions the fact that in 2012, total U.S. economic output ($16.2 trillion) was roughly twice the size of China's $8.2 trillion economy. This makes the average American about 8.5 times more affluent than the average Chinese. Granted, based on purchasing power parity metrics, the gap is not that wide. But this still does not subtract from the fact that early in the 21st century, the U.S. economy remains one of the largest and most dynamic in the world.

The dollar's supremacy mirrors the strength of the U.S. economy and the unappreciated and little-acknowledged attributes that set the economy apart from others. For instance, despite the consensus that the United States has lost its manufacturing prowess, it remains among the top manufacturers of goods in the world, with a global share of over 17% in 2012. The United States is also the world's largest exporter of goods and services and reigns as the world's most favored destination for foreign direct investment and portfolio flows.

Figure 5. U.S. and China Exports of Goods and Services

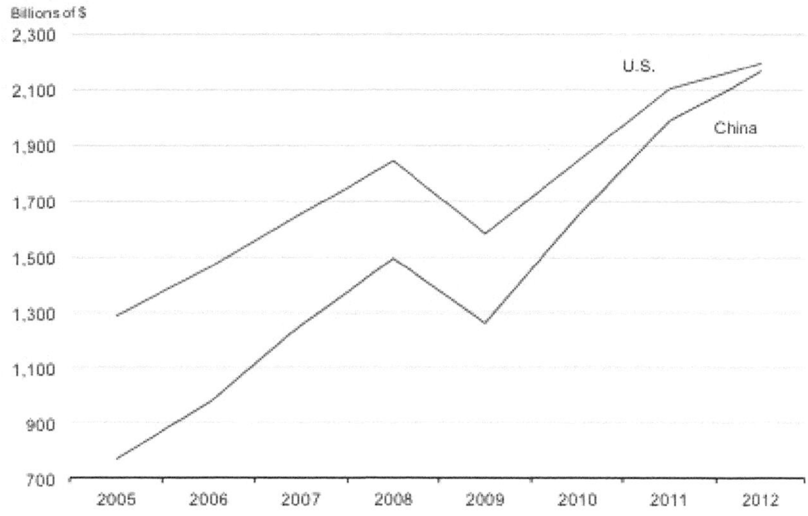

Billions of $

Source: International Monetary Fund.
Data as of July 2013.

The U.S. is a magnet for foreign portfolio investment thanks to its large and transparent capital markets. Meanwhile, America's wealthy consumer base, skilled labor pool, world-class technology capabilities, and protection of intellectual property rights make the United States the prime destination of foreign direct investment. To wit, from 2000 to 2012, for every $1.00 China attracted in foreign direct investment, the United States attracted $2.23. The more global trade and foreign direct investment are conducted with the United States, the greater the demand for and stature of the U.S. dollar.

The dollar is also supported by the fact that when it comes to technological innovation, the United States ranks number one in the world, a competitive advantage supported by America's top-ranked university system. The United States is also home to nine out of the top ten consumer brands in the world (soft power) and the number-one military power in the world (hard power). America's energy revolution, with the United States poised to emerge as the world's largest oil and gas producer by the end of the decade, will only add to the economic and financial strength of the nation.

Figure 6. Foreign Direct Investment Flows, 1970–2012

Source: United Nations Conference on Trade and Development.
Data as of August 2013.

Figure 7. Change in Oil Production: 2012 vs. 2008
(thousands of barrels per day)

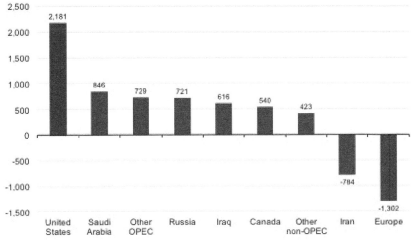

Source: International Energy Agency

Considering all of the above, it is little wonder the U.S. dollar remains the world's primary reserve currency. Today, the greenback is the world's only true international currency, backed by strong economic fundamentals and robust institutions.

The U.S. Dollar: Number One for How Long?

However, the past is not likely to be prologue. Other economies are on the rise and other currencies are likely to gain importance in the years ahead. Global trade and investment flows are shifting towards the developing nations. The emerging markets, collectively, have begun to coordinate policies in attempt to refashion the global financial system. The dollar-centric global monetary order of the past half-century is being reconfigured, with the euro and renminbi poised to become alternative reserve currencies, while a host of other currencies increase in importance over the next decade and a half.

Emblematic of this trend, the dollar's share of central bank holdings has declined by roughly 11 percentage points since 2000, falling to a share of 61% in 2013 from a high of 72% at the start of the century. The decline in dollar holdings reflects many variables, with America's sliding share of world output, trade and foreign direct investment over the past few decades chief among them. Persistent budget deficits and large current account deficits, and the attendant decline in the relative value of the dollar against other major currencies have also eroded the reserve currency status of the U.S. dollar.

So has emergence of Europe's single currency—the euro. While the euro has seen its share of central bank holdings decline over the past few years due to the euro zone crisis, the euro still accounted for roughly 24% of total reserve holdings of central banks in the first quarter of 2013. That is up from 17.5% at the start of 2000 or shortly after the euro was introduced. Meanwhile, according to the last data from the BLS, the euro remains the second most traded currency in the world, with the euro accounting for 33% of all global foreign exchange trading in April 2013.

The euro is also supported by a number of macroeconomic variables. The European Union, a proxy for the euro zone, is one of the largest and wealthiest economic entities in the world, a dynamic that

Figure 8. King Dollar: The Greenback's Share of World Central Bank Reserves

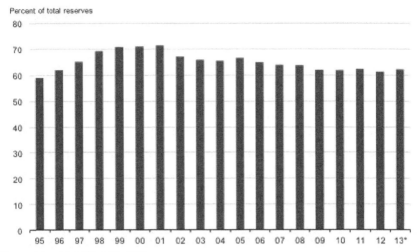

Source: International Monetary Fund.
*Data through Q1 2013.
Data as of June 2013.

Figure 9. Euros Share of World Central Bank Reserves

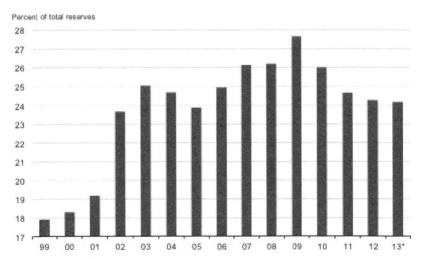

Source: International Monetary Fund.
*Data through Q3 2013.
Data as of December 2013.

will support the financial primacy of Europe for decades to come. Europe is not only rich and large, but also home to some of the most competitive economies and multinationals in the world, a fact that should underpin Europe's leading position in global trade and finance over the medium term.

To underscore Europe's primacy in the global economy, it is worth noting the following: after the sovereign debt crisis in Europe in 2011 and the attendant euro zone recession, bilateral trade and investment flows between Europe and the developing nations contracted significantly, triggering a host of macroeconomic problems in the emerging markets, China included. Trade financing from Europe declined sharply, while import demand in Europe collapsed, leaving many export-dependent developing nations confronting weaker-than-expected real growth.

Assuming that Europe muddles through over the near-term, that the euro zone stays intact, and that Brussels makes some headway in creating some type of banking union over the next few years, the region will remain a key node in the global financial order.

China: Ready for Prime Time?

Beside the euro, the only serious contender to the dollar as the world's reserve currency comes from China and the renminbi (RMB). The growing global importance of the renminbi reflects many variables, including China's expanding role in global trade (the nation is now one of the largest trading nations in the world), China's growing influence in trade finance (the RMB recently replaced the euro as the second most heavily used currency in international trade finance) and the rising use of the RMB in FX trading (the RMB is now the world's ninth most traded currency). Add China's stellar economic performance since 1980, when an economic backwater was transformed into the second largest economy in the world, and the prospects of the RNB becoming a legitimate world reserve currency become more credible.

Beijing has taken a number of steps over the few years to internationalize the RMB. An offshore market, for instance, for RMB transactions has been established in Hong Kong and other global financial centers like London. China has also entered into a number of currency swaps with nations like South Korea, Indonesia, Malaysia and Hong Kong, and has agreed to price bilateral trade with Brazil and Argentina in local currency, moves that will further underpin the global use of the renminbi. In another sign of financial liberalization, U.S. companies like McDonalds and Caterpillar have sold debt priced in RMB, while China's renminbi-denominated debt market is already the largest among the emerging markets. In addition to the above, financial reform and the deepening of the capital markets are top priorities of China's new leadership.

In general, Beijing has charted a course that will ultimately elevate the global stature of the RMB. Less clear is the pace by which all of this will happen. It is going to be some time—another decade at the earliest—before the Middle Kingdom's currency challenges the greenback as the world's top reserve currency.

Much Work Remains to be Done

In order for China's currency to remotely challenge the reign of the greenback, China has to first modernize and open its financial sector, allowing for the build-out of efficient money and capital markets. At the moment, China's banking sector is more closed than opened. The RMB is not convertible, or free to trade in the global capital markets. Not until the mainland fortifies and opens its capital account, strengthens its financial sector, and establishes full convertibility of the RMB will the Chinese currency even have the slightest chance of being a world reserve currency.

The international role of both the renminbi and euro will expand over the coming decade, but the process will be gradual and deliberate. To what extent the euro emerges as a world reserve currency will be determined by Europe's attempts to forge a banking union and create a pan-European capital markets that would pool and allocate capital more efficiently and effectively.

China's influence in the global financial order could be compromised or slowed by the nation's secular slowdown, with the Middle Kingdom, after 10% per annum growth for decades, now struggling to re-set its growth model away from exports and investment and towards consumption and service-led growth. China has hit upon a slow-growth patch; this will slow—not postpone/negate—China's rising influence in shaping the future global financial order.

Meanwhile, beyond the euro and RMB, the use of other currencies in global trade and investment, and as a store of value for central bank holdings, will continue to rise over the next decade, collectively chipping away at the preeminent status of the U.S. dollar. Among this list of secondary reserve currencies will be the British pound, Swiss franc, the Australian dollar, the Brazilian real and perhaps the India rupee.

The Outlook Over the Medium-Term

The shape and character of the global financial architecture over the medium term will be largely determined by three variables: the fiscal/financial health of the United States; Europe's ability to stabilize and fortify the euro zone and therefore the euro itself; and the pace by which China allows the internationalization of the reminibi.

Starting with Europe, policy makers are struggling to craft a coherent and cohesive banking union; the euro's global appeal will go lacking without the latter. In addition, relative to U.S. banks, European banks remain highly leveraged and undercapitalized, making the euro that much more suspect in the eyes of many foreign investors. Notwithstanding these near-term challenges, as long as the euro zone remains intact, the European Union continues to function and muddle through, the euro will remain a key component of the global financial system.

In China, the pace at which China allows its currency to become more global will in turn determine the pace at which the world moves toward a more multicurrency world. The process is expected to be gradual as China slowly shifts from export-led growth to more consumption-led growth. As the Communist Party shifts economic gears, moves on the currency front will be nominal at best over the near term.

That said, it is worth nothing that it is in China's own interests not to see the dollar dethroned in a sudden and unexpected fashion. As one of the largest holders of U.S. dollars, a sharp decline in the value of the dollar would cost the Chinese dearly. Rather, China is all in favor of a steady move toward a more multilateral currency regime since such a scenario would entail the gradual emergence of the renminbi as a top global currency while preserving the value of the U.S. dollar. In other words, it is not in China's interest to see a dollar crisis, contrary to some narratives in the United States.

Finally, no other party will influence the future of the global monetary order as much as the United States. The U.S. dollar and its role as the world's reserve currency hang in the balance. The cost of two wars (Afghanistan and Iraq) and the tab associated with one of the largest financial crises in U.S. history, juxtaposed against soaring entitlement programs, threaten to undermine the financial health of the United States. The financial health of the United States today versus a decade ago is stunning. Recall that the United States entered the new millennium in respectable financial shape. The country enjoyed a budget surplus in 2000, while the ratio of government debt (held by the public) was quite manageable. Reflecting the rather small role of the public sector in the economy, government outlays were below the historic average in 2000. Total revenues were at an all-time high. And Japan, America's ally in Asia, was the largest foreign holder of U.S. Treasuries according to the U.S. Department of the Treasury.

Thirteen years on, America's financial landscape looks radically different. Since the start of the century, the country's level of debt has roughly tripled, rising from $5.6 trillion in 2000 to over $16 trillion in 2013. The latter number includes debt held by the public and debt held in government accounts, and recently exceeded the debt ceiling imposed by Congress.

The massive accumulation of debt reflects near-constant federal budget deficits—since the 1970s, the U.S. has posted deficits in every year but four. Thanks to two tax increases over the 1990s, reduced military spending, and strong federal revenues, the U.S. posted a budget surplus for four straight years, starting in 1998. A decade later, in fiscal year 2009, the United States posted its first trillion-dollar deficit, running a $1.4 trillion federal deficit; that was equal to 9.9% of GDP, one of the highest in peacetime. In FY 2010, 2011, and 2012, trillion-dollar deficits were the norm, although in the fiscal year just ended, the deficit declined to roughly $640 billion.

Looking forward towards 2030, the more the financial health of America declines, the faster the world will shift away from the dollar-centric global economy of the past 60 years. This shift is inevitable, but is expected to play out over decades.

Barring an utter collapse in the finances of the U.S. government, the U.S. dollar will remain first among equals in the gradual movement towards a more multi-financial world. As highlighted above, despite the financial shenanigans of Washington, the U.S. economy, led by a dynamic and hyper-innovative private sector, remains among the most open and competitive in the world. This makes any move or trend to dramatically reconfigure the global monetary system harder to accomplish. Between now and 2030, the United States is expected to remain one of the largest and most competitive economies in the world, and a leading recipient and supplier of trade and investment capital for the world. In the end, in a world where economic growth is becoming more dispersed and less U.S.-centric, it is only natural that a multi-polar global financial order will emerge.

The question is at what speed this transition will take place— gradually and orderly (as expected) or abruptly due to an external shock. The latter would include the breakup of the euro zone, rupturing Europe's financial ties with the United States and developing nations. Another shock could take the form of a second financial crisis in the U.S., and a more debilitating and lasting impact on the U.S. and global economy. Slower-than-expected growth in China that would prompt Beijing to halt or slow the pace of RMB convertibility, could also prove destabilizing for the world financial order.

Another potential disruptive factor to the global monetary order includes a crisis-prone global economy that operates at sub-par levels, triggering more trade and investment protectionism around the world. Under this scenario, capital stays local, or closer to home, and the world financial system becomes more balkanized and looks similar to the interwar years, when capital controls were the norm. A worldwide explosion in income inequality and the attendant backlash against globalization, including the unfettered flow of capital, could have a similar devastating effect on the global monetary system. The rise of a virtual currency ranks as another disruptive element to the world financial order, although this prospect remains slim given investor unease with the concept.

In contrast to the disruptive forces mentioned above, an orderly passage to a multi-polar financial system would help sustain global growth, promote global rebalancing and further integrate the global economy. It would be positive for the United States, Europe and the developing nations. It took two world wars and a Great Depression to radically alter the global monetary system of the 20th century. It will take a similar shock to dramatically reconfigure the current order. Barring such an event, the global monetary order is likely to become gradually more multi-polar in the decades ahead, with the United States, Europe and China at the forefront of this monetary system.

Chapter 7

Global Technology Flows 2030:
Their Impact on Europe and the United States

Bill Ralston, Rob Edmonds, and Carl Telford

Significant social and economic disruption occurs naturally as a technology or set of technologies flows throughout the world. One only needs to consider the advances in communications or transportation technology to appreciate the effects technology flows can have on how societies interact, economies function, and the earth system operates. Currently, *automation* from a particularly interesting set of electro-mechanical and information technologies, stimulated by hitherto unthinkable volumes of data, is poised to drive major disruption in the world.

Traditionally associated with manufacturing, automation technology today is spreading rapidly. Enabled by advanced algorithms, sensors, processing power, user interfaces, and new volumes of data, modern automation involves machines learning, thinking, and performing myriad tasks, both physical and knowledge-based, sometimes with minimal human intervention. These advances have far reaching implications: For example, recent research by the Oxford Martin School suggests that computers could replace humans in 45% of all U.S. jobs within 20 years.[1]

New data is underpinning this spread of automation. Estimates vary, but a reasonable consensus is that the world's data grew by 40-50% in 2013 and is likely to grow even more rapidly over the next two decades due to increasing digitization of work and consumer life, and the growing proliferation of sensors and connected devices (sometimes referred to as "The Internet of Things"). Cloud computing techniques already make huge storage capacities and supercomputer-level processing available on demand to anyone that needs it, and such capabilities will continue to accelerate.

---

[1]Frey and Osbourne, "The Future of Employment" (University of Oxford white paper, September 17, 2013).

A key but often-unrecognized implication of progress in big data and cloud computing is that machine learning is likely to evolve rapidly, leading to new types of automation. Most recent progress in artificial intelligence is driven less by the increasing brainpower of computer programmers (although steady, cumulative progress does occur) and more by the combination of increasing computer power, proliferating data, and cultivation of machine-learning algorithms that perform better the more data they can access. In 2011, Google's chief scientist, Peter Norvig, said, "We don't have better algorithms than anyone else, just more data." Given IBM's suggestion in 2012 that creation of 90% of the world's data took place in the prior two years, rapid progress in the capabilities of machine-learning algorithms in the next decade seems almost inevitable.

While the automation of manufacturing and the use of robots, drones, and driverless trucks have suggested a future where no physical laborers will be required, our personal spaces—the home, office, and car—are also becoming increasingly connected and in the future they will monitor and respond transparently and automatically to everyday human needs and wants.

For Europe and North America the impacts of advanced automation flows in the next 20 years will be particularly acute: Advanced automation will affect the competitive dynamics of many industries, the work tasks done by humans in both the product- manufacturing and knowledge-worker organizations, and how we personally interact with our physical environments and each other. In this chapter, we examine the advanced-automation technology flows and their impacts on the healthcare, financial services, and retail economic sectors in Europe and North American to highlight the possible positive and negative effects of future technology developments on economic and social systems.

Technology-Flow Foresight

This assessment of technology advances on the societies and economies of Europe and North America is based on SBI's analysis of new technologies in the U.S. National Intelligence Council's *Global Trends 2030* report. For the NIC report, SBI technology-commercialization experts applied SBI's scenario-planning and opportunity-discovery methods to identify the most-important new technologies in the next 20 years and assess their influence on the global system and U.S. interests.

We also utilize Tomas Ries' flow-security framework[2] to help explain technology's role and impacts in the global ecosystem.

Technology flows are a result of a complex set of social, economic, political, and ecological forces and drivers where specific outcomes are essentially unpredictable because so many factors are involved. One can shape the conditions, motivations, and costs of technology development, but the range of possible winners and losers will always remain wide. Of the important technological factors that will be shaping the global ecosystem and the particular situation between North America and Europe in the next 20 years, the greatest has been and will be the emergence of the Chinese and Indian economies. As a result, the epicenters of technology innovation are moving toward Asia away from Europe and the United States. The biggest economic growth opportunities in the next 15 to 20 years will be in the emerging markets, where some business experts estimate annual consumption will reach $30 trillion by 2030. This growth will not only stimulate increased technology flows around the world; a shift in the technology center of gravity from West to East will likely occur. The big movement will come as multinationals focus on the faster-growing emerging markets and as Chinese, Indian, Brazilian, and other emerging-economy corporations rapidly become internationally competitive. The speed of this movement will depend on the availability of human and financial capital in the developing countries, rules of law to protect intellectual property rights, and the general desire of developing-economy companies to grow and be globally competitive. As of 2012, China is already the world's largest publisher of patents. This movement of the technology epicenter will change the dynamics of goods and services flows among the regions, but generally lead to increased flows of goods, services, capital, and information around the globe.

Given the present set of political, economic, social, and ecological conditions around the world, the flow of ideas, knowledge, and intel-

---

[2]See Tomas Ries' chapter in this volume.

Figure 1. Global Trends Game-Changer: New Technologies

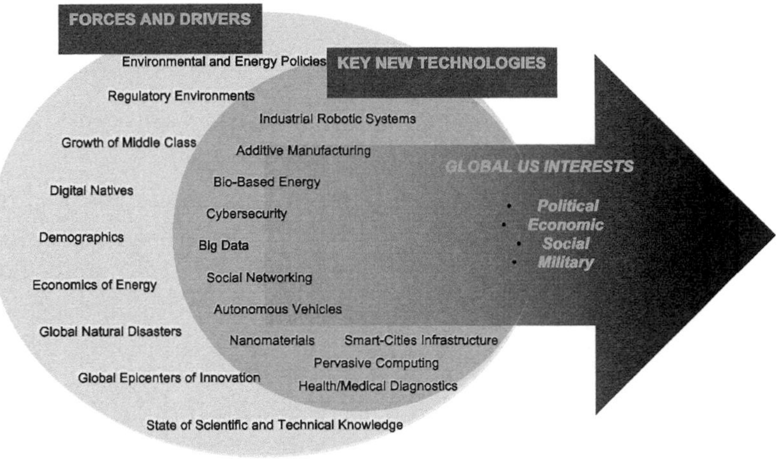

lectual property related to technical advancements and innovations will likely increase in volume and speed in the next 20 years. Technology flows today are already fast and widespread in a global ecosystem because of the internet, mostly open global trade practices, global competition among large multinationals, open national higher education systems that encourage foreign students to attend, academic research conducted by researchers hired on the basis of academic merit, and international commercialization networks of the venture capitalists and other private equity firms. Science and technology research may be centered in the United States today, but teams of mixed nationality conduct it. In the future that research will be increasingly dispersed. Technology flow is a global enterprise, although developed countries led by the United States have dominated the picture because they have the legal systems that support innovation and developed countries are where the initial buyers are. A new technology flow in the last ten years has been reverse innovation, where the innovation initially occurs in an emerging economy and then spreads to the developed world, but this phenomena hasn't affected overall global flows much to this point. But in the next 20 years the sources of technology will increasingly be Asian and innovation could just as likely occur in the United States, Germany, and South Korea, as it could in China, Vietnam, and Turkey.

**Figure 2. Europe/North America Game-Changer:
Advanced Automation**

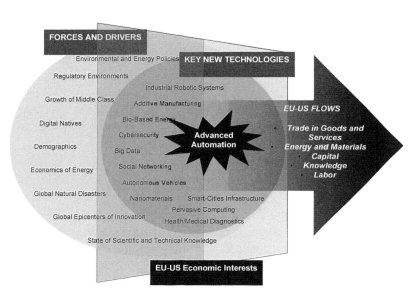

While technology flows stimulate economic flows, they also help expedite fast-moving economic cycles of boom and bust. While technology advances facilitate increased nimbleness by companies and government agencies alike, they also create problems of complexity that few can understand. Thus, an increase in technology flows produces a set of problems that work to undermine the future, and national leaders sometimes find it difficult to support globalization stimulated by technology because of the uncertainties and risks of economic downturns inside their borders.

To develop insight into technology flows and technology's role in shaping social, economic, political, and ecological flows around the world in the next 20 years, it is necessary to develop an integrated international perspective on technology flows and then narrow the focus to specific technologies, in this case advanced-automation technologies, and their influence on economic and social conditions in two geographies, in this case Europe and the United States.

Leveraging SBI's ongoing business-research programs Scan™ and Explorer, we identified the technology building blocks that will drive advanced automation and new automation functions, systems, and capabilities in the next 20 years. We then analyzed the impacts of advanced automation on three key economic sectors for Europe and North America, healthcare, financial services, and retail. Those impacts will likely be very extensive, based on what we're seeing today being commercialized, the resources being invested in new products and services, and market demand. This technology-economic system of advanced automation is reflected in the map below.

Advances in automation technologies will create new human and machine functions and capabilities that will spur productivity, stimulate new markets, and lead to enhanced decision-making, while at the same time forcing change to existing industrial processes, the elimination of many products and services, and the development of new personal routines and connections. Individually, these technology advances are important and interesting, but together they provide the potential for a wide range of new automation functions, capabilities, products, and services that could disrupt every aspect of our lives.

The first key building block for advances in automation is **artificial-intelligence (AI) software.** In pure number crunching and reaction time, machines can already outperform people, and since machine learning will get better the more data it has, and with data growing very rapidly, the prospect is increasing that machines could quickly becoming smarter than humans—Watson was only the beginning.

The extent of machines being able to recognize the content of images and audio and interpreting the meaning of text will depend on advances in pattern-recognition methods. Software today has significant but still limited ability to detect high-level attributes (feature extraction) of sounds, images, and other inputs and to sort inputs into categories (classification), but the potential exists for dramatic improvements in recognition technology, enabling automated analysis of security-camera images, automated generation of machine-readable data from natural-language text, and pattern recognition using fusion of multiple data sources (such as detecting user intent via fusion of sounds, images, and explicit inputs). The goal of learning to become autonomous has inspired large-scale research projects such as the European Commission–funded RobotCub and DARPA's CALO.

Another area of AI that is rapidly evolving is agent software. Agent software can play a humanlike role, or act on behalf of a human user, or substitute for a human user, or act autonomously without human intervention, or present a convincing simulation of a human.

Some researchers believe that rapid increases in computer technology could enable artificial neural networks to achieve the scope and scale of the human visual cortex by 2020. While "humanlike" intelligence is a vague and perhaps unachievable goal, the emergence of machines with considerable insight and capabilities—in many domains, far beyond the capabilities of people—seems plausible.

As an increasing number of devices add data connections and a growing reliance on **mobile and broadband networks** for entertainment content, the capacities of fixed and mobile data networks are being continually stretched, stimulating technology innovation and the development of new business models throughout the world. At the same time, **cloud services** are now accessible and simple to use. The public cloud market—services like Amazon Web Services, Rackspace, and VMWare—is growing at a rate of almost 20% per year and surpassed the $100 billion mark in 2012. Cloud services' multiplatform accessibility gives users a preview of a device-agnostic, synchronization- and version-control-free future, in which their data and services would be available to access and edit any time they have access to the Internet.

Sensors are another technology building block for advances in automation. Sensors for automation applications fall into two distinct categories: internal sensing (monitoring a machine's position and movement while performing a task such as materials handling) and external sensing (monitoring a machine's external environment). Improvements in internal sensing are enabling industrial robots to migrate from their traditional manufacturing role to roles in other industry sectors, while improvements in external sensing are enabling mobile robots to perform highly useful tasks autonomously in many environments. Developments in micromachining and nanotechnology are also leading to smaller and more sensitive sensors.

Other "hard" technology areas that will be important in developing humanlike movement for machines will be **power, motion, and manipulation technologies**. Power technologies are key for nonindustrial, mobile robots. While major breakthroughs are not expected in power technologies (battery and motor technologies or fuel-powered engines), widespread development efforts should result in important advances in rechargeable batteries, charging stations, fuel cells, etc. that will support the many new automation applications. For motion, a wide range of mobile robot options are being developed, from simple wheeled robots to advanced bipedal humanoid robots, while advances in sensors and actuators are enabling increasing degrees of dexterity by machines in handling objects. An exciting area of innovation is using artificial muscles for actuation.

The evolving **internet of things** promises to add new functionalities to an increasingly connected globe. Tagging systems like RFID will give physical objects a persistent digital identity that can appear in a globally accessible registry; they will support an array of integrated tracking services; and they will enable both machine-to-person and machine-to-machine communications. At shipping ports, containers could report their contents to heavy equipment, which could route goods to trucks automatically; at distribution points, pallets and forklifts could similarly communicate and route goods that arrive in stores largely untouched by human hands.

The final important building block for advances in automation is the **user interfaces** that mediate people's relationships with computers, cars, entertainment electronics, office automation, technology in public space, and handheld devices. The advent of natural-language speech interfaces such as Apple's Siri and IBM's Watson suggests people will engage in increasingly natural modes of interaction with machines; some developers even envision hands-free, motionless, silent sensing of a human operator's intentions and thoughts. If successful, research for neural and bioelectric user interfaces could apply to robot control. Honda has already demonstrated limited control of its Asimo robot via a wearable bioelectric-sensor helmet.

New Automation Functions, Systems, and Capabilities

When integrated together, these building blocks create a wide range of new automation functions, systems, and capabilities that will be used by government, industry, and individuals in transformative ways. There's simply no end to the new, and often disruptive, applications of these new ways of doing things. The important new functions, systems, and capabilities include:

Telepresence and Teleoperation

Teleoperation refers to technologies that allow users to have control over distant events, In contrast to teleoperation alone—which includes simply issuing commands that a distant machine fulfills—telepresence entails intimate knowledge of the distant environment and provides users the ability to act at a distance despite major obstacles, including environments that are too hazardous for people and the obstacles faced by people who have impaired use of their limbs. When a doctor-controlled robot performs surgery today, the doctor is normally in the same room. But researchers expect that future robotic surgery will occur via wide-area networks.

Industrial Robots

Advanced automation will enable industrial robots to move into many jobs that currently require skilled labor and eliminate the need for human labor entirely in some manufacturing environments, including many service roles—such as maintenance, logistics, inspection, and cleaning—in industrial environments.

Additive Manufacturing (3D printing)

Additive machines provide a new automation capability for the future that many companies and individuals will find uses for.

Nonindustrial or Personal Robots

A nonindustrial robot is a machine that users can program to perform manipulative and in some cases locomotive tasks under automatic control. Nonindustrial robots already patrol hospital corridors and distribute supplies, while the U.S. military has thousands of nonindustrial robots operating on battlefields. New generations of personal robots for an extremely wide variety of service-sector applications—including cleaning, healthcare, public relations, and maintenance applications—are under development.

Remote-Controlled and Autonomous Vehicles (aka Unmanned Vehicles)

A remote-controlled vehicle refers either to remote-operated versions of traditional land, sea, and air vehicles, or to specialized mobile tele-robotic platforms like bomb-disposal robots and tethered sub-mersibles. Autonomous vehicles are mobile platforms that can operate without any direct human control, and incorporate sensors and control software to orient the vehicle and avoid obstacles.

Collaborative Machines

The development of machines that can work in collaboration with humans and with other machines will be key for being highly efficient at many tasks. Robot swarms, in which groups of robots are controllable through various algorithms, will be able to execute complex behavior in harsh environments, while collaboration between a machine and a human can greatly enhance rather than replace the human because developing a machine that relies mainly on human intelligence is far more practical than developing strong artificial intelligence.

Pervasive Computing

Increasingly, individuals are using information technology and networks to sense and understand variables that relate to that user's needs to which the system can respond. In a most basic example, consider a thermostat that recognizes when the temperature in a room drops below a preset level determined by the user and responds by turning on the heat. In the future, more advanced pervasive-computing environments that are always on, always available, unobtrusive, and self-adjusting to meet people's wants and needs, will shift dramatically the way that people relate to their surroundings and human notions of privacy, safety, and perhaps even liberty.

Automated Knowledge-Work Tasks

The advances in machine learning, big data analytics, pattern recognition, and user interfaces are facilitating the automation of more and more tasks performed by knowledge workers. "E-discovery" software can already analyze legal documents much more quickly than can human labor and for lower cost. In time, machine-learning systems will get better, gaining powerful intelligence from internet and sensor data.

Key Sector Impacts of Automation

The widespread new functions and capabilities from this automation ecosystem will be particularly impactful on Europe and North America and the many connections between the two because they have the industrial and societal needs for change, the means for investing in the new equipment, systems, functions, and capabilities, and the leaders able to take the risks. We've selected three economic sectors to focus on to understand the possible outcomes from advanced automation on Europe and North America: healthcare, financial services, and retail. In determining these possible outcomes, we took into account the many business, social, environmental, and governmental factors that determine what gets commercialized, when, and by whom. A final caveat, these projections are very uncertain and not based on detailed industry, sector, company, or product analyses.

Case Study I: Automation in Health

This section reviews the implications for healthcare automation from three standpoints: the automation of diagnosis and treatment through bioanalytics, automated 3D manufacturing of body parts and tissue, and the automation of care and logistics.

Current Situation

Automation has been an important enabler for accurate, fast and inexpensive testing and measurement in support of healthcare diagnosis and treatment—automated functionalities include sample preparation, fluid dispensing, sensing and detection and pattern-recognition software. Bioanalytical systems can measure the presence of specific molecular components, the existence of particular DNA sequences or the presence of antibodies that indicate infection. With new types of gene and protein microarrays and high-throughput screening platforms, researchers and clinicians have tools that allow massive parallelism in experimentation and testing, providing new leads for drug discovery and clinical diagnostics. The early focus of genetic platforms has been in the diagnosis and treatment of infectious diseases, but personalizing medical treatment using genotype data (pharmacogenomics) is growing in importance as a way of improving healthcare outcomes and avoiding adverse drug responses. Example diagnostics include testing to determine the correct Warfarin dosage (an anticoagulant) or in support of breast cancer treatment.

Additive manufacturing or 3D printing has the potential to create customized body parts. Such machines use computer-aided design (CAD) and a computer-guided laser, extruder, or printer head to construct an object one layer at a time and can generate geometrically complex objects. 3D printing is already in use to make models or temporary objects from plastics in sectors such as consumer products, automotive and aerospace, but it is particularly suited to applications requiring the rapid production of unique or personalized parts. A combination of 3D imaging technology, real-time finite element analysis and computer-guided 3D printing can automate the fabrication of highly customized prosthetics and implants applicable to the medical and dental fields. The field is still in its infancy, and is currently focused on structural components using advanced polymer composites.

Automation also supports clinical and non-clinical care and logistics on the healthcare "shop floor." Today, the functionalities are normally discrete and mostly within structured settings. Simple patient lifts may help within the hospital or at home. Within the field of telemedicine, visual monitoring systems and wireless devices may alert caregivers to patient falls in care centers or at home. In logistics, vacuum-tube pharmacy automation systems are now commonplace and guided vehicles from U.S. and European companies can deliver drugs, linen, food and other supplies. Some autonomous robots with laser navigation and wireless connectivity operate on non-predefined routes and can navigate hospital elevators to carry out deliveries. Today, around two thousand high-value surgical robots operate worldwide carrying out minimally invasive surgery for procedures including prostate removal and hysterectomies; other robots provide automated steering of intravascular catheters.

Potential Outcomes in 2030

Increases in longevity in the United States and Europe, advances in healthcare treatments and the economic strain due to declining support ratios will put a strain on healthcare systems in many countries forcing healthcare and elder-age care sectors to improve efficiency. In Europe, the United States (and Japan), the availability of professional caregivers for elder-age care is likely to become problematic.

Twenty years ago, biochip-based genomic testing did not exist and researchers had not mapped the human genome. Today, a person can obtain an entire map of their human genome for around $1000 and by 2030 human genome mapping may be a routine procedure after birth. By 2030, human genomes from a variety of populations will be stored in the cloud, just as Amazon began hosting the National Institutes of Health 1,000 Genomes Project in 2012. Advances in pharmacogenomics will lead to dramatic increases in the personalization of medical treatment, with more of the value likely to move toward cloud-based computational analytics and diagnostics services, including by non-typical healthcare providers. With early baby boomers reaching 84 in 2030, improving patient outcomes due to more effective personalized therapies has the potential to reduce healthcare provider expenditures by reducing the need for expensive in-patient care. Equally, a danger exists that patients armed with personal genomic information will expect too much from national healthcare systems and begin shopping around for new diagnoses and treatments.

Scientists are already working on a number of approaches for 3D tissue printing for creating cartilage, skin, bone, blood vessels, or for complex mechanical components such as aortic heart valves. By 2030, customized 3D printing could be an established method within the medical and dental device and implant communities, particularly for plastic and biocompatible polymers. Given the regulatory approvals necessary, development in 3D tissue printing will be more limited, but we could see applications in organ repair or tissue implants as part of wider trends in regenerative medicine. In May 2013, doctors in the United States used a 3D-printed tracheal-support implant—using the biopolymer polycaprolactone—to save the life of a young baby. The child was suffering from a severe form of tracheobronchomalacia, in which the trachea collapses because of the lack of supporting cartilage. The biopolymer implant guides the growth of natural cartilage and will gradually dissolve as the child grows.

Autonomous robots are emerging that provide healthcare concierge and registration services, enable patients to communicate with relatives or be the "eyes and ears" of remote doctors, together with onsite nursing staff. By 2030, this new level of automation in unstructured settings could extend to closer physical interaction with patients in hospitals (such as patient lifting, lavatory help), or in the home to support elder care. By 2030, robot hardware is likely to become more standardized, even commoditized, and value will move to robot services, with monitoring and intelligent control of robot swarms moving to the cloud. Multifunctional robots armed with germ sensors and UV beams could kill harmful hospital bacteria, viruses, fungi or pathogens, or equally provide patients with superior non-clinical services that are often the main reason for hospital choice, particularly in the United States.

Case Study II: Automation in Financial Services

Current Situation

Automation of financial services has been ongoing for many years. Automated teller machines first arrived over 40 years ago. Retail banks further automated their operations through call centers and websites. Today, voice recognition systems fully automate much telephone banking, mobile apps make automated financial services available anywhere, and even the bank branches that remain support many automated machines and few bank tellers.

Automation in financial services goes beyond transactional tasks. Consumer finance was among the first sectors to adopt advanced pattern recognition software such as neural networks to automate complex analytical and knowledge-based tasks. For example, HNC Software started selling the neural-network-based Falcon fraud detection software during the 1990s and this software (now marketed by FICO) is now used by 17 of the top 20 credit card issuers worldwide to spot potential fraud.

Automation in investment banking is arguably even more advanced than in retail banking. Over the last twenty years, automation of financial exchanges and back office functions has transformed financial markets. Open-outcry trading (or pit trading) featuring traders in brightly colored jackets issuing hand signals is now a largely a thing of the past and traders now sit in front of banks of computer screens, pressing buttons and relying on automated electronic trading systems to make and fulfill trades.

In recent years, automation software has even started to automate traders themselves. Over the last decade, high-speed financial trading emerged has emerged as an entire new sub-industry with specialist automated-trading firms competing with one another to analyze statistical patterns and make trades in fractions of seconds. Such automated trading has changed markets. In his book *Dark Pools* Scott Patterson reports that some estimates put the average holding period for a stock at four years in 1945, eight months in 2000, two months in 2008, and 22 seconds in 2011.[3]

Automated trading has had some unpredictable effects on markets. In 2010, a "flash crash" occurred when competing algorithms briefly drove down the New York Stock Exchange by around 9%. In April 2013, a news outlet reported a fake Twitter posting about terrorism in the United States and again algorithms caused a short-lived market tumble.

Because of these and other issues regulators and market operators are looking more closely at high-speed trading. For example, in the United States, the New York Stock Exchange has implemented a system limiting sudden price swings. Alongside this increased scrutiny many high-speed trading firms are struggling because increased competition and market changes have driven down profits.

Despite these challenges advocates of automated trading are still trying to develop new systems and strategies, particularly with machine learning algorithms that learn from vast volumes of data inside and outside the financial system to infer information pertinent to trading. For example, Cerebellum Capital's genetic algorithm software analyzes conventional financial data alongside varied Internet data such as restaurant reservations to evolve new trading algorithms. The Cerebellum ATM Fund returned around 7% a year between 2009 and 2011, according to Scott Patterson.

---

[3]Scott Patterson, *Dark Pools*. New York: Crown Business, 2012.

Potential Outcomes in 2030

Long-term trends support increased automation in financial services. Over the last few decades, financial institutions have been among the most enthusiastic adopters of automation technologies and that they would break this pattern over the next two decades seems highly unlikely.

Although automation of transactional finance will have increased by 2030 (perhaps almost fully automating the sector), the bigger change from today will be the increased automation of knowledge work. By 2030, automated systems capable of spotting complex financial patterns will be far more advanced than those of today and routinely outperform human workers. This change is likely because of the combination of increasing computer power, proliferating data, and cultivation of machine-learning algorithms that perform better the more data they have access to (note that in 2012 IBM suggested that creation of 90% of the world's data took place in the prior two years).

Although automation will impact all areas of finance, automated trading perhaps provides the best illustration of the potential impact of new machine learning systems. For example, by 2030, instead of simply carrying out short-term trades, software may be running large and complex long-term trading operations that outperform human-managed investments. Mainstream investment banks are likely to be running such software, not just specialist funds, though they may compete against offshoots of major software firms as well as other banks. With increased automation, human traders may be relegated to a few niche markets, as open-outcry traders are today. Inside financial institutions, human managers and technicians may be supporting and maintaining increasingly autonomous trading software.

In 2030, trading software is likely to be analyzing vast quantities of historical and real-time data on financial systems and on the Internet. This Internet data will be far richer than today's data because developments such as wearable computing and the Internet of Things will yield vast quantities of new data about the activities and conditions of objects, people, businesses, and environments. As well as learning from this raw data, trading algorithms will benefit from an ecosystem of automated software services that pre-process information. Already, services such as MarketBrief automatically create financial news stories in machine-readable formats.

Because many different firms will operate competing automated trading software and because this software will interact with a vast and complex ecosystem of supporting data and services, the complexity of the financial markets in 2030 may be far greater than the complexity of markets today. To keep pace, regulators may themselves turn to automated approaches. Cornell University professors Maureen O'Hara and David Easley have suggested that automated software could monitor markets for reckless behavior in real time.[4]

Case Study III: Automation in Retail

Current Situation

The retail sector has seen massive changes in the past couple of decades. In the United States, retail employment tripled between 1940 and 2000, and during that time emplyed more people than the healthcare and construction sector combined. Since 1990, United States' retail employment has slowed, and the sector now employs fewer people than it did in 1999. This reduction is due to a number of factors, including the economic climate, consolidation, and automation of retail processes. Thirty years ago, people went shopping. Today, automation means that stores effectively go to people. Where once people looked to shop assistants for advice, now consumers turn to retail websites, forums, and online reviews.

Since its emergence, online retail has encroached on physical, or brick-and-mortar, retail. Online retail has become a veritable competitor to real-world retail operations, with serious implications for revenue generation, consumer expectations, and even the design of urban environments. Online retailers such as Amazon can record up to as three times as many sales per full-time employee, in comparison to the retail average. According to Forrester Research, e-commerce already accounts for around 8% of all retail sales in the United States. E-com-

---

[4]See http://engineering.nyu.edu/press-release/2013/04/23/finance-industry-explore-risks-and-rewards-big-data

merce has recently been even more successful in Europe, where the market is now worth in excess of $300 billion per year. Major players such as Amazon (United States) and Otto (Germany) are already household names in many countries. According to Ron Josey, an internet analyst with JMP Securities, shoppers also use the Web to research over 50% of the products that they eventually buy in person. In countries like the United Kingdom, buying groceries online has become commonplace.[5]

Automation has also changed the way physical stores operate. Self-checkouts have started replacing some traditional checkouts. According to research RBR (United Kingdom), around 170,000 self-checkout terminals were already in operation across the world through 2012. Companies such as UK supermarket Tesco have already installed portable scanning equipment that customers take with them around the store.

Automation is already starting to change the way we pay for products and services. For example, consumers can already purchase items at Home Depot (Atlanta, Georgia) using only their mobile-phone number and personal identification number. Start-up Square has also developed a unique form of cashless payment that allows customers to initiate payment through their smart phones, without physically swiping a credit card or signing receipts. The app also organizes rewards points, reviews of companies and stores, and information about past purchases.

Naturally, automation software has also enabled retailers to know more about their customers. Physical retail stores have used credit-card and loyalty-card data to gather consumer information for some time. In recent years, social networks have augmented loyalty-card data. Now, in conjunction with closed-circuit cameras, customer-tracking software records and analyzes shopper behavior. For example, Immersive Labs (New York, New York) has developed video-analysis software that can extract the age and gender of a person in a video feed via face-recognition technology. And Realeyes (London, England) developed a system that can track the position of various facial

---

[5]See http://www.localmedia.org/wp-content/uploads/2014/07/01_830_NativeAdvertisingOutlookfor2014andBeyond_Josey-Compatibility-Mode.pdf.

features—including eyebrows, nostrils, and mouth—and then infer mood from changes in the alignment of those facial features.

Potential Outcomes in 2030

Long-term trends support increasing automation in retail In addition to e-commerce, recent years have seen the emergence of m-commerce—purchases of products and services using smart phones. By 2030, almost every kind of technology needed to support decision-making could become automated. Indeed, advanced software may even automate the decision making process accurately enough for consumers to have confidence in it. E-commerce—and its sibling m-commerce—will quite probably be responsible for a large percentage of total retail sales. Social networks may function as a portal through which those transactions occur. Already, Commonwealth Bank has announced that its customers will soon be able to transfer funds between accounts and receive money electronically through an application on Facebook's social network. By 2030, such activity could become common.

Further automation in physical retail will occur. Market-research company RBR (United Kingdom) forecasts that the global installed base of self-checkout terminals will reach 320,000 by 2018.[6] By 2030, these systems perhaps will be omnipresent. By 2030, automation will make any retail experience highly personalized. Safeway, a large chain of grocery stores in the United States, has already developed an automated personalized price system for its customers. Customers for specific products will pay a price that reflects that customers' past purchasing history. Catalina, a marketing company, has already worked with Stop & Shop's Ahold division to send coupons for specific products to customers via their smart phones while the customers are actually in the store. By 2030, a surprisingly high percentage of retail transactions could become highly personalized.

Other areas of change could see further automation. The product delivery and logistics side of retail could also change considerably by 2030. Manufacturers are already developing autonomous vehicles—for use not only on the ground but also in the air. Event planners and

---

[6]See http://www.rbrlondon.com/retail/RBR_SCO_PR_2013.pdf.

restaurants already intend to use unmanned drones—small eight-propeller helicopters—to deliver beer to crowds at festivals, or perhaps pizzas to customers. Although currently a publicity stunt, the concept is simple: Customers use a smart phone app to order, send payment, and provide geolocation information; the drone returns with the product. Perhaps most significantly, major e-retailer Amazon announced its *Prime Air* concept in late 2013, an R&D project to investigate the use of octocopter delivery drones. By 2030, ground and air autonomous-delivery systems may well be technically and economically possible.

Buying is another important function within retail that could change. While professional buyers currently help retailers find appropriate product lines to sell, and negotiate with suppliers, by 2030 this side of the retail business could see significant automation.

Implications for Europe and North America

Advanced automation will have significant effects on the economies and societies of Europe and North America because Europe and North America both need the new economy/work solutions enabled by automation to remain competitive with emerging-economy solutions and because the citizens of Europe and North America, who have the means, and freedom, to change their lives, will be attracted by the many benefits provided by new automation. But these changes will have both positive and negative impacts on developed-world economies as private-sector competitive environments adjust; as governments try to implement new information management, policy setting, regulatory, and public safety functions and capabilities; and as people adjust to new personal environments. With their high-skilled labor forces, diversity of technical and engineering talent available in their regions, and demanding customers, the Europe and North America are well positioned to lead the development of automation technologies and systems and supply the companies that will serve the new markets. On the other hand, the European and North American regions are already invested in current ways of doing things, and changes to meet future societal needs for connectedness and to remain industrially competitive will be difficult because they will require almost everyone to acquire new skills and live their lives differently. There will be many costs in making these changes.

Conclusion

In summary, the flow of ideas, knowledge, and intellectual property related to technical advancements and innovations will not only increase in volume and speed in the next 20 years, it will be increasingly dispersed in both developed and developing countries. With a global economic system increasingly shaped by emerging markets, the sources of technology will be increasingly Asian.

Stimulated by widespread technological innovation in both information and mechanical/electrical arenas, advanced automation will disrupt many industries, government services, and elements of our social lives in the next 20 years. To understand the potential impacts, we examined three industrial sectors, healthcare, financial services and retail, and considered the flow implications for Europe and North America.

Advances in many automation areas, particularly those related to machine learning and decision making, will probably be applied first in the financial services industry, and since Europe and North America institutions currently dominate this industry, they should be well positioned to implement the new advances first and take advantage of the value created. These effects will flow subsequently to China, and then the rest of the emerging economies. But the balance between labor expenditures and machine expenditures will continue to move toward the machine side.

Automation technology flows will have a very large impact on healthcare because of the urgent needs in developed countries for improved operational efficiency, lower cost, and reduced labor requirements. But we also see the demand for greater personalization or choice as another key factor in the increases in healthcare automation. Up to now, healthcare economic systems have been mostly national with small cross-border flows. But automation technology could change that in a major way. High-end surgical robotics and telemedicine have the potential to stimulate all sorts of international flows, including the provision of medical services by locations where physi-

Table 1. Potential European and North American Flow Impacts from Advances in Automation

Sector	European and North American Flow Impacts
Healthcare	The development of healthcare automation in the next 20 years will stimulate the movement of capital, to invest in new companies, the flow of new products and services, and of expertise and intellectual property. As such, the major flows impacts from healthcare automation will be functional global economic flows and global technology flows. Flow circuits will primarily involve the United States and Europe, but developing countries could play a role in custom manufacturing (China) or software and services (India).
	Global social flows will also be affected by healthcare automation, but the impacts will vary:
	• Healthcare automation will drive greater personalization or choice for individuals, but potentially at the expense of even greater demand on public healthcare systems
	• Some negative impacts on labor are likely as automation is used to improve operational efficiency and reduce labor requirements.
	• Some professional groups in developed countries may be adversely affected as technology reduces the cost of customization and creates greater internationalization of flows of expertise.
	Automation in diagnostics has primarily involved flows of investment capital—to fund startups or make acquisitions mainly in the United States—of capital equipment and of ideas. Diagnosis and treatment has remained mostly localized, but the internationalization of personal genome mapping is now but a DNA test kit and email away. Cloud-based analytical services in areas such as pharmacogenomics could see the circuits, flows and value moving to international centers of computational excellence, away from traditional national healthcare providers, although regulatory influences may slow such a transition.
	Mass customization via additive manufacturing is also part of the trend in the personalization of health and can alter supply chains and flows by breaking down barriers between the manufacturer and final customer. In healthcare, a 3D-printed medical parts supplier and healthcare provider could be co-located, but equally patients armed with electronic records, including 3D imaging data, might order some body parts globally from 3D manufacturing centers of excellence. New more complex circuits and flows could result if patient, medical parts supplier and service provider are all in different regions, with implications for medical tourism. Overall, such healthcare flow circuits could operate with reduced human intervention thereby lowering cost and downward cost pressure is likely on some professions that have benefitted from the high value of medical customization. In contrast, healthcare systems should benefit from lower costs.
	Healthcare-service robots will replace, or augment, low- and medium-skill human labor and the provision of such services could, at least in part, be offshore. For example, robot monitoring or robot remote control services could transfer to low-cost computer literate regions such as India. In regions in which this human labor is in short supply (such as Japan) or where immigration may be contentious, governments are likely to welcome such automation. However, in terms of social flows, workers in some sectors may find their employment positions more precarious. High-end surgical robotics and telemedicine have the potential to move the provision of some medical services to locations where physicians are either better-trained or lower cost. This potential for the internationalization of flows around surgical care is likely to face challenges from national regulatory bodies due to privacy and security concerns and from among local professional bodies.
Financial	The major EU-U.S. flow impacts from future automation in financial services will

Services include the increases in capital flows within and between regions because of better products and services from financial services companies located in the regions, the increased use of information-technology services by financial services institutions, the delivery of services by those institutions to customers, and the movement of talent, expertise, and intellectual property among regions to fill the changing needs. Employment in financial sectors and across consumer finance will be negatively impacted.

By 2030 financial markets are likely to be very different from today, due to increased automation and a furthering flattening of the global financial system. Multinationals and governments from Europe and North America will both likely continue to be major participants in the global system. Singapore and Hong Kong may increase in importance due to better than average mathematical skills in those regions, and the increasing reliance on mathematical skills in finance. Also foreign direct investments in Europe and the United States probably won't grow, as they will in developing countries.

In themselves, European financial markets could remain weak for most of the period. European governments will likely be unwilling to let national private-sector institutions fail, and in the midst of voluminous data and automated financial-transaction capabilities, government regulatory agencies will struggle to develop and implement new laws and regulations to fit the new high-tech environments.

From the perspective of Tomas Ries, the major flow impacts from future automation in financial services will be on the functional global economic flows and global technology flows. Global social flows will also be affected. In particular, increasing automation implies that technology flows (and the accompanying economic flows) will be increasingly independent of people. Potentially, automation software could deal with and create complete flow circuits without human intervention. Today, human fund managers are arguably still the "directing factor" but potential exists for automated software to manage complex portfolios of trading algorithms, taking the human out of this flow circuit altogether.

If the next wave of financial trading automation is successful, then a faster and more efficient technology flow will support greater economic flow. But this could be an environment of winners and losers. Increased automated trading implies fewer human traders (along with their support staff) and trading profits may be shared amongst fewer individuals. At least in theory, increasing automation should drive down fees for investors, making investing more attractive for a wider group of people than it is today.

The flash crash of 2010 and the hash crash of 2013 have demonstrated than highly automated financial systems can be fragile and unpredictable. As complexity increases, a key risk is that regulators fail to stay ahead of technology developments and that automation leads to greater instability in the global financial system. Rogue software (planted by terrorists or other groups) is another risk. For example, rogue algorithms could attempt to deliberately cause market crashes.

The technology to support automation in finance will be primarily operational rather than capital expenditure, due to the increasing reliance on cloud services rather than in-house hardware. The flows of this expenditure will include those from the United States to Europe (perhaps particularly to financial centers) but primarily from Europe to the United States. Information flows all around the world will increase as automated systems track myriad Internet data. Sometimes this data will be licensed, increasing financial flows, though often the data will be freely available.

Changes in the financial sector are likely to create increased demand for technical staff, particularly those that can combine machine-learning expertise with an understanding of the finance sector. Expertise and intellectual property flows are likely to be fairly fluid between Europe's, Asia's, and the United States' main financial centers.

Table 1 (continued). Potential European and North American Flow Impacts from Advances in Automation

Sector	European and North American Flow Impacts
	Countries whose students perform well in numerate subjects, notably China, Hong Kong, Singapore, and South Korea, are likely to make increasing inroads into the new, more mathematical financial sector. Financial sectors in Hong Kong and Singapore are likely to grow in importance. Whether new financial sectors will emerge in China, South Korea or elsewhere or whether students will migrate to existing financial centers is uncertain.
	Employment in consumer finance is likely to decline across the world as automation of transactional and knowledge-based work in the sector gathers pace. Financial centers in Europe, Asia, and the United States may also see reduced demand for traders and related support staff as automated traded operations become commonplace. It's uncertain how the need for navigation or auxiliary services might change, and possibly increase.
Retail	The flows that new automation in retail will stimulate are likely to be extremely wide in scope. In particular, the flow of information will increase as automated retail systems track and analyze consumers' data. Information will flow between retailers, payment-systems companies, cloud-computing providers, and social networking services. Many companies developing some of the novel enabling technologies, software, apps, and digital infrastructure, for use in retail, are based in the United States. The activities of large players such as Google, Facebook, Amazon—and perhaps new service-providers that emerge in the interim—will increasingly overlap with any retail transaction.
	If automation approaches prove successful in retail, economic and social change could result. Retail flow circuits could operate with minimal human intervention, potentially driving down operating costs and increasing retailers' margins. Economic flows would increase.
	Currently, a large number of people are employed in the retail sector—not only in customer-facing roles, but also in areas such as management and logistics. Potential exists for significant change: For example, future retail warehouses could be controlled entirely automatically—using management software and robotics. In other words, humans could leave this part of the retail flow circuit completely.
	Social change could also occur: Globally, the nature of employment in the retail sector in the will be affected; fewer retail workers (in particular, store assistants) will be needed at showrooms and retail outlets. However, workers that do remain will likely be higher skilled than many of today's workers, with specialty knowledge. Changes in the retail sector are likely to create opportunities for technical personnel. Expertise and intellectual-property flows are likely to prove fluid, involving players both in Europe and the United States.

cians are either better-trained or lower cost to anywhere in the world, the movement of patients to large-volume, high-tech surgical centers, and the export of high-tech hardware developed and developing countries. This potential for the internationalization of surgical care is likely to face challenges from national regulatory bodies due to privacy and security concerns and from among local professional bodies.

Automation innovations in retail in response to market needs will be implemented rapidly in both Europe and North America. The retail situations in Europe and North America are quite similar vis-à-vis the challenges retail companies face and the buying behaviors of their populations. As a result, the flow of ideas, products, and services in retail between the continents should be heavy.

Notwithstanding the increased social and economic flows the two regions will realize from more automation, the automation of work and new ways in which organizations use human labor will have enormous social and economic implications, perhaps particularly in areas like retail and lower-level healthcare services. Labor employment could generally decline as many labor categories and positions will be eliminated, while wages of lower-level service workers may be stagnant for many years. At the same time, there will be some potential worker shortages in some areas, like nursing. A complicating factor could be that some jobs associated with automation would be more mobile than those they replace. In response a major flow we might see could be in education and training services to fill the new needs for skills, expertise, and adjusting to new work environments.

Future workplace automation and the new machines that can process the vast new quantities of data will likely alter significantly the costs of producing the goods and services demanded around the world and thus how businesses are organized and operate. While advanced-automation changes will stimulate increased demand for products and services because of lower costs, and thus overall prosperity, they will require new business models and connections among individuals and between individuals and firms and be disruptive for everyone.

Chapter 8

Shock Therapy:
Building Resilient International
Industrial Systems in 2030

Barry C. Lynn

The "globalization" of industry and commerce, we are often told, is the surest path to universal peace and prosperity. If so, this would mean the world should be a far safer and richer place than two decades ago, when world leaders largely unleashed the business corporation to operate across national borders. Yet the "global" *systems* of industry and finance built by the masters of these institutions are increasingly the source of both political conflict and economic disruption. Indeed, the world today—although in some respects richer—is in many ways a far more perilous place than before we established the World Trade Organization (WTO) regime in the 1990s. And it grows more so by the day.

Shock after shock, and political showdown after political showdown, threaten to trigger wide if not global-scale catastrophe. Perhaps it is a natural disaster, like the Tohoku Quake of March 2011—events that are entirely outside the power of any rational actor in any state to control. Perhaps it is a contagion like the avian flu scare of 2009, or a financial panic like the Lehman Brothers crash of 2008. Perhaps it is a crude territorial face off, such as the ongoing conflict over the Senkaku/Diaoyu Islands south of Japan. Whatever the triggering event, where only 15 or 20 years ago the result would have been a merely local disruption or local discord, today we see crashes that cascade swiftly across the whole face of the earth.

Worse, many if not most of us believe these problems derive from forces largely or even entirely beyond our control. For some, the culprit is technology. For others, it is the mechanics of the marketplace or something in the nature of capitalism. For yet others, "globalization" itself is a "force" that has largely determined this fragility. And so, as a society, we stumble from one crisis to the next, wavering between moments of bafflement and terror. Why, we wonder, is our world so much more dangerous than only a few years ago? And what new risks have we missed? What new events—like cyber attacks or crop failures—loom in the offing?

But what if we could trace both the source of these dangers and our confusion to a relatively simple set of intellectual mistakes? What if the problem is merely that we have used the wrong ideological frames, hence the wrong principles, to establish the rules that guide the actions of our bankers, executives, and engineers? Further, that these same mistaken ideas also block our ability as a society to understand the problem and act to fix it?

As this chapter makes clear, we possess all the skills and tools we need to solve the problem. We can for instance easily identify—and at least in theory enact—a simple set of fixes that would greatly reduce the likelihood of almost all conceivable sudden crashes of vital, cross-border flows of goods, money, and information. Once identified, enacting these changes is a matter of political will only.

If anything, the immensity of this new threat actually presents us with an immense opportunity—to lay a foundation for a more cooperative, more inclusive world political economy. This is a pertinent task as we look towards 2030. Perhaps, indeed, we can achieve exactly what the founders of today's global system expected to achieve seven decades ago, at the end of the Second World War, which is to build a truly perpetual peace and prosperity, one made to last through our 21st century.

An Entirely New Threat

In recent years we have witnessed numerous cascading "crashes" of industrial activity, in which a small and local breakdown in the flow of physical goods or finance triggers a shutdown of systems across the world.

The most dramatic of these "supply chain" crashes took place after the Tohoku earthquake in March 2011 off the north coast of Japan. The event shuttered Japanese industrial giants like Toyota and Honda for nearly half a year, and resulted in extremely powerful economic downdrafts across Asia, Europe, and North America. (In the United States, the Philadelphia Federal Reserve reported the largest three-month drop in industrial activity ever.) Similarly, we saw unprecedented levels of industrial disruption from the "demand shock" after the collapse of Lehman Brothers in September 2008. Within weeks this financial crash brought the entire U.S. automotive industry to the verge of physical paralysis, and resulted in a truly phenomenal drop off of industrial activity in Japan and other Asian nations, with activity often plunging more than 50%.[1]

These were but two of many similar events. We saw cascading shut-downs of industrial activity after the Thai floods of 2011, the Icelandic volcano blast of 2009, the Niigata earthquake of 2007, the SARS epidemic of 2003,[2] and the September 11, 2001 attacks in New York, among others. We have also seen many near misses, in which a natural or political disaster that threatened to disrupt some complex system simply failed to reach critical state. This includes the avian flu epidemic of 2009 and the two near wars between India and Pakistan a decade ago.

Although we have known since the second half of the 19th century that financial collapses can swiftly cascade from country to country, these *industrial* crashes are largely a new phenomenon. The first major international supply chain crash took place in September 1999 after an earthquake in Taiwan cut off the flow of highly specialized semiconductors from foundries concentrated in the city of Hsinchu. Within days this resulted in the sudden closure of factories across Asia and the United States.[3] Within the business community, these crashes have resulted in a boom industry devoted to identifying ways to lessen the impact of a sudden supply shock on individual companies. One of most sophisticated such efforts is run out of the Massachusetts Institute of Technology by the systems engineer Yossi Sheffi, author of the book *Resilient Enterprise*.[4]

---

[1] See Kiyoyasu Tanaka, "Trade Collapse and International Supply Chains: Japanese Evidence," *Vox*, Centre for Economic Policy Research, November 27, 2009.

[2] Michael T. Osterholm, "Preparing for the Next Pandemic," *Foreign Affairs*, July/August 2005.

[3] Barry C. Lynn, *End of the Line: The Rise and Coming Fall of the Global Corporation*, Doubleday, 2005.

[4] Yossi Sheffi, *The Resilient Enterprise: Overcoming Vulnerability for Competitive Advantage* (Cambridge: MIT Press, 2005).

What became clear from these early studies is that there are sharp limits to what individual companies can accomplish on their own. Every large and structurally important company today depends on outside suppliers for many key components and materials. Competitive pressures—and the actions of mercantilist governments and monopolistic corporations intent on concentrating a particular industrial capacity—can make it difficult or even impossible for even the most safety-minded of management teams to keep an alternative source of supply always at the ready.[5]

What is also clear is that, despite the fact that 15 years have passed since the first modern industrial crash, and despite the evident limitations on what private sector actors can accomplish on their own, national governments and multilateral organizations have only barely begun to analyze how a major industrial crash might affect national communities or human society as a whole. Even less effort has been devoted to the study of whether and how nation states and other political actors might seek to exploit these structural flaws for political ends, or how to limit the dangers they pose.

The Proximate Sources of the Threat— Mercantilism, Monopolism, and Speed

There are a few important exceptions to this all-but-willful effort to ignore the new phenomena of cross-border industrial crashes. This includes a team of WTO economists who studied how supply chains transmitted and amplified the Lehman stock market crash.[6] It also includes Japan's Ministry of Economy, Trade, and Industry, which in 2012 published a groundbreaking study that introduced a new concept, that of "diamond structure" manufacturing systems.[7]

---

[5]Peter Marsh, "Industry Left High and Dry." *Financial Times*, April 12, 2011.

[6]Hubert Escaith, Nannette Lindenberg, and Sebastien Miroudot, "Global Value Chains and the Crisis: Reshaping International Trade Elasticity?" in *Global Value Chains in a Post-Crisis World* (World Bank, Washington, DC, 2010).

[7]In 2012, Japan's Ministry of Economy, Trade, and Industry became the first state institution to acknowledge publicly that this revolutionary new structure of industrial activity poses fundamental and grave dangers to society. METI also provided a useful image to illustrate the problem. Whereas until recently production was organized in the structure of a pyramid, with the products of many companies feeding up towards a single chokepoint, METI officials say the earthquake "revealed" that the manufacturing industry today "has a 'diamond structure' in which parts/material supply at tier 2 or deeper in the supply chain is concentrated in a certain

From these private and public studies we see a growing consensus that the fragility of these systems poses a potentially "existential" problem for human society, in the words of Tomas Ries. To be sure, no industrial crash has yet resulted in the complete shut down of an entire global production system for more than a few days. But, obviously, the mere fact that a catastrophic event has not happened yet does not mean that such a system-wide collapse is not entirely possible today or even likely to occur in the near future. We also see a general consensus forming as to what factors are most responsible for these cascading, cross-border industrial crashes.

The most obvious factor is international industrial integration. It is plainly evident that the radical liberalization of trade in the mid-1990s cleared the way for private firms to tie nation states together industrially in far more intimate ways than ever before. Well into the 1990s, every large industrialized nation remained largely self reliant. The only exceptions were for low-end products, like apparel, and very high-end technological devices and software, the production of which was carefully regulated by the governments themselves. Today by contrast, we see a single immensely intricate world-spanning industrial system, on which all peoples now depend for almost all day-to-day necessities, including drugs, food, and information, but over which no group of businesses nor any group of nations exerts control.

A second factor is the rapid concentration of production capacity in most industrial systems over the last 25 years. Many factors have played a role in this concentration—including the emergence of digital technologies. Most important, however, is the radical relaxation of antimonopoly law beginning in the early 1980s in most industrial nations, especially the United States. The concentration of ownership that has resulted does not necessitate concentration of capacity; governments could require industrial monopolies to build redundant plants. But absent such regulation, the real-world result in industry

---

supplier." It is no surprise that Japan was the first state not merely to recognize the problem but to publicize it. For one thing, METI employs one of the world's most sophisticated teams of industrial experts. For another, in recent years Japan has been the site of some of the most dramatic industrial disasters. This gives officials there the ability to, say, compare the lessons of the Aisin brake valve fire of 1997 to the lessons of the Riken piston ring shut down of 2007, or the lessons of the Kobe earthquake of 1995 to those of the Tohoku Earthquake of 2011.

after industry has in fact been a dramatic concentration of physical capacity, hence of risk.[8]

A third factor is the rise of "just-in-time" and "lean" production techniques designed to speed the flow of materiel and capital through manufacturing systems. Although we can trace such techniques to the 1920s, the emergence of the internet and of modern data management systems over the last 20 years has enabled corporate managers both to extend such systems across much wider geographies and to speed them up dramatically. The key result for our purposes has been to enable production managers to reduce sharply the inventories of both raw and processed materials that until recently were available to cushion against supply chain disruptions.

In combination, the effects of these three changes upon the physical structure of most of our important industrial systems is economically and politically revolutionary. For millennia, groups of people have aimed at a general self sufficiency for most vital industrial goods, to ensure their independence of action in times of economic or political emergency. For most of the last century, the international distribution of productive capacity that resulted from this policy was reinforced by domestic antimonopoly law, which was used by many states to promote competition and to further distribute capacity. Yet what the Tohoku quake and the Lehman crash revealed was that, for all intents, many of our most important industrial activities are now organized into tightly integrated, world-spanning networks marked by great and growing degrees of concentration and specialization.[9]

Although concentration of ownership does not *necessitate* concentration of capacity, in industry after industry the real world result has in fact been a dramatic concentration of physical capacity. In many instances, the entire world supply of some keystone component now takes place in a single industrial zone, even a single factory. The immediate *and necessary* result of such physical concentration of production is

---

[8]Kei-Mu Yi, "The Collapse of Global Trade: The Role of Vertical Specialisation," in The Collapse of Global Trade, Murky Protectionism, and the Crisis: Recommendations for the G-20, Centre for Economic Policy Research, 2009

[9]See Kei-Mu Yi, "The Collapse of Global Trade: The Role of Vertical Specialisation," in *The Collapse of Global Trade, Murky Protectionism, and the Crisis: Recommendations for the G-20*, Centre for Economic Policy Research, 2009.

an extreme concentration of risk that leaves production managers with little or no ability to respond to even predictable disruptions.[10]

The ultimate result is a new global industrial *commons* that, from the point of view of a systems engineer, suffers from extreme if not fatal structural flaws. As a system, this new global industrial commons is characterized by numerous single points of failure, innumerable active tectonic and political fault lines, and (in the words of Charles Perrow, the pioneering expert on systemic risk) by extremely "tight coupling."[11] It is, in short, a system that is not merely "built to break" but that is all but designed to ensure that a relatively small disaster in one place will one day result in a massive disaster every place.

The Ultimate Source of the Threat—Laissez Faire Politics

Ask almost any engineer how to eliminate the fragility in these cross-border systems and you will likely receive a simple answer— geographically distribute all keystone industrial capacities and create real-time redundancy in every important production systems. Ask most any member of the public, and the answer will be even simpler— don't put all our eggs in one basket.

Nevertheless, as a society, not only have we failed to address this industrial fragility, we have largely failed to inquire whence it came and what it means. Before discussing what exactly to do, we therefore have to address why we as a society have so much difficulty seeing the problem. And why, among the few who do see the problem, there is little faith that we can fix it.

Much of the answer traces to a revolution in U.S. and European politics that began more than three decades ago. This was the rise of the corporate libertarian—or "estatist" movement.

---

[10]For a more detailed explanation of the structure and history of this system, see my articles "Built to Break: The International System of Bottlenecks in the New Era of Monopoly," *Challenge*, March/April 2012; Barry C. Lynn, "How Detroit Went Bottom Up: Outsourcing Cleared the Way for a Discreet but Dangerous Monopolization of the Automotive Industry," *The American Prospect*, October 2009.

[11]Charles Perrow, *Normal Accidents: Living With High-Risk Technologies* (Princeton, 1999).

The first generation of industrial interdependence, established in early post-war Europe through the Marshall Plan and the Coal and Steel regime, is widely recognized as a grand political achievement. Not only did the generation that rebuilt Europe after the War use industrial interconnectedness to bridge the centuries-old divide that separated France from Germany, they used industrial interconnectedness to provide a foundation for a period of unprecedented peace and prosperity across much of the "Western" world.

That international economic regime required very close regulation of trade and investment flows. This regulation was provided by multilateral institutions such as the Organization for Economic Co-operation and Development. And it was provided by the U.S. government in Washington. As Geir Lundestad has written, although this first generation "global" system was entirely "imperial" in its nature. But it was also a uniquely liberal form of imperialism; the U.S. Executive's vision of empire required it to work hard to distribute fairly among many nations not only skills and capital but also access to market. And, thereby, industrial capacity.

In the 1970s and 1980s, however, first the Thatcher government in Britain and then the Reagan Administration in the United States reacted strongly against such intrusive regulation by the state. In this initial stage of the corporate libertarian movement, however, the main targets were purely domestic—such as labor unions and antitrust laws. The result was also mainly domestic—in the form of greater concentrations of economic and political power in private hands.[12]

Internationally, the U.S. government continued to use its power to break up efforts to overly concentrate wealth or power in a single country. This included successful efforts to revalue Japan's currency and to place strict limits on how much control over the international computer industry Japan could acquire.

After the collapse of the Soviet Union in 1991, however, the corporate libertarians moved swiftly to extend their revolution into the international realm. The key tool for this revolution was the Uruguay Round of the General Agreement on Tariffs and Trade, which established the World Trade Organization.

---

[12]Barry C. Lynn, *Cornered: The New Monopoly Capitalism and the Economics of Destruction*, Wiley, 2010.

On the surface, the WTO regime was designed only to take the grand success of first-generation globalization to the next level, by extending the system to China, Russia, and the nations of Eastern Europe. More important for our purposes, the WTO regime was also designed to shift the power to regulate the international industrial and financial systems away from the U.S. government and institutions like the OECD, to the giant industrial corporation and banking estate.

In combination, the revolution in the governance of domestic political economies of the 1970s and 1980s, and the revolution in the governance of the international political economy in the 1990s, cleared the way for the rise of today's monopolists and mercantilists.

Perhaps even more damaging, these twin revolutions undid the public institutions, regulatory practices, and ways of thought that had enabled the United States and its European allies to ensure the safe distribution of industrial and other economic activity, and the stability of complex cross-border systems.

Political Origins & Ideological Obstacles

Our inability to see the threat and to respond practically is also due to ideological and intellectual factors. Some of these obstacles derive from the rapid rise in the influence of the economics academy over international trade and industrial policy, hence to the ideologies that shape the thinking of many professional economists. Other obstacles derive from the ways in which concentration of control and capacity has disrupted many of the traditional ways we manage risk in our political economy, and apportion responsibility and liability.

Of the many factors that have played a role in hiding the fragility of our industrial systems, the following four stand out.

The Fetishization of Efficiency

Economists believe their prime task is to promote the "efficient" use of natural and human resources. There is nothing new about this; we can trace this thinking far into the 19th century. What is new is the degree to which other academies have come to accept this same basic goal and have ceased to offer competing ideas of what we, as a society, might desire or require.

Consider competition policy, which for 200 years in the United States was the single most powerful determinant of industrial structure. From the founding of the nation, the goals of our many anti-monopoly laws and policies were the liberty of the individual citizen, the democratic distribution of voice and responsibility, the maintenance of a rough equality of opportunity, and the security of the nation. Efficiency, although it was sometimes taken into account, was never held to be the foremost goal.

This all changed in the 1970s and early 1980s when legal scholars of the "Chicago School," led by Richard Posner and Robert Bork, succeeded in convincing policymakers to embrace an "economic analysis of law." The result, almost overnight, was a radical simplification of competition policy around a single goal, "efficiency," theoretically in order to better serve the interests of the "consumer." The main consideration now became not the distribution of power, the maintenance of competition, the openness of markets, nor the stability of systems. Instead it was only whether any particular proposed "economy of scale" would drive down the price of a particular good or service.

One result of this radical change in competition policy and law (and I would argue, an intended result) has been a revolutionary concentration of power, especially in the United States but in other countries as well. Another (apparently unintended) result has been a rapid concentration of human thought around the goal of efficiency, in ways that have all but blinded us—as individuals and as a society—to the *physical* dangers posed by the extreme concentration and reorganization of human industrial activity over the last generation.

The Socialization of Risk

Economists assume, as a foundational principle of their system, that rational actors will always identify and mitigate risk. This assumption is entirely logical, given that economists also assume the existence of open markets in which multiple companies compete to deliver the same basic goods and service. When capacities and skills are compartmentalized in such a way, the failure of any one company is always an option society as a whole will be willing to accept. This enables a compartmentalization of responsibility, which leaves it entirely up to the individual owners and operators of these firms to guard against any failure—including the cutoff of supplies—that would destroy the value of their assets.

The main problem with this theory is that it no longer reflects the reality of today's industrial and financial structures. Over the last two decades we have witnessed a revolutionary reorganization of industrial activity around the world. In addition to the extreme consolidation of control over many marketplaces already noted, this restructuring also includes the *dis-integration* of many industrial systems that for the last century were highly vertically integrated. In sector after sector, managers have chosen to "outsource" key production activities to outside suppliers, many of which in turn have captured control over the production of vital components, and which have also often concentrated the capacity to produce these components.

The practical result is that where once we had many companies competing in real time to, say, manufacture windshield wipers or piston rings, today we increasingly see one company managing the bulk of such production. This in turn entirely alters how the managers of top-tier companies view risk. When production of vital components is the responsibility of each company individually, and that company faces robust competition, managers of that company are all but compelled to guard against supply chain disruptions. By contrast, the *pooling* or *communalization* of production largely eliminates any impetus to invest time and resources in identifying and mitigating supply chain risks. Such pooling of capacity affects the incentive for any one corporate actor to devote time to identifying and mitigating potential bottlenecks.

The Resurrection of Metaphysics

One of the key ideas of the Enlightenments is that all economics is political, hence human beings enjoy the capacity to restructure all economic relationships within society and all economic relationships among different peoples. In America, over the last generation, we have witnessed a phenomenal—yet all but unaddressed, even unremarked—resurrection of the belief that our economy is shaped by powers largely or completely outside human control. The basic idea here is that some force—such as "technology" or the "market" or "capitalism"—mechanically drives actors within the economy towards certain ineluctable outcomes.

Most important for this discussion is the belief that "globalization" itself is a natural, even inevitable force, rather than a carefully structured product of political decisions.

Over the years, many actors have sought to inject deterministic thinking into political debate. A century and half ago, the richest man in United States, Andrew Carnegie, literally imported Herbert Spencer to preach the metaphysics of "Social Darwinism" to voters who might otherwise be tempted to view Carnegie's assets as ill gotten. In the 20th Century, the economist Joseph Schumpeter promoted a form of biological determinism that owed much to Spencer's teachings

What is new, and directly pertinent to our problem, is how fully such metaphysical thinking and analysis has come to dominate not merely the social sciences but the thinking of policymakers. Nowadays, we see such deterministic thinking not only in popular works of journalism such as the books of Thomas Friedman. We also see such deterministic thinking in the statements of important politicians; U.S. President Barack Obama recently defined "globalization" as a "force" that shapes us at least as much as we shape it. And we see such deterministic thinking in the economics academy and throughout the social sciences.

What is also new is how dangerous such thinking can be. A century ago the main dangers of believing in such metaphysics was that some would-be plutocrat would use such tales to concentrate economic and political power. Today, such metaphysical thinking—by hiding the political acts of the human builders of these systems—can also prevent us from acting in pragmatic and practical ways to ensure the stability of even our most vital systems.

A Flawed Understanding of InterDependence

Among those who do understand the fragility of systems, many argue that such extreme industrial interdependence forces political leaders to walk peaceful paths in any dispute. Perhaps the best known purveyor of this argument is *New York Times* columnist Thomas Friedman, especially in his 2005 book *The World is Flat*. The basic thesis of Friedman and similar thinkers is that the dangers of systemic disruption are more than counterbalanced by the ways in which such mutual dependence on the same systems forces different peoples to avoid conflict and to cooperate harmoniously.[13]

---

[13]Thomas, Friedman, *The World is Flat* (New York: Farrar, Straus and Giroux, 2005).

But there are two large problems with Friedman's line of thinking. First, such extreme industrial interdependence is simply not necessary to keep the peace. There are many other very potent checks against armed conflict among industrial nations today—such as the fear that any hot conflict might lead to the use of nuclear weapons. Further, as we learned from the first half century of America's postwar empire, the main political benefits of industrial interdependence can be achieved with a far more limited sharing of capacity—in energy, metals, and advanced electronics for instance.[14]

Second, today's extreme industrial interdependence poses dangers that in many respects far outweigh even the potential benefits imagined by Friedman and other "globalists." And these dangers grow worse by the day. It is, indeed, all too easy to imagine "normal," everyday disasters that would effectively end economic—and hence political—life as we know it.

The most obvious flaw is that the structure of the system leaves us entirely exposed to natural disasters, which obviously are entirely outside the power of any rational actor in any state to control. Two of the biggest industrial crashes—in September 1999 and March 2011—were triggered by earthquakes. Similarly, the incipient shut down of trade flows during the SARS scare of 2003 was averted only when the disease suddenly ceased to spread.[15]

Third, the structure of today's system leaves us entirely exposed to political disasters in third states, as well as within states. Even if leaders in Beijing and Washington forged the most perfect of ententes, they would not be able to exert complete control over the human beings who control other states. They would not, for instance, be able to guarantee that North Korea would never disrupt South Korea's highly concentrated DRAM industry, for instance. Nor could they guarantee that Pakistan will never disrupt the flow of processed information from India to the back offices of corporations in the United States, Europe, Japan, and China.

Similarly, neither China nor the United States is itself a monolith, and there is no guarantee whatsoever that leaders in either Beijing or

---

[14]Lynn, "The Industrial Policy that America Has Forgotten," *Europe's World*, Autumn 2013.
[15]Michael T. Osterholm, "Preparing for the Next Pandemic," *Foreign Affairs*, July/August 2005.

Washington can always prevent factions within their nations from disrupting vital industrial and financial flows. In 1989, the Tiananmen uprising had little effect on any economic activity outside China. Any similar event today would conceivably shut down business as usual through much of the industrialized world.

Worse, in some cases extreme industrial interdependence appears actually to tempt powerful factions within a state to various forms of adventurism. This is certainly one way to view China's cut off of shipments of rare earth minerals to Japan in 2010, following a flareup of tension over the Senkaku/Daiyudao islands.

Such High Noon-style political face-offs between two nations joined at the industrial aorta pose two huge dangers to the United States and Europe. First is that one of the parties will miscalculate and make a military or political move that triggers exactly the sort of catastrophic industrial shut down we most fear. The second danger is that China (or some other nation) will manipulate the face off in a way that forces the United States (or one of our key allies) to back down politically, much in the way the United States forced Britain and France to retreat from the Suez in 1956. The political and economic effects of such a humiliating loss of prestige—and such a complete demonstration of the impotence of military power—are almost incalculable.

Finally is the fact the hyper concentration of capacity we see in so many of today's international industrial system also provides numerous highly tempting targets for non-state actors like terror groups as well as factions within a state who are playing for power. In September 2001 al-Qaeda struck at what it viewed as the symbolic heart of the capitalist system—Wall Street. Today, if al-Qaeda or some other group really wanted to wreck havoc, it need merely strike some vital concentrations of industrial capacity located somewhere around the world, in Hsinchu, or Seoul, or Bangalore, or maybe Shenzhen. Last, there is the danger that the United States, or one of our allies, might respond to some provocation in an unwise or untimely fashion.[16]

---

[16]Barry C. Lynn, "Glitch in the Matrix: Why the Pivot to Asia Has No Clothes," *Foreign Policy*, September 2012.

Toward Simple Rules

Human societies can be highly flexible and resilient, and often adapt with remarkable speed to new physical realities. So too the human mind, which can swiftly turn the truths of today into the stuff of ridicule tomorrow. That's why, despite the fact that economic power and thought have been so fantastically concentrated, we can still look to the day when the perils we face will become starkly clear. The only question is whether this truth will reveal itself via insight or catastrophe.

Our most immediate practical challenge then is twofold: to determine what sorts of rules would result in a safe physical distribution of keystone industrial capacities; and to determine how to begin a political discussion that will prepare us for this task before a truly devastating crash does the work for us.

In any discussion of making rules, it helps to clarify up front exactly what role government would play. I myself am very confident of the ability of private sector actors to work out the basic details all on their own. The task they face is actually quite simple. The constituent pieces of these systems—be it machines, or servers, or debt—are all man-made, and can be arranged however we wish. For such a challenge, today's industrial engineers and corporate managers have all the technical expertise our society requires.

That said, governments will have to set basic ground rules that ensure that all these private actors are treated alike. Regulators do not need to figure out every last detail of our supply chains. But they do have to establish an environment that empowers engineers to secure these systems, without fear of putting their individual companies at competitive risk.

The following three observations may be of use in helping policymakers set such rules. These three observations address the three factors that—as noted in the first section of this chapter—are widely regarded as the primary sources of the growing fragility of our international industrial systems. They are based on 15 years close study of supply chain crashes and of the history of interdependence among nations, and distill much of the reporting I have done elsewhere.[17]

---

[17]See, for example, Barry C. Lynn, *End of the Line: The Rise and Coming Fall of the Global Corporation*, Doubleday, 2005; Barry C. Lynn, "War, Trade, and Utopia: Economic Interdependence Leads to Peace, say the Globalists. Think Again, and Examine the U.S.-China Connec-

Just-In-Time Logistics Practices Are Not a Fundamental Source of Fragility

After the Tohoku quake, many in the news media and in the investment community blamed the subsequent disruptions on overly "lean" supply chain practices. But we also know from previous industrial crashes that JIT practices can themselves be compartmentalized, hence that even in extremely lean systems, disruptions can be kept local.[16] Further, focusing too much attention on JIT practices poses dangers of its own. It will likely lead us to aim at the wrong fixes; bigger inventories of components, for instance, may cushion the shock, but the effects are at best only temporary. Worse, placing too much blame on JIT may lead us to discount the role that information technologies can play in providing more supply chain transparency.

Industrial Integration Among Countries Is Also Not a Fundamental Source of the Danger

After every industrial crash, a staple of news coverage is that "globalization" has put us in danger. Yet there is no sound basis whatsoever for such a conclusion. We can in fact imagine many forms of highly complex international industrial systems that would be, from an engineering point of view, all but fully safe against both natural and political disaster. As we saw during the first era of globalization between 1947 and 1993, it is possible to engineer systems that promote high degrees of international cooperation, yet also do not bind peoples so tightly that disaster in one place instantly becomes disaster everywhere. Worse, blaming integration poses perils of its own. The fix it implies—i.e. a retreat from "globalization"—means abandoning a policy that at least in its first iteration proved immensely successful. Further, blaming integration for fragility runs the risk of exacerbating tensions between nation-states in ways that threaten to spin out of our political control.

---

tion," *The National Interest*, Winter 2005/2006; Barry C. Lynn, "How Detroit Went Bottom Up: Outsourcing Cleared the Way for a Discreet but Dangerous Monopolization of the Automotive Industry," *The American Prospect*, October 2009; Barry C. Lynn, "How Detroit Went Bottom Up: Outsourcing Cleared the Way for a Discreet but Dangerous Monopolization of the Automotive Industry," *The American Prospect*, October 2009; Barry C. Lynn, *Cornered: The New Monopoly Capitalism and the Economics of Destruction*, Wiley; Barry C. Lynn, "Built to Break: The International System of Bottlenecks in the New Era of Monopoly," *Challenge*, March/April 2012; Barry C. Lynn, "Glitch in the Matrix: Why the Pivot to Asia Has No Clothes," *Foreign Policy*, September 2012.

Geographic Concentration of Keystone Production Capacity Is, In Fact, a Fundamental Source of Fragility

My reasoning here is simple. This is the one factor that is entirely new; we have never before seen such high degrees of concentration of vital capacity. We can clearly measure the effect of concentration by comparing two events that took place in the 1990s—the Kobe earthquake and the Aisin fire—to two events that took place more recently—the Niigata and Tohoku earthquakes.[18] The principles here are the same ones responsible for the growing fragility of our financial system, where much of the problem is the over concentration of debt of storage and processing capabilities. Perhaps most important, not one of these industrial crashes would have happened had alternative sources of production been available in real time.

If these three observations are in fact true, the key to ensuring the resiliency of our international production systems is to build up real-time redundancy by physically distributing the capacity to produce keystone components, be they electronics chemicals or information. This, in turn, points us immediately to all sorts of pragmatic, practical rules and laws that would promote such distribution. We could, for instance, require that all firms dual source supplies in real time. We could, for instance, require firms to report all bottlenecks and potential bottlenecks to investors, governments, and the public. We could, for instance, alter the goals of competition policy (which, properly understood, includes trade policy) to ensure that the resiliency of vital systems is a main goal.

The one thing we need never do is adopt protectionist policies designed specifically to shift production to our own home countries. The fragility of these systems derives not from the fact that production is located off shore, but from the fact that all production of many keystone components is located in one or a couple places only. It is, if anything, a direct product of our failure to deal with such protectionist and mercantilist policies—in places like Beijing, Tokyo, Taipei, and Berlin—in a realistic fashion.

---

[18]See my comparison of the disruptions caused by the Aisin fire of 1997 and the Niigata earthquake of 2007 in Barry C. Lynn, "Built to Break: The International System of Bottlenecks in the New Era of Monopoly," *Challenge*, March/April 2012, pp. 94-96.

Looking to 2030—Fragility and Volatility.

The Atlantic Community faces a choice as it looks forward towards 2030. We can stumble numbly on towards an economic and/or political disaster of the first magnitude. Or we can work, honestly and realistically, with the leaders of the dominant nation-states and dominant corporate and banking estates to reestablish these systems on a more stable and resilient footing.

This is not a problem that will "heal" itself; nor will some new technology emerge to solve the problem for us. The origins of the problem are entirely political in nature, hence can be fixed only through political action. Absent such political will, the fundamental structural flaws in the industrial system will, in many cases, simply grow more dire. To make matters worse, the concentration of political and economic power that is the source of this danger poses many other closely related threats to our political and economic wellbeing.

The stakes could not be higher. Failure to act now to restore coherent, rational, democratic, public institution-based control over our international political economy means that, as we look to 2030 we can expect:

More industrial and financial crashes. The present industrial system is already radically unstable. Every day the actions of monopolists and mercantilists—by promoting an ever greater concentration of keystone capacities—make it more so. Given that natural and political disasters are inevitable in our world, it is only a matter of time until some event triggers another cascading shutdown, perhaps far more damaging than any we have yet experienced.

An ever more provocative and assertive China. Factions within China have already proven willing to use various forms of embargo to project power on other nation states and on individual international corporations. They will continue to use this power until the United States, Europe, and Japan mount a coherent, coordinated response.

A sudden collapse of U.S. and European prestige and authority. The Iraq War, the financial meltdown, the eurozone crisis, and the revelations of NSA spying have all severely reduced U.S. and European standing in the world but have not destroyed it. However, another financial crash or a humiliating retreat before a Chinese provocation has the potential to shatter the political foundations of the postwar system once and for all.

More economic volatility. Over the last decade, the increasingly giant companies that control the flow of grains, energy, and metals have become far more sophisticated at manufacturing volatility in commodity markets, mainly to drive up trading profits. This volatility will increasingly disrupt the ability of states, businesses, and individuals to plan and act in any coherent fashion.

Worsening economic stagnation. Over the last decade, a few increasingly large and powerful companies like Monsanto, Oracle, Google, Microsoft, GE have captured control over entire realms of technology. This concentration of control appears already to have reduced innovation and growth, and will only do so more dramatically over time.

Collapse of Checks and Balances. Today's regulators tend to respond to crises mainly by further concentrating power and by integrating state regulatory functions more intimately into theoretically "private" institutions. This blurring of public and private economic realms will increase the corruption of our democratic political system even while it greatly increases the likelihood of bigger crises in the near future.

A dis-integration of public information systems. One of the most important products of competition in open markets is trustworthy information that allows us—as a society and as individuals—to react and adapt to a constantly changing world. The monopolization of control over entire production activities by private corporations and foreign states radically reduces the flow of trustworthy information through our society, and hobbles our ability to understand and manipulate the world around us.

Towards a 21st Century International System

The greatest threat to the stability of the complex systems on which we all depend is posed not by any terrorist group or foreign state but by the corporate libertarian movement in the United States. It was their assault on competition policy that transformed the international industrial system from a source of resiliency and strength into what is now perhaps the single most powerful transmitter of shock from nation to nation. It was their assault on the institutions of public knowledge and empiricism itself that has all but destroyed our ability—as individuals and as a society—to understand and respond to these dangers.

This is not only an American problem. The extreme and growing instability in our international industrial and financial systems, caused by this reckless dismantlement of the U.S. state's ability to police against efforts to concentrate industrial capacity and other forms of risk threatens all nations. The threat is not merely to the grand achievements of Monnet, Schuman, Marshall, and Eisenhower. It is to human society as we know it.

The good news is we have two reasons for hope. First is that the public attitude towards concentrated power is changing fast. We saw this in the United States with the Tea Party and Occupy movements. We see this among a growing number of experts and policymakers, in places like the Bank of England and the Federal Reserve. We see this increasingly around the world, such as in Brussels and Berlin, where competition authorities are taking more aggressive stances than in years.

The second reason for hope is that we now face an immanent and eminently understandable threat—in the form of renascent militarism. We see this in Europe, in Russia's adventures in the Ukraine. And we see it most dramatically in Asia, where China in recent years has engaged in military face offs with the United States, Japan, Vietnam, and the Philippines.

The stakes in Russia are relatively small, as few complex cross-border systems are threatened by sanctions there, or even hotter war. The South China Sea is another matter entirely. Across these waters pass the physical and digital components that go into making almost every device on which modern society depends, and to a large degree on which our international financial system stands.

China's growing belligerence, despite more than two-decades of phenomenal economic growth, is stark proof of the failure of the corporate libertarian vision to deal with real-world threats. And catastrophe here does not even require a hot conflict. Any showdown that results in a simple embargo of goods would inevitably, and almost immediately, result in the seizing up of vitally important cross-border flows of goods, cash, and information around the entire world.

Our opportunity, then, is to take advantage of the high and growing danger of some sort of conflict in the seas around China—and of the fact that such a conflict has the potential to wreck massive economic and social devastation across the entire world—to force a fundamental reassessment of the policies and ways of thinking responsible for today's unstable cross-border systems. The promise is not merely to avoid disaster. It is also to reestablish our world on a foundation that truly helps to promote peace, widespread prosperity, and stability across the long expanse of this next century.

Chapter 9

The Global Illicit Economy 2030

Peter Andreas

This chapter offers some brief, speculative, and wide-ranging thoughts on what the world of illicit flows might look like in 2030. By definition this exercise in crystal ball gazing is tentative and cautious. Bold, sweeping predictions beyond confidently asserting that the world of illicit flows will remain alive and well would be foolish. Nevertheless, it is worthwhile to try to think ahead to where we might be in the coming years based on past and present patterns and trajectories.

Global illicit flows can simply be defined as the clandestine cross-border economic exchange of people, goods, money, and information unauthorized by the sending or receiving country. Typically this means flows that are prohibited (such as drugs and endangered species), regulated (such as cigarettes, arms, people), stolen (such as art, antiquities, and intellectual property), or counterfeit (such as prescription drugs or currency). Together, these flows reflect the illicit "underside" of globalization and the global economy. It is reasonable to conclude that in the next decade and a half or so we are not likely to see some sort of fundamental shift in the illicit global economy. Instead, we can expect to see both significant continuity and change, with considerable variation across places and flows.

This is a more cautious and nuanced account of the future of global illicit flows than the "doom and gloom" alarmism that dominates much of the policy debate.[1] The Washington pundit Moises Naim, for example, has recently sounded the alarm bells about the proliferation of what he labels "mafia states" that make it their business to promote and profit from global illicit flows, and even warns of the possible

---

[1] See especially, Moises Naim, *Illicit: How Smugglers, Traffickers, and Copycats are Hijacking the Global Economy*. More recently, see Michael Miklaucic and Jacqueline Brewer, eds. *Convergence: Illicit Networks and National Security in the Age of Globalization* (National Defense University Press, Washington, DC, 2013).

emergence of nuclear mafia states.[2] Transnational crime expert Phil Williams projects that the 21st century will be defined by a continuing weakening of states in which illicit non-state actors and activities spread in an increasingly violent, lawless, and out of control world. For Williams, a gathering storm of illicit flows that may turn into the "perfect storm" is a dark and dangerous future characterized by chaos and disorder.[3]

These scary accounts tend to see almost everything as fundamentally new and unprecedented. The actual newness of the trend is typically asserted rather than empirically demonstrated.[4] History tends to be bracketed rather engaged to generate comparative insight and analytical leverage.

Rather than pointing to trends that all lead in one direction—a more lawless and illicit-flows saturated world—I suggest that a more realistic and complex picture of the near future takes into consideration countertrends and ambiguous trends. The trends, I argue, are often double-edged, both encouraging and inhibiting global illicit flows of various sorts. Instead of expecting some sort of fundamental shift in global illicit flows in the coming decade and a half (as part of what Tomas Ries provocatively calls the larger "paradigm shift of the human condition"[5]), the main lesson of history is that we are far more likely to simply experience the latest chapter in an age-old story of continuity and change.

I am certainly not suggesting that the problem of global illicit flows is not serious, and may even worsen, especially in some parts of the world. It will likely continue to be a defining source of tension

---

[2]Moises Naim, "Mafia States," *Foreign Affairs* (May/June 2012), and Andreas/Naim exchange, "Measuring the Mafia State Menace," *Foreign Affairs* (July/August 2012).

[3]Phil Williams, "Lawlessness and Disorder: An Emerging Paradigm for the 21st Century," in Michael Miklaucic and Jacqueline Brewer, eds., *Convergence: Illicit Networks and National Security in the Age of Globalization* (Washington, DC: National Defense University Press, 2013).

[4]It should be recognized that the aggregate data available is of such poor quality (given the hidden nature of illicit flows) that it is often of questionable utility, though this does not stop some analysts from making confident sweeping claims. For a discussion, see Peter Andreas, "The Politics of Measuring Illicit Flows and Policy Effectiveness," in Peter Andreas and Kelly M. Greenhill, eds. *Sex, Drugs, and Body Counts: The Politics of Numbers in Global Crime and Conflict* (Cornell University Press, 2010).

[5]See Tomas Ries' chapter in this volume.

between developed and less developed regions (such as the EU in relation to its immediate neighbors to the east and south, and the United States in relation to its southern neighbors). Illicit flows may become more and more difficult to "weed out" of the growing volume of flows that define the process of globalization. But we should take a deep breath and resist hyperventilating—especially when such hyperventilating can lead to knee-jerk policy responses that may do more harm than good and may even contribute to the very problem they are supposed to solve. The sky is not falling. The global economy is not being hijacked by the illicit dark side of globalization and is unlikely to be in the foreseeable future (and indeed, as the 2008 financial crisis powerfully demonstrated, the bigger threat may ultimately come from perfectly legitimate actors behaving irresponsibly even if not necessarily illegally[6]). Moreover, even if there is an overall increase in illicit flows, this does not necessarily mean they will be increasingly global, let alone be controlled by global organized crime. Indeed, some illicit flows may become both more domestic and less organized.

In the first section of this chapter I look at some of the leading megatrends and their implications for illicit flows. I then examine the case of the illicit drugs—considered the leading "sector" of the illicit global economy. The connection between illicit flows and armed conflict is then briefly evaluated. Finally I discuss the implications of U.S. decline for international crime control efforts, given that Washington has been the world's leading policeman fighting illicit flows such as drug trafficking and money laundering.

How do Global Megatrends Impact Global Flows?

The standard approach to projecting future developments is to identify key "megatrends"—as evident in the November 2012 *Global Trends 2030: Alternative Worlds* report from the National Intelligence Council. Although these type of reports typically do not focus much on global illicit flows, we can certainly try to extend the analysis to

---

[6]The fact that much of such behavior remains legal reflects corporate lobbying power to avoid greater regulation rather than the severity of social consequences. Nikos Passas and Neva Goodwin, eds. *It's Legal but it Ain't Right: Harmful Social Consequences of Legal Industries* (University of Michigan Press, Ann Arbor, 2005).

include this. For instance, the *NIC Report* points to the growth of middle classes in the developing world that could add as many as two billion consumers—which has all sorts of implications for accessing raw materials and for the production and trade in manufactured goods. Many of these consumers, of course, will no doubt also be consumers of illicit flows (ranging from drugs to counterfeit goods).

The *NIC Report* also points to the importance of growing migration. The demand for both skilled and unskilled labor is expected to increase in the coming years—and if legal channels are not sufficient to satisfy this demand it is reasonable to predict that illicit channels will continue to provide an attractive substitute (and in the process continue to enrich migrant smuggling organizations). The extraordinary political difficulty in making progress on comprehensive immigration reform in the United States to date suggests that the illicit channel option will likely remain an important alternative mechanism to meet labor needs—which can be expected to grow as the U.S. economy continues to recover.

Unauthorized labor flows between developing countries—already a serious issue but too often overlooked—may also accelerate further.[7] China, for instance, has also started to have its own illegal immigration problem (such as from North Korea), and this can be expected to grow as well. Climate change may further fuel a distinct and growing form of unauthorized migrants—"environmental refugees"—who flee from the most stricken areas but are not welcomed by receiving countries as legitimate refugees.

The growth of middle classes in the developing world that could add as many as two billion consumers—which has all sorts of implications for accessing raw materials and for the production and trade in manufactured goods. Many of these consumers, of course, will no doubt also be consumers of illicit flows (ranging from drugs to counterfeit goods). Urbanization is also expected to increase substantially by 2030. Already some half of the world's population lives in an urban area, and this is expected to grow to nearly sixty percent by 2030. The UN estimates that by 2030 the urban population in China will grow

---

[7]See especially Kamal Sadiq, *Paper Citizens: How Illegal Immigrants Acquire Citizenship in Developing Countries* (Oxford University Press, 2008).

by 276 million and in India by 218 million—accounting for more than a third of the total projected increase in the world's urban population. Bangladesh, Brazil, the Democratic Republic of Congo, Indonesia, Mexico, Nigeria, Pakistan, the Philippines, and the United States are also expected to experience major urban growth spurts. As has long been the case, urbanization and criminality often go hand in hand— and this includes criminality related to illicit flows such as drugs, unauthorized migration, and sex workers. Based on past patterns, it is therefore not difficult to predict a continued close connection between urbanization and the proliferation of illicit flows.

The development and spread of new technologies, especially information technologies, is often identified as having a particularly profound impact on future trends. But again, this is hardly new, and should be thought of as simply the latest chapter in a very old story— including in the world of illicit flows. The revolutions in transportation and communication associated with globalization have been a major source of change for both licit and illicit flows, and there is every reason to expect this to continue to be the case in the years to come. President Barack Obama noted in July 2011, "During the past fifteen years, technological innovation and globalization have proven to be an overwhelming force for good. However, transnational criminal organizations have taken advantage of our increasingly interconnected world to expand their illicit enterprises."

There is much truth in this statement. But as important as new technologies have been and will continue to be, it would be difficult to argue that these new technologies have had a more profound impact than earlier technologies—such as the rise of transoceanic commerce, the development of the telegraph, and the proliferation of train travel and the invention of the automobile all long before globalization became a buzzword. In other words, new technologies do matter, often profoundly, but this is also an old story that dates back not just years and decades but centuries.

Law enforcement authorities have long grumbled about how new technologies advantage criminals—and this is certain to be a continued source of frustration. But less noticed is that law enforcement has long been a major beneficiary of technological change—consider, for instance, how much the invention of photography and fingerprinting enabled criminal investigations and the development of government-issued identification documents. The invention of the telephone aided not only criminals but also cops—including the use of wiretapping as a crucial tool in undercover investigations.

Thus, if the past is any guide to the future, new technologies will continue to be exploited to facilitate the movement of illicit flows but also by government authorities tasked to deter and disrupt such flows. Consider, for example, the development and proliferation of unmanned aerial vehicles (UAVs), otherwise known as drones. Future commercial applications of drones—such as proposed by Amazon ("Amazon Air Prime") for extra fast delivery of packages[8]—can also presumably be exploited for domestic and international illicit commerce, including for both surveillance of law enforcement and for unmanned GPS-guided aerial delivery of illicit goods. At the same time, drones will no doubt become an increasingly popular tool for policing and surveillance of illicit flows—as is already the case along the U.S.-Mexico border—though there has been growing popular resistance to domestic drone use due to privacy concerns in some places.

New technologies will continue to increase government capacity to track and police the cross-border flow of people, cargo, money, and information. We are likely to especially see this in the further development of tamper-resistant travel documents and "smart" IDs with biometric identifiers (such as digital fingerprints and facial and retinal scans), the creation of more expansive and sophisticated databases for "data mining," and the proliferation of high tech cargo tracking, monitoring, and inspection devices. Cargo inspections traditionally done at ports of entry will continue to be pushed outward through prescreening and preclearance, facilitated by the development of "smart containers" and the use of new cargo tagging and tracking devices.

These technological developments will not only continue to enhance the policing of illicit cross-border flows but also contribute to (and necessitate) the continued growth of international policing cooperation, most developed in Europe and in U.S.-EU relations. As in the past, increased policing cooperation can also bring with it increased

---

[8]Steve Banker, "Amazon and Drones—Here Is Why It Will Work," *Forbes*, December 19, 2013.

friction between governments over policing agendas, methods, and strategies—as evident in U.S.-EU tensions over data privacy. More generally, efforts to "push borders outward" create pressures on other countries to facilitate pre-inspection and pre-screening.

Technology has so far enabled governments stay one step ahead of currency counterfeiters. Currency counterfeiting will remain a serious problem in the years ahead, but is likely to pale in comparison to the much more rampant counterfeiting in earlier eras (most notably 19th century America).

We can especially expect to see a rapid growth of both cybercrime and cyberpolicing in coming years. Policing cyberspace will continue to develop as a new frontier of law enforcement that coexists and intermingles with traditional terrestrial policing. This will no doubt also continue to provoke intense political battles and concern over privacy and civil liberties issues, both domestically and internationally.

In some cases, scientific and technological breakthroughs may not only facilitate illicit trade but create entirely new types of illicit trade. New scientific advances may enable DNA theft and illicit cloning in the not-too-distant future—but this can also be expected to open up new forms of policing through more advanced genetic testing and tracing. The black market for human organs, especially kidneys, can be expected to keep growing in the immediate term thanks to growing access to the advances in organ transplant procedures. Yet we should keep in mind that future scientific advances in the development of artificial organs could greatly reduce black market demand. The emergence of 3D printing, for instance, even includes "bioprinting" that is expected to produce human organs.[9]

At the same time, as 3D printing improves and becomes less expensive and more accessible, it will have all sorts of troubling illicit applications, such as the production of plastic guns that can evade airport metal detectors—not to mention production and distribution of illicit conventional guns.[10] Printing items that violate intellectual property

---

[9]Sophie Novack, "The Next Frontier for 3-D Printing: Human Organs," *National Journal*, December 27, 2013.

[10]Steven Kotler, "Vice Wars: How 3-D Printing Will Revolutionize Crime," *Forbes*, July 31, 2012.

laws also has enormous legal and financial consequences, ranging from fake fashion to fake pharmaceuticals.[11] The quality of cheap counterfeit goods, which is already often quite high, will likely get much better and much cheaper.

But the most important repercussion of 3D printing for illicit flows may be much greater domestication—after all, why illicitly import something that one can replicate on a 3D printer at home? This may mean that even as the overall quantity, quality, and range of illicit flows could increase in the future through 3D printing, *global* illicit flows—flows that cross borders—may actually decrease. And one crucial consequence of this may be to reduce the role of transnational criminal organizations in the provision of illicit goods. In other words, illicit flows may proliferate, but transnational organized crime may not—and may even shrink. This is certainly a positive development even if the consumption of illicit flows may increase.

Although the full repercussions of the development and spread of 3D printing on the world of illicit flows remains to be seen, we can certainly predict the coming of a "war on 3D printing" by law enforcement targeting its illegal applications. And 3D printing can also be expected to aid law enforcement—as already evident in the forensic use of this new technology, such as replicating crime scenes.[12] The importance of new scientific and technological developments in shaping future illicit flows may be nowhere more evident than in the illicit drug trade, which is discussed in detail below.

Case Study: Illicit Drugs

Although extremely difficult to measure (and questionable quantitative claims are often made without reliable evidence[13]), there is widespread agreement that illicit drugs are the single largest and most profitable "sector" of the illicit global economy—and therefore highlighted in this discussion.

---

[11]Dennis Draeger, "3-D Printing's Radical New World," *Salon*, May 16, 2012.

[12]Eugene Liscio, "Forensic Uses of 3D Printing," *Forensic Magazine*, June 4, 2013.

[13]For a discussion, see Peter Andreas, "The Politics of Measuring Illicit Flows and Policy Effectiveness," in Peter Andreas and Kelly Greenhill, eds. *Sex, Drugs, and Body Counts: The Politics of Numbers in Global Crime and Conflict* (Ithaca: Cornell University Press, 2010).

It is safe to predict that the current trend toward the development and availability of a wide range of new synthetic substances will continue to accelerate—and that these will increasingly compete with and substitute for natural-based drugs such as heroin and cocaine. We are already seeing this in the meth trade, but could become more generalized. As part of the move toward synthetics we can also expect a continuation of the trend toward greater abuse and black market diversion of prescription pills (already a serious and growing problem with drugs such as Adderall and Oxycontin)—greatly facilitated by the Internet and the proliferation of online pharmacies.[14]

Along with the shift in types of drugs consumed we can also expect some shifts in the location of drug consumption. Europe has in recent decades emerged as a cocaine market nearly as large as the U.S. market, though has recently stabilized and even fallen slightly.[15] With the U.S. market saturated and cocaine prices higher in Europe, it is no surprise that cocaine trafficking organizations have since the 1990s shifted some of their focus to the European market.

Much has been made of the use of West Africa as a cocaine transshipment point to Europe, including shipments from Brazil to Nigeria, provoking alarm and anxiety in some policy circles. However, this response seems to have been overblown and overly alarmist. The problem is certainly serious, but it should be noted that the West Africa route appears to have significantly declined in importance in recent years[16]—and there is little to suggest that this will change greatly in the coming years. Traffickers have long exploited a diversity of routes into Europe by land, sea, and air, and there is no reason to believe this will not continue to be the case. For Latin American cocaine traffickers, this includes continuing to use Spain as a logical access point to the European market using a wide range of conveyances and transportation methods, but also includes expanded use of other transshipment routes such as through Bulgaria and the Western Balkans.[17]

---

[14]See especially Mike Power, *Drugs 2.0: The Web Revolution that's Changing How the World Gets High* (Portobello Books, 2013).

[15]*World Drug Report* (UN Office on Drugs and Crime, 2011).

[16]See especially *World Drug Report* (UN Office on Drugs and Crime, 2013).

[17]On the dynamics of transshipment in general, see especially H. Richard Friman, "Just Passing Through: Transit States and the Dynamics of Illicit Transshipment," *Transnational Organized Crime*, Vol. 1, No. 1 (1995): 65-83.

But while United States and Europe will remain core illicit drug markets, the real growth markets may be places such as Brazil and especially China. Brazil is already estimated to be the world's second largest consumer of cocaine (behind the United States). With China expected to become the world's single largest economy a few years before 2030, we can also expect China's parallel emergence as the world largest illicit economy—including in the drug trade. China is already a major producer of counterfeit drugs. However, China's emergence as both a leading consumer and exporter of synthetic drugs may prove far more consequential. It is important to recall that in the mid-19th century China was under siege by western opium pushers (with the power of the British East India Company dwarfing that of any so-called "drug cartel" today), and China's efforts to shut them out resulted in the opium wars. Now we may see a very different dynamic, in which China is a major consumer country and a major source country—but in black market synthetic drugs.

Even as we can expect the spread of synthetic illicit drugs to accelerate, a countertrend may be the decline of the illicit marijuana (cannabis) trade if current moves toward decriminalization and legalization continue. This is particularly striking in the United States, where several states (Colorado and Washington) have recently legalized marijuana for recreational purposes, and other states may soon follow. With the United States as the most important player in creating and sustaining the global drug prohibition regime, the challenge to marijuana prohibition from within may have powerful regional and global ripple effects. After all, how can the United States continue to pressure and insist that other countries crackdown on the marijuana trade when it is turning a blind eye to legalization initiatives within its own borders? Uruguay has been the first Latin American country to legalize marijuana, but far more consequential would be for producer countries such as Mexico and Colombia to also do so. Extended globally, this could eventually take cannabis mostly out of the realm of illicit flows and into the realm of licit flows such as tobacco. Are legal exports of Moroccan hashish to Europe all that unrealistic in the medium term (if not near future)? Or legal high-quality "boutique" cannabis exports from the Netherlands to the rest of Europe?

We are already seeing a growing domestication of the marijuana trade in the United States—the world's largest market. Domestic growers already have distinct competitive advantage over foreign illicit suppliers. Tighter border interdiction will continue to serve as an unintended form of "pot protectionism" (since marijuana is a bulky and smelly product it is the easiest drug to interdict and indeed the vast majority of border drug busts involve marijuana seizures). More intensive interdiction in coming years would only reinforce this. With highly uneven domestic marijuana laws, some states such as Colorado and Washington are likely to become major black market exporters to other states across the country. In other words, the illicit marijuana trade persists, but with domestic supply increasingly outweighing foreign imports.

Domestication could also extend to other drugs. The development of new synthetics, including potentially synthetic cocaine, could reduce imports if the barriers to entry for producers and the law enforcement-induced risks are sufficiently low. Of course, we may also simply see a repetition of the methamphetamine story, in which law enforcement pressure within the United States has pushed much of the production across the border to Mexico. In that case, we would simply have yet another illustration of history repeating itself.

At the same time as we may see the continued decriminalization and even legalization of marijuana, it is not so far-fetched to speculate that tobacco may become more criminalized than it is today. The consumption of tobacco is the single greatest cause of preventable deaths in dozens of countries. It is indisputably linked to the premature deaths of millions of people every year. Norms with respect to tobacco consumption, especially in public, have changed rapidly in some countries in recent years. We can well imagine that some countries will choose to ban production and sale of tobacco and therefore propagate their prohibitions to others, and that anti-tobacco activists will lobby for a global prohibition regime. Whether these efforts will follow on the footsteps of the stillborn alcohol prohibition regime promoted by the United States in the 1920s or be incorporated into the larger drug prohibition regime is hard to say.

Just as there will be a continued shift in the types of drug consumed and in who is consuming the drugs, we can also project shifts in the transportation methods used to reach drug markets. Take the case of the United States. Currently the U.S.-Mexico border is the main entry point for illicitly imported drugs. It is partly due to efforts by traffickers to control entry to this market—amidst government crackdowns—that has fueled such high levels of drug violence in Mexico. We can speculate that the drug violence that has overwhelmed Mexico in recent years will eventually subside but without a substantial reduction in the flow of drugs to the United States. One possibility is a partial shift in trafficking routes back to the Caribbean—but via growing use of GPS-guided submersibles and semisubmersibles.

This is an alarming development from a national security perspective, since such delivery mechanisms can also deliver other things (including terrorists and weapons of mass destruction). But this is actually a positive trend from the perspective of reducing drug corruption and limiting the collateral damage of the drug trade along transshipment routes. After all, the more removed the illegal drug trade is from legal commerce, population centers, and transportation channels the better. For example, many Central American countries, such as Honduras, are battered and overwhelmed by being transshipment points for the flood of South American cocaine bound for the U.S. market. This would be a change for the better if the trade were pushed out to sea (and even under the sea). Of course, if the use of submersibles and semisubmersibles really takes off (we are still at a fairly early stage), perhaps this will provide a rationale to adapt and deploy the U.S. Navy's latest submarine detection technologies for counternarcotics purposes.

To date, these submersibles and semisubmersibles have typically required a small crew, but one can easily imagine the development of unmanned remotely controlled vehicles, not only by sea but also by air. For instance, as previously noted, the current government monopoly over drone technology can be expected to loosen in the coming years—and drones have the potential to not only provide surveillance and targeted strikes but also carry high-value illicit cargos such as drugs.

We are also already witnessing important shifts in how illegal drugs are purchased and distributed to consumers. Internet pharmacies have already eased illegal access to prescription drugs such as Oxycontin, but the Internet also facilitates distribution of illicit drugs such as cocaine and ecstasy—most strikingly evident in the case of Silk Road, an online black market that started in 2011 using Bitcoin as digital currency and the anonymity tool Tor to protect user identities. Some have dubbed the site the "Amazon of illegal drugs." Although Silk Road was shut down by the FBI in October 2013, and its founder, Ross William Ulbricht, has been arrested on drug trafficking charges, a month later there were reports that Silk Road 2.0 was already online and administered by a new manager.[18]

Yet the sustainability of sites like Silk Road is unclear. Silk Road was just one of a number of sites that suddenly shut down, including BlackMarket Reloaded, shaking consumer confidence. And while online anonymity provides some protection, anonymity can also be exploited by law enforcement—including by setting up sites that are actually sting operations.

Moreover, the viability of Bitcoin, which has provided the crypto-currency for Silk Road and other online black market exchanges, remains highly uncertain. Bitcoin transactions leave digital bread-crumbs that can expose users who do not know how to cover their trail. The most convenient ways of using Bitcoin are also the most traceable. And Bitcoin services like Coinbase are subpoenable.[19] Fur-thermore, law enforcement crackdowns have started to target leading players in the Bitcoin universe. For example, Charles Shrem was arrested in January 2014 on charges of helping people convert money into virtual currency for the purpose of buying illegal drugs. Shrem was chief executive of a popular website set up to convert dollars into Bitcoins. He was also on the board of the Bitcoin Foundation, a non-profit created to educate the public about digital money.[20]

The international drug trade may also be shaken up by new techno-logical breakthroughs in production methods. Most notable in this regard is the potential revolutionary impact of 3D printing. As 3D printing improves and becomes cheaper and more accessible, drug production could become much more democratized and local—and therefore less and less in the hands of international drug trafficking

---

[18]Andy Greenberg, "'Silk Road 2.0' Launches, Promising a Resurrected Black Market for the Dark Web," *Forbes*, November 6, 2013.

[19]Andy Greenberg, "Follow the Bitcoins: How We Got Busted Buying Drugs on Silk Road's Black Market," *Fortune*, September 5, 2013.

[20]Nathaniel Popper, "Bitcoin Figure is Accused of Conspiring to Launder Money," *New York Times*, January 27, 2014.

organizations. The same may be true of prescription drugs.[21] In other words, in the not too distant future, consumers may be able to download and print both their meds and their recreational drugs. For the illicit drug trade, this would greatly facilitate consumer access—but with the upside of also greatly reducing the transnational organized crime and violence associated with the trade. Supply-side drug control efforts would become even less effective than they already are, leading to more pressure to focus on the demand side of the problem.

In this regard, it should be noted that even as new drugs, new drug markets, new drug routes, and new drug transportation and production methods can be expected to proliferate, scientists are reportedly working on an "addiction vaccine" which could greatly curtail both licit and illicit drug flows. And even if this proves illusive, scientists will likely continue to unlock the mysteries of addiction in ways that could greatly improve treatment.

The Illicit Flows and Conflict Connection

A great deal of scholarly and policy attention has been given in recent years to the relationship between illicit flows and armed conflict, leading some to speculate that this will increasingly become a defining feature of warfare in the 21st century.[22] Much of the focus has been on how violent non-state actors, ranging from insurgents to terrorists, have exploited profitable illicit flows to fund and sustain rebellion.

It is commonly asserted that this is a distinctly post-Cold War phenomenon—even a defining characteristic of so-called "new wars."[23] A frequent argument, for example, is that in the absence of formal external sponsorship from the United States and the former Soviet Union, insurgents have increasingly turned to alternative forms

---

[21]Tim Adams, "The 'Chemputer' that could print out any drug," *The Observer* July 21, 2012; "3D Printers for Prescription Drugs Could be in Homes Within 20 Years," *Huffington Post*, April 24, 2012.

[22]See, for example, Vanda Felbab-Brown, "Crime-War Battlefields," *Survival*, June-July 2013; and John P. Sullivan, "Future Conflict: Criminal Insurgencies, Gangs, and Intelligence," *Small Wars Journal*, May 31, 2009.

[23]See Mary Kaldor, *New and Old Wars: Organized Violence in a Global Era* (Stanford University Press, 3rd ed. 2012).

of material support. This includes illicit exports dubbed "conflict commodities," such as drugs, timber, ivory, diamonds, and so on. Thus, partly thanks to the campaigns of international NGOs such as Global Witness, diamonds from conflict zones in West Africa have been labeled "blood diamonds." Illegal drugs such as opium and cocaine have come to be particularly associated with armed conflict, given their role in ongoing insurgencies in Colombia and Afghanistan.

Much of the attention to the illicit political economy dimensions of conflict is welcome and long overdue—all armed conflicts, after all, have a political economy, and this includes an illicit side. Too often, however, the end result of this new attention has been to distort and exaggerate more than to explain and inform. And one must always ask, what is fundamentally new here? The contemporary novelty of the illicit flows and conflict connection is too often simply stated rather than empirically proven.

We need look no further than the American historical experience to show that illicit flows have been an essential ingredient in conflict not just for decades but centuries. Indeed, illicit flows profoundly shaped the nature, duration, and outcome of the country's early military engagements. In the case of the War of Independence, illicit flows of arms successfully supplied the rebellion. In the case of the War of 1812, illicit trade in the form of "trading with the enemy" extended the conflict, helped to turn it into a stalemate, and subverted U.S. efforts to annex Canada. In the case of the Civil War, illicit cotton exports via blockade running helped to prolong the conflict, allowing the Confederacy to persist far longer than would otherwise have been the case. No contemporary "conflict commodity" has been more important in sustaining a conflict than was the case of cotton in the American Civil War. We could even call it "blood cotton."[24]

Based on past and present trends, it is safe to assume that illicit flows will continue to be deeply complicit in many future conflicts, especially in some resource-rich parts of the developing world. At the same time, there is no reason to assume that their importance will actually increase. Moreover, it is important to keep in mind that, contrary to

---

[24]For a more detailed account, see Peter Andreas, *Smuggler Nation: How Illicit Trade Made America* (Oxford University Press, New York, 2013).

popular impression, the overall global trend in recent decades has been toward fewer and less deadly armed conflicts.[25] Of course, this does not necessarily mean that this trajectory will continue, and there are all sorts of reasons—environmental, economic, and political—to expect armed conflict, especially within countries, to persist even if it doesn't necessarily increase. Here, the distinction between crime and war, and between soldiering and crime fighting, may be blurry.

U.S. Policing Power and Hegemonic Decline

Along with being a military and economic superpower the United States is a policing superpower. No other country has been as globally aggressive in policing illicit flows in recent decades. Foreign governments have reacted to U.S. pressures, inducements, and examples by creating new criminal laws targeting drug trafficking, money laundering, and organized crime and by reforming financial secrecy laws as well as their codes of criminal procedure to better conform to U.S. legal needs.

As we look towards 2030, the question is how long U.S. policing hegemony will last and who will emerge as the most likely challengers in the coming years. In other words, when will the fingerprints of U.S. negotiators fade in the creation of international agreements, and the footprints of U.S. law enforcement officials overseas become less pronounced? The EU may be a viable challenger in some international law enforcement arenas, especially if member states can strategically behave as a collective bloc. But for the most part, EU efforts are likely to complement more than challenge U.S. policing hegemony. At least in the short term, we can expect that the U.S.-European law enforcement relationship will continue to be based on a mixture of competition and collusion, reflecting an uneasy combination of political tension and regional divergence amid broader policy convergence and cooperation at the global level in policing the illicit flow of people, goods, and money.

---

[25]Joshua Goldstein, *Winning the War on War: The Decline of Armed Conflict Worldwide* (Dutton: 2011). For an earlier account, see John Mueller, *The Remnants of War* (Cornell University Press, 2004).

Based on past historical patterns and trajectories, we can expect that as power centers shift, so too will international crime control priorities and practices. The diffusion of power away from the United States is likely to have important consequences for policing illicit flows as policing preferences become more varied, priorities change, and coordination becomes more cumbersome. In this regard, the rise of China and other potential regional challenges in coming years may erode the hegemony of U.S.-sponsored international crime control initiatives and approaches. For instance, China is likely to continue to place far greater emphasis on policing the Internet to enforce strict censorship laws (aided by security tools, firewalls, and information provided by U.S. companies) rather than enforcing intellectual property rights laws. This, in turn, may become a growing source of international friction as China flexes its policing muscle and uses market access as a powerful leverage to pressure foreign governments and companies to cooperate in carrying out its own law enforcement agenda.

At the same time, U.S. policing influence may outlast its waning power. Some U.S.-backed international initiatives, such as the anti-money laundering efforts of the Financial Action Task Force, have taken on a life of their own and generated their own momentum. Major international agreements that the United States played an instrumental role in creating have built on and reinforced each other and provided models for future agreements. For example, the Palermo Convention Against Transnational Organized Crime very much built on the Vienna Convention Against Illicit Traffic in Narcotics and Psychotropic Substances, and the more recent UN Convention Against Corruption, in turn, has built on the Palermo Convention. If this pattern continues, we can expect future multilateral crime control agreements to at least partly borrow from these earlier models regardless of the level of U.S.-sponsorship and influence.

Finally, it is worth noting that U.S. decline may also mean the decline of the U.S. dollar as the currency of choice not only in the licit global economy but also the illicit global economy. The future of the dollar is of crucial importance for the architecture of both licit and illicit financial flows. This could include a shift in the principal focal points of world finance away from New York, London and Frankfurt. But regardless of U.S. decline, it would not be surprising to see continued pressure on tax havens due to the fiscal crisis and necessity of increasing tax collection. Just as Switzerland led the way in pioneering bank secrecy, it is now leading the way in bowing to pressure to curtail tax evasion (which has implications for hiding illicit money more generally). This may be just the beginning of a much broader trend in government efforts to track and curtail tax evasion. At the same time, we can expect continued evolution of methods of undercutting techniques designed to curb or control or just monitor illicit financial flows because the apparatus was designed with traditional international banking methods and institutions in mind. In other words, changes in legitimate finance will lead to parallel opportunities for illegitimate finance. The rise (and possible demise) of Bitcoin as an alternative "digital currency," discussed earlier, is just one particularly prominent example of this.

Conclusion

As has always been the case, there will continue to be inherent limits to how much governments can deter, detect, and interdict illicit flows, especially while maintaining an open society and keeping borders open for legal trade and travel. Facilitating the enormous volume of licit cross-border flows while attempting to enforce laws against illicit cross-border flows is and will remain an inherently cumbersome and frustrating task. And nowhere are the difficulties of this task felt more intensely than in the efforts to manage the growing transactions between developed and less developed regions of the world, whether across the southern and eastern edges of Europe or the southern edges of the United States.

Illicit flows will persist, as they always have—what will vary is their location, organization, method, and content. More police agents will continue to be deployed, new detection and interdiction technologies will continue to be developed, but illicit flows will also continue to go around, through, over, or under the policing barriers. Policing campaigns will continue to shape the methods, organization, and location of illicit flows, yet are unlikely to completely deter.

The future certainly looks bright both for those who profit from the business of illicit flows and for those in the business of policing such flows. On the policing side, this will likely include building on

The Global Illicit Economy 2030 225

the ever-thickening cross-border law enforcement networks that have become a crucial—even if often overlooked—dimension of transatlantic relations and regional and global governance.[26] Declining U.S. leadership may present new opportunities for the EU to play a bigger global, and not just regional, role in this realm. However, EU officials are unlikely to find the policing challenge to be any less formidable than it has been for their American counterparts, though they may have more realistic expectations of what can reasonably be achieved.

---

[26]See Peter Andreas and Ethan Nadelmann, *Policing the Globe: Criminalization and Crime Control in International Relations* (Oxford University Press, 2006).

Chapter 10

Global Trends 2030 and Illicit Flows

Louise Shelley

The illicit flows observed in the transatlantic region are just part of a larger phenomenon observed globally. Precisely as Tomas Ries notes that transnational corporations are acting on a global scale moving goods and people, a parallel phenomenon is occurring in the illicit arena. The illicit often moves along with the licit. Sometimes as with illicit financial flows such as that from kleptocrats or large-scale tax evaders, the money flows through the legitimate banking system and is not the domain of the criminal world. They are facilitated by individuals of high social status who are often not connected with the illicit world that characterizes some of the flows analyzed here. These large-scale financial flows have been the subject of major criminal and civil investigations in recent years and have resulted in the payment of large scale fines by banks.

This chapter will focus on more tangible movements—people and goods which often travel the same routes where there is legitimate movement of technology, people and trade. These routes often have deep historical precedents and their continued use over centuries suggests that they will be employed in coming decades for the benefit of legitimate actors as well as illicit non-state actors. Illicit actors are moving people illegally and a variety of goods that are either illegal (like narcotics) or are not authentic like counterfeit goods. Counterfeits and diverted goods assume a significant share of international trade even in the affluent and well-regulated countries of North America and Western Europe. Often illicit trade is not detected because the illicit moves along with licit commodities or with large-scale human flows across borders.

This chapter focuses on common forms of illicit trade—the narcotics trade, human smuggling and trafficking and the counterfeit trade. The first two are criminal activities that receive significant law enforcement attention in developed countries. But the massive trade in counterfeit is a less policed forms of criminal activity in both North

America and Europe despite the harm that some of these counterfeits cause to public health and safety. As we look towards 2030, global megatrends will impact these illicit flows in a variety of ways.

Current Trends in Global Illicit Flows

Why the Growth in Illicit Flows?

There are important drivers of these illicit flows and they are tied to very fundamental forces in the contemporary world such as growing incoming inequality across and within regions, the population bulge in many developing countries, climate change, the rise of regional conflicts in recent decades and the increasing competition that has accompanied globalization. The displacement that comes with climate change and conflict fuels the illicit movement of people. Europe has seen many desperate people try to arrive on its territory fleeing the conflicts in Afghanistan, Syria, and the upheavals accompanying the Arab Springs and the instability of regions south of North Africa.[1] The United States is less close to some of the greatest conflicts but still has individuals seeking to enter to avoid the violence in Central America and drug-dominated regions of Mexico.

Significant income disparities characterize the borders of Europe on the Mediterranean Sea with those on its southern shores having a fraction of the income of those on its northern borders. The countries on the southern rim of the Mediterranean are now characterized by high levels of disorder and receive migrants from even poorer countries to the south, such as from sub-Saharan Africa. The same can be said for the United States and Mexico. The northern part of Mexico has very high rates of violence, much higher than in the more affluent United States, and receives migrants trying to enter the United States from poorer countries to the south of Mexico, particularly Honduras, El Salvador and Guatemala.[2]

---

[1]Global Initiative, "Smuggled Futures: The Dangerous Path of a Migrant from Africa to Europe," May 7, 2014, http://www.globalinitiative.net/smuggled-futures/; Phillip Connor, "Illegal immigration by boat: A dangerous, but common way of entering Europe," April 30, 2014, http://www.pewresearch.org/fact-tank/2014/04/30/illegal-immigration-by-boat-a-dangerous-but-common-way-of-entering-europe/.

[2]By Daniel González and Bob Ortega, "Central American Immigrants on the Rise," September 23, 2013, http://www.azcentral.com/news/politics/articles/20130923central-americanmigrantson-rise.html.

The economic disparities in many authoritarian states are particularly profound as officials of states are able to loot tens if not hundreds of millions of dollars or euros from their countries and transfer these assets into bank accounts and real estate in many desirable financial centers.[3] This enriches the financial centers of the developed world in North America and western Europe and drains the assets needed for development from the developing world. [4]

The desire to compete economically in a global market forces a brutal competition. As competition increases in the coming decades under population pressures and economic disruptions of climate change, the brutality of the workplace may be increased. Despite some consumer concern in both Europe and North America for ethical sourcing of products, there is precious little attention to the supply chains of imported goods or even those that are produced in the region.[5] The fire in Prato near Florence in Italy in which many illegal Chinese died is illustrative of the problem, that the high labor costs in the developed world have made it hard for some manufacturers to compete. Therefore, they employ individuals in dangerous conditions and pay substandard wages in order to manufacture goods at competitive prices.[6] This Chinese-owned factory served as a supplier to Italian-based firms.

This problem of exploitative conditions of immigrants also exists in North America but in a slightly different form as so much of production has shifted offshore. Difficult and dangerous work conditions exist in some of the maquiladores, factories in Northern Mexico, and the same can be said for factories in Asia, as exemplified by the recent deaths in textile factories in Bangladesh that supply both European and North American markets.[7]

---

[3]Louise Shelley, "Money Laundering into Real Estate," in *Convergence: Illicit Networks and National Security in the Age of Globalization*, eds. Michael Miklaucic and Jacqueline Brewer (Center for Complex Operations, Institute for National Strategic Studies, National Defense University Press, Washington, DC, 2013), pp.131-46.

[4]See the website of Global Financial Integrity and its numerous reports on this topic, http://www.gfintegrity.org/.

[5]The organization, Verite, is trying to raise awareness and work with companies that seek to improve their supply chains, www.verite.org.

[6]"Italy Prato fire kill seven in Chinese-owned factory," , December 1, 2013, http://www.bbc.co.uk/news/world-europe-25180500.

[7]Ruma Paul and Serajul Quadir, "European and US Retailers Split on Bangladesh Reform Plan," March 14, 2013, http://www.reuters.com/article/2013/05/14/us-bangladesh-building-idUSBRF94C0BL20130514.

In both North America and western Europe, illegal migrants work in hazardous conditions particularly in the agricultural sector and in construction. Often housed in sub-standard conditions by those who control them, they are sometime subject to abuse and the spread of disease.[8] Many are injured or some even die in these unregulated or poorly regulated environments. There has been limited response by the legal system and regulators to these abuses and the failure to focus or finance regulation suggests that this problem will grow in the coming decades.

The conditions that have fueled illicit trade in the past decades will only compound the problem in the future. Those who perpetrate these crimes are major beneficiaries of globalization. At the same time that these groups are able to operate flexibly and innovatively to circumvent the regulations of the state, the financial crises of recent years in North America and Europe have reduced the capacity of states to address these illicit flows. Fewer personnel, reduced budgets and stovepiped bureaucracies have failed to counter the rise of these organizations. Therefore, illicit trade will be a significant financial, public health and political stability concern in the coming decades. The ever present supply of people to be smuggled and trafficked and the increased manufacturing capacity in the developing world means that there will be ample supplies of people and goods ready to be trafficked.

Significant Forms of Illicit Trade

The different forms of illicit trade discussed here provoke very different policy responses by states. Counterfeiting, an increasingly pervasive and lucrative crime for the counterfeiters, is generally accorded relatively low priority by the state even though revenue losses in the United States and western Europe are increasing significant and thereby commanding more attention in this time of fiscal constraints. Therefore, it is anticipated that there will be further growth in this phenomenon by 2030.

---

[8]John Bowe, *Nobodies: Modern American Slave Labor and the Dark Side of the New Global Economy* (New York: Random House, 2008); Nsenga Burton, "Illegal Immigrants Abused as Domestics," July 5, 2011 http://www.theroot.com/articles/culture/2011/07/illegal_immigrants_abused_as_ domestics.html; "Migrant Smuggling," http://www.unodc.org/toc/en/crimes/migrant-smuggling.html.

Human smuggling and trafficking are much higher priorities not only because of the crime involved but because of the impact of these crimes on both American and western European society. It is not only the state that is responding but citizens, both from human rights and nationalist communities, that are demanding responses by the state. In both Europe and the United States, citizens have responded violently to migrants, some of them illegal migrants, and this trend may increase as evidenced by the backlash against migrants evident in the European parliamentary elections of May 2014 [9] and the violence by diverse groups against illegal immigrants on the southern border of the United States that has been a problem for many years already.[10]

Both North American and Europe spend significant amount of their law enforcement responses addressing the international drug trade. It is in this area that there is the greatest transatlantic cooperation as governments and organizations such as Europol share information on international drug organizations and routes. These markets have stabilized or even declined in both North America and Europe and as there may be a trend to increased legalization in the coming decade in both regions, countering illicit drug flows may not be the primary priority of illicit trade as it has been.

The area of illicit financial flows has, until recently, been an area that commanded too little attention from both the U.S. government, individual European states and the EU. The problem is not just one of offshore locales but of money flowing into major international financial centers without due diligence by financial institutions. The absence of regulation of shell companies has just compounded the problem. Revelations from leaked financial records have shown the enormous volume of this activity, some of it in offshore branches of major financial institutions.[11] But the U.S. policies that have made some banks "too big to fail" [12]and the penalties to institutions in both

---

[9]"Rise in Illegal Migration in 2014,"May 30, 2014, http://www.bbc.com/news/world-europe-27631192

[10]Jesus A. Trevino, "Border Violence against Illegal Immigrants and the Need to Change the Border Patrol's Current Complaint Review Process," *Houston Journal of International Law*, vol.21, no.1, Fall 1998.

[11]See http://www.publicintegrity.org/news/Offshore-bank for a discussion of this problem.

[12]Emily Stephenson and Jonathan Spicer, U.S. banks enjoy 'too-big-to-fail' advantage: Fed study, March 25, 2014, http://www.reuters.com/article/2014/03/25/us-usa-banks-systemic-idUSBREA2O19320140325.

North America and Europe are "merely a cost of business,"[13] suggesting that this phenomenon will not decline significantly in the coming decade but may increase.

Counterfeits

The highly regulated markets of Europe provide some controls on the entry of counterfeits. Europe, however, has a long and vulnerable coastline, historical trade routes that date back to the Ottoman Empire. Furthermore there are significant problems of corruption in the eastern part of Europe, especially along the historic Balkan route that links Europe with Turkey.[14] The conflicts in the former Yugoslavia and the extensive problems of organized crime in Italy, where criminal groups such as the Naples-based Camorra have significant controls over major ports,[15] contribute greatly to the growth of illicit trade. Their influence over illicit trade should continue in the coming decades as little has been done by the Italian state to counter their growth.

The sheer volume of trade, such as arrives at the port of Rotterdam in the Netherlands, limits the ability to ensure quality control at the entry points to Europe.[16] Therefore, imports of counterfeits are growing in frequency. In "2008, the European Customs Union detected over 3,200 attempts to import bogus drugs, involving almost 9 million items, over half of which originated in India."[17]

The prime criminal actors in the European counterfeit trade are the Camorra, who may earn "more than 10 percent of its roughly $25 billion annual profit through the sale of counterfeit and pirated goods—such as luxury clothing, power tools, CDs, DVDs, and software."[18] They are also active in the trade in counterfeit pharmaceuti-

---

[13]Richard McGregor and Aaron Stanley, "Banks Pay Out us $100 bn in fines," March 25, 2014, http://www.ft.com/cms/s/0/802ae15c-9b50-11e3-946b-00144feab7de.html#axzz33Iajso7r.

[14]Aida Hozic, "Between the Cracks: Balkan Cigarette Smuggling," *Problems of Post-Communism* 51, no. 3 (2004), pp. 35–44 discussed the corruption that facilitates this trade.

[15]Tom Behan, *The Camorra: Political Criminality in Italy* (Routledge, New York, 1996); Roberto Saviano, *Gomorrah* (Farrar, Straus, and Giroux, 2007).

[16]UNODC, *Globalization of Crime: Transnational Organized Crime Threat Assessment*, pp. 177, 179, see map of European seizures.

[17]Ibid., p. 184.

[18]Daniel L. Glaser, *Combating International Organized Crime: Evaluating Current Authorities, Tools, and Resources*, 2011, p. 3, http://www.treasury.gov/press-center/press-releases/Pages/tg1346.aspx.

cals. As a less traditional crime group than the Sicilian-based mafia they also cooperate with terrorists. A recent parliamentary investigation in Italy has raised serious concerns as to the extent and diverse costs of their significant role in importing and disseminating counterfeits.[19] Italian governmental corruption is a key component in their ability to operate on such a large scale.[20]

Two conflict regions in Europe have been at the center of the trade of counterfeit DVDs—Northern Ireland and Bosnia-Herzegovina.[21] The production and sale of counterfeits benefited both republican and loyalist paramilitary factions during the conflicts in Northern Ireland. During the Balkan conflicts of the 1990s the Arizona market in Brcko in Bosnia-Herzegovina was a major provider of counterfeit DVDs and other commodities. Behind this market were a diverse variety of criminals, terrorists and insurgents benefiting greatly from the sale of these products to the peacekeepers. In this way, those sent into stabilize the situation were providing operating funds to those who were intentionally destabilizing the political environment.[22]

These problems persist. Data on the consumption of counterfeit cigarettes indicate that an estimated 49% of cigarettes consumed in Bosnia-Herzegovina are illegal, amongst the highest recorded level in the world.[23] The war years and massive illicit trade that occurred have

---

[19]Discussion at a WAITO board meeting in Geneva, Switzerland, February 2012 with a member of the UNICRI staff that did research on this topic that was discussed in the Italian parliament. See research of UNICRI http://counterfeiting.unicri.it/, accessed December 26, 2012.

[20]Donatella della Porta, *Lo Scambio Occulto Casi di corruzione politica in Italia* (Bologna: Società Editrice Il Mulino, 1992); *Mafia e Potere* (l'Unità, Rome, 1993) discusses governmental corruption; UNODC, *Globalization of Crime: Transnational Organized Crime Threat Assessment*, p. 180.

[21]BCC, "Border Raid on Fake CD Plant," BBC News, December 17, 2000, http://news.bbc.co.uk/2/hi/uk_news/northern_ireland/1074672.stm, accessed December 26, 2012; Susan Watts, "Counterfeit CDs Threaten the Record Industry: Northern Ireland Terror Groups Believed to Be Involved in Importing Discs from China and Eastern Europe," The Independent, August 8, 1994, http://www.independent.co.uk/news/uk/counterfeit-cds-threaten-the-record-industry-northern-ireland-terror-groups-believed-to-be-involved-in-importing-discs-from-china-and-eastern-europe-1382140.html, accessed December 26, 2012; Peter Andreas, "Symbiosis Between Police Operations and Illicit Business in Bosnia," *International Peacekeeping*, 16, no. 1 (2009), pp. 233–246.

[22]Andreas, op. cit.

[23]Melzer provides international data on the percentage consumption of illicit tobacco in many countries based on Euromonitor data. A caveat needs to be applied to this data as there is no clarity on the methodology used by Euromonitor to assess illicit trade penetration. Recent

established a large and permanent second economy that shows no sign of abating.

The counterfeiting of DVDs, software and other multimedia is rampant in Russia. This is the type of organized crime that post-Soviet organized crime excels at, because of the many technically sophisticated criminals within their ranks. But in the North Caucasus, a highly corrupt region where both terrorists and criminals operate, there is the involvement of both groups in the DVD trade. A decade ago, according to Interpol, Russian law enforcement officials disrupted the operation of a Chechen-run counterfeit CD manufacturing plant. The Russian security service estimated that the criminal organization earned $500,000-700,000 and sent some of the funds to Chechen rebels.[24] This is an example of the indirect involvement of terrorist groups receiving funds from criminals who are directly engaged in this activity.

More recently, Russian researchers in Stavropol in the North Caucasus have observed the continued involvement of both terrorist and criminal groups in counterfeiting in the highly unstable region of the North Caucasus. Analysis of many court cases in the region reveal that illicit trade benefit terrorists, as well as criminal groups, as in the case of the Chechen DVD factory.[25] But the sampling of cases may be skewed, because of the widespread corruption and the complicity of government officials in this trade. They may only be ready to act against counterfeiting when there is a terrorist component.

The illicit counterfeit trade in the United States combines the theft of intellectual property from the United States, as well as the importation of counterfeits produced largely in Asia. Intellectual Property stolen in the United States will be counterfeited both in the United States and abroad, and will be marketed both domestically and internationally. The recent report of the state Attorney General for California on the future of crime, focusing much on high technology crime, as well as charging of Chinese computer criminals for targeting American innovation housed on computers are both indicative of the

---

analyses by the cigarette industry, according to an interview with an industry expert on illicit trade, identify Brunei as presently the largest market for illicit cigarette trade.

[24]Noble, op. cit.

[25]Discussions with Tatiana Pinkevich of the Stavropol Center on organized crime, see their website. http://cspkitraccc.skforussia.ru, accessed August 18, 2012.

crimes in the coming decade.[26] Despite the regulation and enforcement capacity in the United States, it has proven increasingly difficult to control the trade in counterfeit clothing, pharmaceuticals purchased through the Internet,[27] and the illicit sales of counterfeit DVDs and software in large metropolitan areas. Counterfeit and diverted cigarettes are an additional concern, particularly in states with high tax rates on cigarettes.[28] Illustrative of this is the case of New York, with the highest tax rates per pack, where 60% of cigarettes sold are smuggled.[29]

There are several important locales in the United States where theft of Intellectual Property is a particular concern. The theft of Intellectual Property related to software and technology is a particular concern on the west coast, particularly in Silicon Valley and Seattle areas.[30] Most of the pirated movies that are disseminated worldwide on DVDs originate from California, as does music from the Latin recording industry that is disseminated through counterfeit CDs.[31] Key parts of the American recording industry whose artists' recordings are subject to counterfeiting are based in New York City. In Los Angeles, Russian Organized Crime, Eurasian Organized Crime, Asian Organized Crime, Latin American and Lebanese Organized Crime groups as well as criminal gangs have been identified as benefiting from intellectual property crimes.[32] Counterfeits have been identified

---

[26]California Attorney General, "Gangs Beyond Borders, California and the Fight Against Transnational Crime," March 2014, http://oag.ca.gov/transnational-organized-crime; Michael S. Schmidt and David E. Sanger, "5 in China Army Face U.S. Charges of Cyberattacks," May 19, 2014, http://www.nytimes.com/2014/05/20/us/us-to-charge-chinese-workers-with-cyberspying.html

[27]Damon McCoy et. al., "PharmaLeaks: Understanding the Business of Online Pharmaceutical Affiliate Programs," august 2012, https://www.usenix.org/conference/usenixsecurity12/technical-sessions/presentation/mccoy.

[28]Diverted cigarettes are untaxed cigarettes that enter into the black market, see U.S. Department of Justice, *The Bureau of Alcohol, Tobacco, Firearms and Explosives Efforts to Prevent the Diversion of Tobacco* (DOJ: Washington, DC, September 2009), p. 92.

[29]Aaron Smith, "60% of cigarettes sold in New York are smuggled: report," January 10, 2013, http://money.cnn.com/2013/01/10/news/companies/cigarette-tax-new-york/index.html, accessed August 17, 2013.

[30]California Attorney General, "Gangs Beyond Borders, California and the Fight Against Transnational Crime," March 2014, http://oag.ca.gov/transnational-organized-crime.

[31]Stedman, op. cit., p. 7.

[32]Ibid., p. 7; National Gang Intelligence Center, National Gang Threat Assessment: Emerging Trends, 2011, 43, http://www.fbi.gov/stats-services/publications/2011-national-gang-threat-assessment, *accessed December 26, 2012.*

in what should be the most secure of supply chains. The US military has identified 1800 cases of counterfeit parts entering into US military combat hardware.[33]

Only a small share of counterfeits is intercepted in the United States because this is not a law enforcement priority. New York City, a major port of entry for the United States, faces significant imports of counterfeits, apart from its local production. Law enforcement in New York estimated that they confiscated only 2.5 million of the 19.5 illicit sound recordings destined for the streets of New York, or approximately three illegal CDs per capita.[34]

As a member of the Los Angeles' Sheriff Office for countering Intellectual Property crime admitted in Congressional testimony, IPR (Intellectual Property Rights) crime is attractive to gang members, because of the high profit and minimal jail sentences." In the parlance of one suspect, "It's better than the dope business, no one's going to prison for DVDs."[35]

The supply chains for the counterfeits connect countries of production in Asia with countries of demand in North America or Europe. The illicit counterfeit trade does not at present extensively to link the transatlantic region. This may increase in the future as some recent cases may be harbingers of future trends. For example, the largest case of illicit cigarettes in the United States involved the Real IRA that was marketing these illegally imported cigarettes from Panama to Europe.[36] The significant divergence in price between pharmaceuticals in the United States and Western Europe may lead to the illicit trade in diverted pharmaceuticals from Europe into American markets.

---

[33]Merrill Goozner, "U.S. Military Equipment Built with Counterfeit Parts," The Fiscal Times, May 22, 2012, http://www.thefiscaltimes.com/Articles/2012/05/22/US-Military-Equipment-Built-with-Counterfeit-Parts.aspx#page1, accessed December 24, 2012.

[34]City of New York, Office of the Comptroller, "Bootleg Billions: The Impact of the Counterfeit Goods Trade on New York City," 2004, 12, www.comptroller.nyc.gov/bureaus/bud/.../Bootleg-Billions.pdf, *accessed December 24, 2012.*

[35]U.S. Senate Committee on Homeland and Security and Governmental Affairs, *Counterfeit Goods: Easy Cash for Criminals and Terrorists* (Testimony by John C. Stedman, 109th Cong, 1st sess, May 28, 2005, purl.access.gpo.gov/GPO/LPS66671, accessed December 26, 2012.

[36]Paul Thompon, "US Businessman" funded Real IRA soldiers killing smuugling cigarettesh into Ireland,'" March 12, 2009, http://www.dailymail.co.uk/news/article-1161530/U-S-businessman-funded-Real-IRA-soldier-killers-smuggling-cigarettes-Ireland.html.

Human Smuggling and Trafficking

Human trafficking and smuggling into Europe have grown since the 1980s. Emigrants are attracted by generous welfare support and perceived economic advantages, as well as the demand in Western Europe for "three-d" workers—those willing to take dirty, dangerous, and/or degrading jobs that national citizens are unwilling to do. The increase can also be attributed to a number of converging global factors in the past few decades: economic crises in Asia; the conflicts in Iraq, Afghanistan, and Pakistan; and poverty in the global south have all encouraged emigration. Finally, options for legal entry to Europe are limited. In 2011, Europe accepted approximately 1.7 million legal migrants—a small percentage of those seeking entry—from outside the European Union.[37] Meanwhile, Frontex detected 141,000 illegal border crossings during the same year.[38] In 2008 an estimated 1.9 to 3.8 million unauthorized migrants resided in the European Union.[39] Given the numbers of people who wish to travel to the European Union, it is no surprise that the problem of human smuggling has grown relative to that of human trafficking.[40] The European Statistical agency in 2013 reported that there was an 18% growth in identified victims between 2008 and 2011 although the number represents just a small fraction of the problem.[41] The problem is growing in Europe in 2014 as a result of the conflicts in Africa, Syria and other regions of the world, placing particular pressure on the states of Southern Europe such as Spain and Italy.[42]

---

[37]Eurostat, "Migration and Migrant Population Statistics," http://epp.eurostat.ec.europa.eu/statistics_explained/index.php/Migration_and_migrant_population_statistics; Kristiina Kangaspunta, "Mapping the Inhuman Trade: Preliminary Findings of the Human Trafficking Database," *Forum on Crime and Society* 3, no. 1 (2003): p. 81, www.unodc.org/pdf/crime/forum/ forum3_note1.pdf.

[38]Frontex, *Annual Risk Analysis 2012* (Frontex, Warsaw, 2012), http://frontex.europa.eu/assets/Attachment_Featured/Annual_Risk_Analysis_2012.pdf.

[39]Clandestino Project, *Policy Brief: Size and Development of Irregular Migration to the EU* (Athens: Hellenic Foundation for European and Foreign Policy, 2009): 4, http://irregular-migration.net//typo3_upload/groups/31/4.Background_Information/4.2.Policy_Briefs_EN/Co mparativePolicyBrief_SizeOfIrregularMigration_Clandestino_Nov09_2.pdf.

[40]John Salt and Jennifer Hogarth, *Migrant Trafficking and Human Smuggling in Europe: A Review of the Evidence* (International Organization for Migration, Geneva, 2000), chapter 8.

[41]Eurostate, "Trafficking in Human Beings, 2013, http://ec.europa.eu/anti-trafficking/download.action?nodePath=%2FPublications%2FTrafficking+in+Human+beings+-+DGHome-Eurostat_EN.pdf&fileName=Trafficking+in+Human+beings+-+DGHome-Eurostat_EN.pdf&fileType=pdf

[42]"Rise in Illegal Migration into European Union."

Human smuggling and trafficking are not evenly distributed across Europe. According to the United Nations, five countries of western Europe—Belgium,[43] Germany, Greece, Italy, and the Netherlands— have recorded the highest number of trafficking victims. These same countries are also principal destinations for individuals who enlist the services of human smugglers.[44] The next-largest hubs of human trafficking are Austria, Denmark, France, Spain, and Switzerland.[45] Greece and Spain are not only recipient countries for unauthorized migrants but also have been exploited by transnational smuggling organizations because of their key geographic locations on the periphery of Europe.[46] These destination countries are among the most affluent and populous countries in Europe. They also have large sex markets, either due to domestic demand or tourism industries (such as in the south of Spain).[47] Moreover, many have large immigrant populations, ports, and extensive coastlines that facilitate the entry of both trafficking victims and smuggled migrants.

The trafficking landscape within the European Union is diverse (as it is in other developed countries). While most of the attention has been focused on sex trafficking of women from eastern Europe, the former Soviet Union (particularly after the fall of the Berlin Wall), and Africa, victims come from all regions of the world. UNODC reports a greater variety in the national origins of human-trafficking victims in Europe than in any other part of the world.[48]

---

[43]Stef Janssens, Patricia Le Cocq, and Koen Dewulf, *La Traite et Le Trafic des êtres humains: Lutter avec des personnes. Et des ressources Rapport Annuel 2008* (Centre pour l'égalité des chances et la lutte contre racisme, Brussels, 2009).

[44]Khalid Koser, "Why Migrant Smuggling Pays," *International Migration* 46, no. 2 (2008): pp. 3–26; Gao Yun and Véronique Poisson, "Le trafic et l'exploitation des immigrants chinois en France," (Organisation International du Travail, Geneva, 2005): pp. 70–2, www.ilo.org/sapfl/Informationresources/ILOPublications/WCMS_082332/lang—fr/index.htm.

[45]UNODC, *Trafficking in Persons: Global Patterns* (UNODC, Vienna, 2006): 92, www.unodc.org/pdf/traffickinginpersons_report_2006-04.pdf.

[46]Akis Kalaitzidis, "Human Smuggling and Trafficking in the Balkans: Is It Fortress Europe?" *Journal of the Institute of Justice and International Studies* 5 (2005): pp. 3-4.

[47]Alejandro Gómez-Céspedes and Per Stangeland, "Spain: The Flourishing Illegal Drug Haven in Europe" in Cyrille Fijnaut and Letizia Paoli, eds., *Organised Crime in Europe* (Springer, Dordrecht, 2004), pp. 402-404. http://link.springer.com/chapter/10.1007/978-1-4020-2765-9_14.

[48]UNODC, "The Globalization of Crime." op cit.

Different regions of Europe receive victims from different source countries. In its 2012 assessment, Europol identified five major hubs of organized crime. Each is connected to particular source countries, and specializes in certain types of labor placement. The five hubs are: in the northwest, the Netherlands and Belgium; in the northeast, the Baltic states and Kaliningrad; in the southeast, Bulgaria, Romania, and Greece; in the south, southern Italy; and in the southwest, Spain and Portugal.[49]

The southwest hub (Spain and Portugal) receives victims from the Iberian Peninsula and redistributes them throughout Europe according to market demand. Chinese victims often work in textile sweatshops, Eastern Europeans in agriculture, South Americans in the sex industry, while Roma children are forced to beg and commit thefts.[50] The southern criminal hub (southern Italy) is a transit and destination area for individuals who come from North and West Africa, Eastern Europe, the Balkans, and China.[51] They work in the textile industry, entertainment sector, elder and child care, and construction.[52]

The major source countries of smuggling and trafficking victims were identified by Europol in 2008 as Moldova, Ukraine, Bulgaria, Romania, the Russian Federation, and Nigeria. In many cases, trafficking to Europe is facilitated by members of victims' own migrant communities.[53] Identified source countries include some of the poorest nations in Europe. Meanwhile, Europol fails to mention several source countries that were once European colonies. These include Morocco and Algeria in North Africa, and Brazil, the Dominican Republic, and Colombia in Latin America. Citizens from these former colonies are increasingly identified as victims of trafficking, both for sex work and general labor, particularly in Mediterranean countries. Large numbers

---

[49]Europol, *Trafficking in Human Beings in the European Union*, p.12.

[50]Ibid, pp. 11-12.

[51]For more on the Southern and Eastern European region see Rebecca Surtees, "Traffickers and Trafficking in Southern and Eastern Europe: Considering the Other Side of Human Trafficking," *European Journal of Criminology* 5, no. 1 (2008): pp. 39–68.

[52]Europol, *EU Organised Crime Threat Assessment (OCTA) 2011* (The Hague: Europol, 2011): p. 12, www.europol.europa.eu/content/press/europol-organised-crime-threat-assessment-2011-429.

[53]Europol, *Annual Report 2008* (The Hague: Europol, 2008): pp. 17–9, www.europol.europa.eu/sites/default/files/publications/annual_report_2008.pdf.

of women from the Dominican Republic, a Spanish colony until the early 19th century, are trafficked to Spain.[54] Women from Brazil and Colombia are increasingly identified as victims of sex trafficking in Europe.[55] Italy, home to the second-largest Nigerian diaspora community in Europe, had 12,500 trafficked Nigerian women working as prostitutes in 2006, representing approximately half of the prostitutes in Italy.[56] In the UK in 2011, a man was arrested and successfully prosecuted for attempting to traffic two Nigerian teenage girls to Greece and Spain from Great Britain.[57] Therefore, the patterns of trafficking have grown more complex over time, a trend that will continue.

Among child victims, leading source regions are Eastern Europe, North Africa, and Asia.[58] A significant number come from the Middle East and the Indian subcontinent by way of Turkey and often the Balkans. Most of these children, defined as trafficking victims, will work in illegal labor markets, but not the sex markets that have received the most attention.[59]

---

[54]International Organization for Migration (IOM), Migration Information Program, *Trafficking in Women from the Dominican Republic for Sexual Exploitation* (Geneva: IOM, 1996), www.oas.org/atip/country%20specific/TIP%20DR%20IOM%20REPORT.pdf;   US Department of State, "Dominican Republic," in *Trafficking in Persons Report 2009* (Department of State, Washington, DC, 2009): 123–34, www.state.gov/j/tip/rls/tiprpt/2009/123136.htm.

[55]Liz Kelly, *Journeys of Jeopardy: A Review of Research on Trafficking in Women and Children in Europe* (IOM, Geneva, 2002): p. 26, www.iom.int/jahia/webdav/site/myjahiasite/shared/shared/mainsite/published_docs/serial_publications/mrs11b.pdf.

[56]John Picarelli, "Organised Crime and Human Trafficking in the United States and Western Europe," in *Strategies Against Human Trafficking: The Role of the Security Sector*, ed. Cornelius Friesendorf (National Defense Academy and Austrian Ministry of Defense and Sport, Vienna, 2009): p. 134; Jørgen Carling, "Trafficking in Women from Nigeria to Europe," July 2005, *Migration Information Source*, www.migrationinformation.org/Feature/display.cfm?ID=318; Jørgen Carling, *Migration, Human Smuggling and Trafficking from Nigeria to Europe* (Geneva: IOM, 2006), www.iom.int/jahia/webdav/site/myjahiasite/shared/shared/mainsite/published_docs/serial_publications/mrs23.pdf.

[57]"Man jailed for trafficking Nigerian girls out of UK," July 7, 2011, http://www.bbc.co.uk/news/uk-england-14065838.

[58]United Nations Children's Fund (UNICEF) Innocenti Research Center, *Child Trafficking in Europe: A Broad Vision to Put Children First* (UNICEF, Florence, 2008), www.unicef-irc.org/publications/pdf/ct_in_europe_full.pdf.

[59]Financial Action Task Force (FATF), *Money Laundering Risks Arising from Trafficking in Human Beings and Smuggling of Migrants* (FATF and OECD, Paris, 2011): p. 34, www.fatf-gafi.org/dataoecd/28/34/48412278.pdf.

European policymakers have made great efforts to restrict illegal immigration. This is an enormous challenge given the nature of EU borders — the Mediterranean coast is lightly guarded, and the long border that many Eastern European countries share with the former Soviet Union is notorious for its often-corrupt border patrol personnel.[60] Given that Eastern Europe includes porous, lawless regions through which many migrants and trafficked people from other regions transit, the lack of control along this eastern border is especially significant.[61] The Arab Spring had a significant impact on illegal immigration into Western Europe. Many migrants from sub-Saharan Africa who were working in North Africa when the unrest started escaped to Europe. Frontex, the European border control agency, noted that in the first nine months of 2011 there were 112,000 illegal migrants detained compared to 77,000 for the same time period in 2010, although not all from sub-Saharan Africa.[62] As routes across the Mediterranean were shut off through interdiction at sea, more individuals came through Turkey. Consequently, Greece noted an upturn in smuggled migrants.[63]

The business of human smuggling and human trafficking is possibly more ethnically diversified in the European Union than in North America. Of various national and ethnic criminal groups, several in particular are associated with the trafficking of human beings. Nigerian and Chinese groups are probably the most threatening to society, according to a 2011 Europol assessment.[64] Bulgarian, Romanian, and Roma criminal groups are also particularly active, as are Albanian, Russian, Turkish, and Hungarian groups. Such criminal groups—especially the Chinese, Nigerian, and Romanian ones—work with diaspora communities overseas to limit detection. Bulgarian, Hungarian,

---

[60]Human Rights Watch, "Hopes Betrayed: Trafficking of Women and Girls to Post-Conflict Bosnia and Herzegovina for Forced Prostitution," *Human Rights Watch* 14, no. 9 (2002): pp. 26–34, www.unhcr.org/refworld/docid/3e31416f0.html.

[61]Frank Laczko, Irene Stacher, and Amanda Klekowski von Koppenfels, *New Challenges for Migration Policy in Central and Eastern Europe* (Cambridge University Press, Cambridge, 2002).

[62]Agence France-Presse (AFP), "Arab Spring Prompts Surge of Illegal Immigrants to EU," AFP, November 16, 2011, www.timesofmalta.com/articles/view/20111116/local/arab-spring-prompts-surge-of-illegal-immigrants-to-eu.394158.

[63]EurActiv, "Greece Measures Arab Spring Immigration Impact," EurActiv, November 22, 2011, www.euractiv.com/justice/greece-measures-arab-spring-immigration-impact-news-509109.

[64]Europol, *Trafficking in Human Beings in the European Union*, op. cit., p. 20.

and Turkish groups are often facilitators, moving individuals from the east through the Balkans to Western Europe. Balkan traffickers operate within family groups, often functioning within diaspora communities. For example, French police discovered through wiretaps that a sister of a French-based Balkan trafficker was operating a cell in Belgium.[65] But such groups also hire individuals outside their communities to reduce suspicions. Belgian and Dutch women have been hired by Balkan clans to help run day-to-day operations and minimize risks.[66]

Women are more active in human trafficking than other areas of transnational crime.[67] That said, they still number less than half of traffickers. According to a UN analysis of identified offenders in Europe, women rarely compose more than one-third of identified suspects in human-trafficking cases. Minors have been suspected as traffickers in some Western European countries. The majority of identified traffickers work within their own countries, but in some countries the presence of foreign traffickers is much higher.[68]

Combating the transnational criminal groups that facilitate trade in humans has become a high priority for the member states of the European Union. Policymakers have allocated significant resources to Europol, the European police agency, and established Frontex, a European agency devoted to border control.[69] Despite such steps, and mass media coverage of the issue, human smuggling and trafficking continue unabated. The financial crisis in 2008 only exacerbated the situation by increasing economic hardship in source countries and

---

[65]Jana Arsovska and Stef Janssens, "Human Trafficking and Policing: Good and Bad Practices," in *Strategies against Human Trafficking: The Role of the Security Sector*, ed. Cornelius Friesendorf (National Defense Academy and Austrian Ministry of Defense and Sport, Vienna, 2009), p. 213.

[66]Ibid, p. 184.

[67]Dina Siegel and Sylvia de Blank, "Women Who Traffic Women: The Role of Women in Human Trafficking Networks — Dutch Cases," *Global Crime* 11, no. 4 (2010): pp. 436–47; Alexis Aronowitz, *Human Trafficking, Human Misery: The Global Trade in Human Beings* (Praeger, Westport, 2009): pp. 52–5.

[68]UNODC, *Global Report on Trafficking in Persons* (UNODC, Vienna, 2009): p. 56, www.unodc.org/unodc/en/human-trafficking/global-report-on-trafficking-in-persons.html.

[69]Letizia Paoli and Cyrille Fijnaut, "General Introduction," in Fijnaut and Paoli, op. cit. Frontex is a specialized and independent body based in Warsaw to provide operational cooperation on border issues; see Frontex, "Origin," www.frontex.europa.eu.

placing businesses in Europe under severe pressure to cut costs. According to Europol, this has increased demand for unauthorized migrants and trafficked victims in the economy as companies under financial pressure struggle to survive.[70]

Trafficking in the United States is different from that in Europe in several ways. Its sex trafficking victims are younger, more often native-born, and more mobile. The United States, with a higher birthrate than Europe, has more children. Without the significant social safety net which exists in Europe, many children are unsupervised and are born to single or unwed parents who are forced to work two or three jobs to sustain their families. It is, therefore, hardly surprising that a majority of American trafficking victims began their careers before they were 18.[71] This pattern of sexual exploitation of native-born minors of both sexes is a pattern not found in Europe but is more often associated with the developing world and is found in Asia, Latin America, Africa, and the Middle East.

Although the preponderance of trafficking cases in the United States concern sex trafficking, there are many other forms of trafficking that exploit the millions of illegal immigrants in the United States. Some of the labor trafficking became more pronounced after the financial crisis of 2008. Trafficking exists in every state of the United States. Victims of trafficking are exploited in diverse environments including rural, urban, and suburban communities and at truck stops across the country. American trafficking victims originate from all regions of the world including Latin America, Asia, Africa, Europe, and Eurasia. Almost all identified forms of human trafficking except for child soldiers exist in the United States.

Over a decade after the passage of the trafficking in person legislation, human trafficking still survives on a significant scale with large numbers of native born citizens and foreigners subject to labor, sexual and other forms of exploitation in the United States. There is an

---

[70]Europol, *Trafficking in Human Beings in the European Union* (Europol, The Hague, 2011), www.europol.europa.eu/sites/default/files/publications/trafficking_in_human_beings_in_the_european_union_2011.pdf.

[71]Attorney General's Annual Report to Congress and Assessment of U.S. Government Activities to Combat Trafficking in Persons Fiscal Year 2011, http://www.justice.gov/ag/annualreports/agreporthumantrafficking2011.pdf.

increasing state and federal response to the problem but the number of prosecuted cases in no way reflects the severity of the problem. Federal prosecutions in 2011 totaled 118 defendants in forced labor and adult sex trafficking cases," representing a 19% increase over the number of defendants charged in the previous year and the highest number ever charged in a single year. The same year DOJ prosecuted 125 total human trafficking cases (including sex trafficking of minors) and convicted 70."[72]

A disproportionate share of American-born victims of sexual trafficking are black and Hispanic,[73] but the problem is not confined only to minority group members as victims of sex trafficking are recruited from diverse locales across the United States. The profits from the illicit sex trade are significant.[74] In some markets in the United States, pimps can make up to $33,000 in a single week.[75]

Labor trafficking victims are engaged in everything from street peddling to housekeeping, from child care to construction, agricultural labor, and landscaping. Guest farm workers who enter from Latin America, the Caribbean, Asia and Eastern Europe on H-2 visas are routinely cheated or short changed on their wages. In extreme cases, they are forced to live in squalid conditions; and, denied medical benefits for on-the-job injuries.[76]

Indictments of human traffickers reveal that multiple forms of exploitation may occur simultaneously with women forced to prostitute themselves at night and clean houses or engage in agricultural work during the day.[77] There is also a problem that individuals who are smuggled into the United States may be forced to carry drugs or may be trafficked into labor exploitation. The prevalence of large-

---

[72]National Center for Victims of Crime, "Human Trafficking," http://www.victimsofcrime.org/library/crime-information-and-statistics/human-trafficking#ftn1.

[73]Ibid.

[74]Meredith Dank et al., "Estimating the Size and Structure of the Underground Commercial Sex Economy in Eight Major US Cities," March 12, 2014, http://www.urban.org/publications/413047.html.

[75]Ibid.

[76]Kevin Bales and Ron Soodalter, *The Slave Next Door: Human Trafficking and Slavery in America Today* (University of California Press, Berkeley and Los Angeles, 2009).

[77]"Former Wrestler Sentenced to Life on Federal Sex Trafficking and Forced Labor Charges, April 1, 2008, www.justice.gov/opa/pr/2008/April/08_crt_259.html.

scale gangs in human smuggling and trafficking, a phenomenon different from that observed in Europe, has resulted in the convergence of different forms of exploitation.[78]

Illicit Drugs and Trade

The drug trade is one of the most profitable and rapidly growing forms of trade in the world. The United Nations Office on Drugs and Crime latest estimate is that the profits from narcotics trafficking out of Afghanistan is estimated at a total of $13 billion annually for the northern route through Central Asia to the Russian Federation. The market that heads in a more southerly direction through Turkey and on to the Balkans and Western Europe is $20 billion.[79] Add to this the sales for cocaine, synthetic drugs and marijuana and there are many more billions in sales. This sum far exceeds the profits from any other area of illicit trade.

The European drug market is increasingly complex. Cocaine remains the most used drug in Europe. Heroin use has declined but there is a growth in synthetic drugs. The rise of cocaine within Europe is a relatively recent phenomenon and is a consequence of the decline of cocaine consumption in the United States and the search for alternative markets by the drug traffickers.[80] The new narcotics trade route that goes from Latin America to Africa, for sale in Europe, is the converse of the slave trade of previous centuries. Now, Latin Americans control a trade that runs through Africa and where Europeans purchase its production at a premium because of their addiction.[81] This trade route is critical to European supply. A 2007 estimate

---

[78]FBI, National Gang Threat Assessment: Emerging Trends 2011, 24-25, http://www.fbi.gov/stats-services/publications/2011-national-gang-threat-assessment/2011-national-gang-threat-assessment-emerging-trends.

[79]United Nations Office on Drugs and Organized Crime, "Drug Trafficking," http://www.unodc.org/unodc/en/drug-trafficking/index.html, accessed January 8, 2012.

[80]"Drugs in a changing European market — EMCDDA analysis 2014. European Drug Report out today — Europe's drugs problem 'increasingly complex'", May 27, 2014, http://www.emcdda.europa.eu/news/2014/3.

[81]Information on the source of the factories comes from published reports, see R. Hudson and Library of Congress Washington D.C. Federal Research Division, "Terrorist and Organized Crime Groups in the Tri-Border Area (TBA) of South America" (Defense Technical Information Center, 2003), http://www.loc.gov/rr/frd/pdf-files/TerrOrgCrime_TBA.pdf; A. R. Sverdlick, "Terrorists and Organized Crime Entrepreneurs in the 'Triple Frontier' Among

placed 60% of Europe's cocaine transiting through West Africa, a figure that declined to 30% by early 2009 because of the greater external attention to this route.[82]

New routes have been found for the cocaine trade into the United States. The trade no longer centers on Colombia, other states have assumed a key role in the cocaine trade. In what may be called "the fudge effect," the devastation of the drug trade has merely been moved northward to Central America and Mexico, undermining the quality of life and governance in what were once transit regions for the Colombian drug trade

The drug trade may have stabilized in Europe and the United States but it still remains a key part of the illicit economy and affects diverse sectors of the economy. There is every indication that both North America and Europe will remain important markets for drugs although the trade may not link these two regions. Both regions have different routes for the entry of drugs.

The present efforts to legalize marijuana in parts of the United States[83] will result in a patchwork of policies within the country because many states will not authorize any forms of illegal drugs. Consequently, this trend to partial legalization will have diverse consequences in the coming decades. Effective responses to crime are based on the harmonization of legislation and the diversification of responses may have unexpected criminogenic consequences.

Argentina, Brazil, and Paraguay," *Trends in Organized Crime* 9, no. 2 (2005), 84–93. Other sources are interviews with individuals in the cigarette industry following illicit trade, and the investigative project of Public Integrity. One of the few times I have been threatened was after I reported on our TraCCC Georgia center's research on illicit cigarette factories in the country tied to Iraqi investment. This was later confirmed through interviews with anti-illicit trade specialists in the cigarette industry. See also, Sharon Anne Melzer, "Counterfeit and Contraband Cigarette Smuggling: Opportunities, Actors, and Guardianship" (American University, dissertation, 2010).

[82]Ashley Neese Bybee, "The Twenty-First Century Expansion of the Transnational Drug Trade in Africa," *Journal of International Affairs* 66, 1 (Fall/Winter 2012), p. 75.

[83]http://www.governing.com/gov-data/state-marijuana-laws-map-medical-recreational.html.

Illicit Flows in Europe and United States in 2030

The most important global trends are all going to impact illicit trade. The rise of non-state actors, conflict regions, increased ethnic and sectarian violence, displacement of populations, economic disparity, climate change are all going to impact the nature of illicit trade in the developed countries of North America and Europe through the displacement of people, the need for individuals to survive and the absence of legitimate opportunities.

The decline of state power, the retreat of the state, and the embedding of non-state actors in the power and governance structures of many regions[84] suggest a different organization of power in the future in the future that will make many countries outside the affluent states of Europe and North America unable to control the illicit trade at its origin.

The developed economies must deal with threatening non-state actors, who are not their symmetric opponents. Much more diverse elements of government are needed to counter these actors than just traditional military forces. But many states' integrity and capacity where these problems are most pronounced have been compromised by corruption; they are not capable of opposing illicit actors. Corruption is particularly acute in many states in the developing world, particularly in Africa and the Middle East, that have had their boundaries defined by colonial powers and lack any inherent integrity or citizen loyalty to state institutions that transcend the clan or the tribe. Therefore, the instability in these regions will have many consequences for Europe and the United States in the coming decades in the form of more illegal migration and illicit trade and financial flows.

An entangled threat of crime, corruption, and terrorism will require more attention from the leadership of North America and Western Europe because of its endemic nature in many diverse regions of the world, especially in conflict regions; the financial success and extensive influence of non-state actors on governments, often by means of corruption; the increasing economic role of criminals and terrorists both

---

[84]Camino Kavanagh, "Getting Smart and Scaling Up: Responding to the Impact of Organized Crime on Governance in Developing Countries," June 7, 2013, http://cic.nyu.edu/content/responding-impact-organized-crime-governance-developing-countries.

as employers and participants in the local and global economy; the deleterious impact of crime and terrorism on communities and the political order; and the incapacity of state and multinational organizations to successfully challenge transnational criminals and terrorists at the national, regional, and global levels.

Yet no comparable effort exists in the United States or Europe to understand the rise of non-state actors who pose a different, but very diverse, challenge to the contemporary order, far different from that of the superpower conflict. Functioning below the state level, they require as great, if not greater, understanding of history, geography, culture, demography, and society than in the past. Yet to counter these potent non-state actors also requires a knowledge of networks, economics, business, and technology. This approach is far different from merely studying terrorists and insurgents or transnational criminals and has not been sufficiently applied.

Rather than a grand strategy, the international community needs a holistic approach. American officials assert that to address crime and terrorism, we need a whole-of-government approach integrating military, law enforcement, and financial countermeasures with development assistance.[85] But this is too narrow a response for the entangled problem of crime, corruption and terrorism, which requires much more than a state response.

A whole-of-society approach is needed by both North America and Europe that must work together more closely to address these problems by identifying the trajectory of these current problems. Yet these problems cannot be left to governments alone. They require the participation of multilateral organizations, international and local business, consumers, religious and secular civil society, journalists and international online communications (which have replaced much print journalism), researchers, and educational institutions. Without the participation and cooperation of different communities outside of government forming strategic partnerships, it will prove impossible to counter the corrosive impact of crime, corruption and terrorism[86.]

---

[85]Jim Garamone, "New National Strategy Takes 'Whole-of-Government' Approach," May 27, 2010, http://www.defense.gov/news/newsarticle.aspx?id=59377.

[86]Louise Shelley, *Dirty Entanglements: Corruption, Crime and Terrorism* (Cambridge University Press, New York and Cambridge, 2014).

Chapter 11

The United States, the West, and 21st Century Global Flows of Ideas

Bruce W. Jentleson

Oh, how euphoric it all seemed at the end of the Cold War. "The triumph of the West, of the Western *idea* is evident," in Francis Fukuyama's iconic proclamation, "an unabashed victory of economic and political liberalism . . . [and] the total exhaustion of viable systematic alternatives." Similar triumphalism was trumpeted by globalization-*istas* such as Thomas Friedman with among other things his "golden arches theory of conflict prevention" by which no two countries with McDonald's franchises within their borders go to war against each other. While acknowledging the need for some adaptation, John Ikenberry confidently predicted "liberal internationalism 3.0" following on the 2.0 of the post-World War II order and 1.0 of Wilsonianism. Even the "rise of the rest" in Fareed Zakaria's post-American world was largely Americanized in nature and with the United States still as the central player.[1]

Similar themes have come through in policy. The "enlargement" conception with which the Clinton administration began saw democracy spreading globally. George W. Bush's post 9/11 "evildoers" and freedom agenda, while deploying American power quite differently, followed from a similar set of ideas. So too Barack Obama's first-term emphasis on restoring America's reputation by making the United States truer to its core values. In Europe as well, whether with Tony Blair or David Cameron, Nicolas Sarkozy or Francoise Hollande, or Angela Merkel, the core worldview has been a Western-centric one.

---

[1]Francis Fukuyama, "The End of History," *The National Interest*, 16 (Summer 1989), 16; Thomas Friedman, "Foreign Affairs Big Mac I," *New York Times*, December 8, 1996, http://www.nytimes.com/1996/12/08/opinion/foreign-affairs-big-mac-i.html; G. John Ikenberry, *Liberal Leviathan: The Origins, Crisis and Transformation of the American World Order* (Princeton University Press, Princeton, 2011); Fareed Zakaria, *The Post-American World* (New York: W.W. Norton, 2008).

The prevailing assumption in these and other articulations is that there principally continues to be an outward flow of ideas about how best to organize national societies and the international system from the West to rest of the world. That assumption has not held up. Instead what has been emerging is a "global marketplace of ideas" marked by three main dynamics: (1) greater doubts about Western models at both the international system and national domestic levels; (2) increasing affirmation across the non-Western world for ideas rooted in their own history, culture and identity, as well as their own national and regional politics; and (3) technology as a driver of a profoundly different discourse and competition of ideas enabled by a digital infrastructure that increasingly connects everyone to everyone.[2]

This is not a lament about "declinism." Rather it is a corrective against "denialism," acknowledging profound changes shaping the 21st century world as an essential mindset for strategizing for the world as it is, not as it used to be. Peace, security, prosperity and justice are best served by ideas that give shape to institutions and policies that can effectively address the challenges posed both internationally and domestically. To the extent that ideas from non-Western nations and cultures can do that more effectively than Western ones, in themselves or as adapted, there is "winning for losing" in the global competition of ideas.

The 21st Century International System in Transition

Forget the pole-counting: uni-, bi-, multi-. And the G-counting: G-2, G-8, G-20, G-0. The most useful conceptualization of the 21st century international system, with a nod to Carl Sagan, is the transformation from a "Ptolemaic" to a "Copernican" world. The Cold War system of the second half of the 20th century was a lot like the ancient philosopher-astronomer Ptolemy's theory of the universe. For Ptolemy the Earth was at the center with the other planets, indeed all the other celestial bodies, revolving around us. And so too was the United States at the center of the Cold War world. It was the wielder

---

[2]This article draws on Steven Weber and Bruce W. Jentleson, *The End of Arrogance: America in the Global Competition of Ideas* (Harvard University Press, 2010), and Bruce W. Jentleson, "Global Governance in a Copernican World," *Global Governance* 18 (2012), pp. 133-148.

of power. The economic engine. The bastion of free world ideology. When the Cold War ended with the demise and defeat of the Soviet Union, American centrality seemed even more defining. It was the sole surviving superpower. The American economy was driving globalization. Democracy was spreading all over. The world seemed even more Ptolemaic.

Not anymore. The 21st century world is more like Copernicus' theory of the universe in which the Earth is not at the center but like the other planets each has its own orbit around the Sun. So too here in the 21st century the United States is not at the center. It has its own orbit. Other countries do too with their own sources of influence, their own national interests, their own identities, their own domestic politics. This Copernican world is evident geopolitically with other powers rising (China), recovering (Russia), seeking to reinvigorate (European Union), emerging (India, Brazil, Turkey, South Africa, others), and engendering their own political revolutions and counterrevolutions (Tunisia, Egypt, Syria, et al). It is evident economically with globalization having what the U.S. National Intelligence Council assessed as a "less of a 'Made in the USA' character." It is evident culturally as with the comment by a New York art dealer after an auction dominated by newly moneyed non-Western collectors that "for the first time in nearly two hundred years the Western world doesn't make the decisions about our future." And it is evident ideologically amidst what my colleague Steve Weber and I have called the "global marketplace of ideas."[3]

Two main forces have been driving this transformation. One is the shifting international distribution of power through diffusion (spread to many more actors) and dilution (traditional sources becoming less potent). Power diffusion is especially evident in the eastward and southward shift in economic dynamism. Chinese economic growth has fallen out of double digits, but 7-8% is still substantial. More broadly, as General Electric CEO Jeffrey Immelt put it, "the billion people joining the middle class in Asia"—not U.S. consumers— "are the engines driving global growth."[4] Nor is it just Asia. The $150 bil-

---

[3] Weber and Jentleson, *End of Arrogance*, op cit., pp, 10-11.
[4] Chrystia Freeland, "GE's Immelt Speaks Out on China, exports, and competition," *Reuters*, January 21, 2011, http://blogs.reuters.com/chrystia-freeland/tag/jeff-immelt

lion in aircraft orders recently placed by the Gulf Arab monarchies set industry records. Between 2000 and 2010 six of the ten fastest growing economies in the world were in Africa. Whereas in 1950 the United States, Canada, and Western Europe accounted for 68% of global GDP, by 2050 this will likely be less than 30%.

Nor does the U.S. have the diplomatic stage as much to itself anymore. While it still takes on lead diplomatic roles more often than anyone else, there's been a "pluralization of diplomacy." There are more states with more relations with one another on a wider range of issues than ever before. As a study by the London-based International Institute of Strategic Studies put it, "countries small, medium and large are all banking more on their own strategic initiative than on formal alliances or institutional relationships to defend their interests and advance their goals."[5] Relatedly, very few states today are defining their foreign policies principally in pro- or anti-American terms. This was the point of the statement by the Indian national security advisor on the eve of President Obama's 2010 visit that while India seeks better relations with the United States its foreign policy remains one of "genuine non-alignment."[6] The point was even more pointed in the criticism expressed by Brazilian Foreign Minister Antonio Patriota at a joint press conference with Secretary of State John Kerry that revelations of Brazil being one of the most spied-on countries by the National Security Agency "cast a shadow of distrust" over bilateral relations.[7]

While military power has been less diffused—the United States still has ample superiority over any other state or potential coalition—it is being diluted in two respects. First is that the military balance is much less central to overall systemic structure than during the Cold War-strategic nuclear deterrence era. In a world in which there is much less of a shared and overreaching threat, the currency of military power is less convertible to other forms of power and influence than when such

---

[5]International Institute for Strategic Studies, *Strategic Survey 2010: The Annual Review of World Affairs* (London: Routledge, 2010), p. 417.

[6]*The Hindu*, November 2, 2010.

[7]Simon Romero, "In Brazil, Kerry is Told Spying Sows Distrust," *New York Times*, August 14, 2013, A10; Henry Farrell and Martha Finnemore, "The End of Hypocrisy," *Foreign Affairs*, *November/December 2013*; Mark Leonard, "The NSA and the Weakness of American Power," (European Council on Foreign Relations, November 1, 2013), http://ecfr.eu/content/entry/commentary_the_nsa_and_the_weakness_of_american_power

threats were more defining. Second is the "capabilities-utility" gap between military superiority as traditionally measured and the utility of that superiority for achieving strategic objectives, as all too graphically demonstrated in the Iraq and Afghanistan wars.

The other key shaper of this Copernican world is a 21st century version of nationalism which, while not as conquest-oriented as in other eras, is quite assertive of national interests and identities. For centuries-old civilizations like China and India it is the return of history, great pride in the re-emergence of their cultures and nations to the prominence they once had.[8] So too with Turkey. As one official responded when asked the typical question of whether his country was turning East instead of West, Turkey is "pursuing its own national interest. The debate about whether Turkey has become anti-Western and pro-Islamism misses the ways in which, as a Turkish foreign ministry official expressed the nationalist logic, "We have waited for the big powers to make up their minds on big issues and we just follow them. For the past several years we have made up our own minds."[9] With Brazil, while some anti-Americanism is sprinkled in, the drive is much more about its own national narrative of greatness as yet unfulfilled going back to its founding. Many other countries also are out there with a sense of being on the world stage for the first time after eras of colonialism and superpower dominance.

One of the paradoxes of our globalized world is the mix of integration and fragmentation, countries being pulled together into various webs of interconnectedness while also being pushed apart by various manifestations of identity. For all the proclamations of the universalization of Western liberalism, we see many tensions between universality and uniqueness of those norms, practices and priorities that are widely held and those which are more particularistic and differentiated. These and other dynamics have belied Western liberal internationalism's positing of international cooperation as principally a collective action problem for maximizing shared global public goods. The aspirational is confused with the actual in three respects: state interests are more divergent than asserted; even when interests are

---

[8]Patrick Smith, *Somebody Else's Century: East and West in a Post-Western World* (Random House, New York, 2010).

[9]*New Republic*, April 29, 2010.

shared, prioritizations vary among states; and even when interests shared and priorities in synch, there often are significant substantive differences over strategy.

Indeed what's unclear in our Copernican world metaphor is what the "Sun" is, keeping planets/states from crashing into each other. For all that it achieved for so many decades, the post-World War II international system is showing increasing strains in effectiveness and decreasing global consensus on its legitimacy. This doesn't mean full system failure or fully revisionist powers. But it also is not just a matter of integrating emerging and other powers while institutional structures and core missions change only minimally. The thrust, as Charles Kupchan puts it, is to "revise, not consolidate, the international system erected under the West's watch." Many outside the West do not see the system as value neutral as the West claims, but rather reflecting Western ideological dispositions (e.g., laissez faire economics, liberal democracy politics) and biased towards Western interests. It follows the same logic that as their power increases non-Western powers will "recast the international order in ways that advantage their interests and ideological preferences."[10]

Consider UN Security Council (UNSC) expansion. If the UNSC is to play the role that it needs to play—not the whole Sun, but a key component of it—it must be reformed to better reflect 21st century distributions of power. To be sure, it is not just the West that is resisting change. China opposes a seat for Japan; Pakistan against India; Argentina and Mexico compete with Brazil; various African countries make their cases for why they should get any seats allocated to their continent. Nor is the need for expansion the only factor affecting UNSC effectiveness. But it is a crucial one without which the most global of all international institutions will not be up to the role it needs to play. The global marketplace of ideas is open.

There also are real questions about the viability of the Bretton Woods international economic system. The Doha Round is well into its second decade, the issues more complex and difficult than as cast in the standard free trade-protectionism dichotomy. The international

---

[10]Charles A. Kupchan, *No One's World: the West, the Rising Rest and the Coming Global Turn* (Oxford University Press, New York, 2012), p. 7.

financial system has had two huge global crises within a few years, one emanating from one of the ostensible paragons (the United States) and the other from the other (Europe). The United States is the only country not to approve International Monetary Fund reforms that would give China and emerging powers greater voice in IMF policy. While Europe has supported these reforms, it still guards its hold on the IMF Managing Directorship. The United States continues to do the same on the World Bank President. While the G-20's role in the 2008-09 global financial crisis exemplified the kind of cooperation the liberal order can produce, this was a "fellowship of the lifeboat" which ensuing G-20 summits have made look more like the exception than the rule. Both scaling up and generalizability of the G-20 are questionable. Moreover, while the dollar isn't going to be replaced, it's not going to retain its quasi-monopoly position. The BRICs (Brazil, Russia, India, China, and now BRICS with South Africa added) are pushing increasingly hard on these issues. As stated at its 2011 summit, "Recognizing that the international financial crisis has exposed the inadequacies and deficiencies of the existing international monetary and financial system, we support the reform and improvement of the international monetary system, with a broad-based international reserve currency system providing stability and certainty."[11] Whether this transition is stabilizing or destabilizing is its own question: the point here is trend lines towards systemic change.

Even more wide open are questions about norms of global responsibility. Who defines it? On what terms? Through which processes? With what accountability? A major version of this debate is over the scope and limits of state sovereignty and the corresponding rights and responsibilities that come with sovereignty. Whereas during the Cold War much of global instability was "outside in"—i.e., the internalization into states with their own tensions and conflicts of the East-West bipolar global rivalry—the 21st century dynamic is more an "inside out" one of the increased susceptibility of the international community to threats and other disruptions that emanate outward from inside states. Thus while it may be true that "what happens in Vegas stays in

---

[11] Sanya Declaration, Hainan, China, April 14, 2011, http://news.xinhuanet.com/english2010/china/2011-04/14/c_13829453.htm. See also "Enhancing International Monetary Stability—A Role for the SDR?. (2011, January 7). *IMF—International Monetary Fund Home Page*. Retrieved September 10, 2011, from http://www.imf.org/external/pp/longres.aspx?id= 4523

Vegas," as the tag line of a catchy American commercial had it, what happens inside states doesn't stay inside states. Not popular uprisings against repressive governments that transmit to other countries and scramble regional geopolitics, nor failed states that become safe havens for terrorist groups with global operations, nor mass atrocities that cause refugee flows across borders that then feed into neighbors' ethnic and other conflicts, nor inadequate public health capacity to prevent disease outbreaks from becoming pandemics. This "Vegas dilemma" of the domestic locus yet transnational effects of so many contemporary era threats makes the state sovereignty rights-responsibilities balance a critical issue over a broad array of policy areas.

This comes through especially strongly in the "Responsibility to Protect" (R2P). First developed in 2000-01 in the wake of Bosnia, Rwanda and Kosovo by the unofficial International Commission on Intervention and State Sovereignty (ICISS), and accepted in principle by the UN at the 2005 World Summit, R2P affirms that governments and any other group within states have a responsibility not to commit atrocities against their own people. When they fundamentally violate that responsibility, the international community has its responsibility to protect endangered peoples, including through military intervention. "What is at stake here," as the ICISS report stressed, "is not making the world safe for big powers, or trampling over the sovereign rights of small ones, but delivering practical protection for ordinary people at risk of their lives, because their states are unwilling to protect them."[12] Easier said than consensus built, though, as brutal leaders have continued to exploit the anti-imperialist card for their own nefarious purposes, and China and Russia have had their own interests for pushing state sovereignty strict constructionism.

Questions of historical justice and who benefited how much from past international systems also are part of the debate. Global environmental issues and the norm of "common but differentiated responsibility" (CDR), affirming that all states share responsibility for addressing present problems but with respective shares varying based on historical legacies of relative contribution to the problem and relative capacity to contribute to amelioration, is a major example. On the one

---

[12]International Commission on Intervention and State Sovereignty (ICISS), *The Responsibility to Protect* (International Development Research Centre, Ottawa, 2001), p. 11.

hand the 1987 Montreal Protocol on Ozone Depletion had some success in working out a CDR formula. It required differential cost-bearing and remedial action based on who bore the greatest responsibility for causing the ozone depletion problem and reaped the greatest benefits from atmospheric damage being a production externality, while requiring all states to bear some costs and be in compliance with non-depletion regulations going forward in the name of the common responsibility of averting a future crisis. On global warming and climate change, though, while CDR was inscribed in the UN Framework Convention on Climate Change and the Kyoto Protocol, it has not worked as well. How differentiated the responsibility should be, as set in actual costs and tasks, has been both more substantively complicated and more politically contentious.

On these and other questions about the optimal norms, institutions, and policies for the 21st century international system, the global marketplace of ideas is open for competition.

Beyond Western Democracy and Capitalism: Diverse Domestic Political and Economic Models

At the domestic level, the marketplace of ideas is even more robust and diverse. Two main dynamics are at work: increasingly critical assessments of Western models, and greater affirmation by non-Western states and peoples of their own "cultural and socioeconomic foundations."[13] As Patrick Smith, a journalist with many years' experience in Asia, puts it, "to be modern no longer means to Westernize at the cost of one's past."[14] While some ideas and practices have been adopted from the West, modernization has not meant homogenization. Culture and identity are powerful and enduring forces.

Given the combination of the U.S.-precipitated 2007 global financial crisis, persistently poor policy performance of the U.S. gridlocked political system, the eurozone crisis and intensifying stresses in European social compacts, the critical view of Western political and economic systems is not hard to understand. While the strengths of lib-

---

[13]Kupchan, *No One's World*, op. cit., p. 6.
[14]Smith, *Somebody Else's Century*, op. cit., p. 99.

eral democracies in protecting civil liberties and individual rights remains unrivaled, their policy capacity to deliver on the crucial problems their societies face is increasingly being questioned. The United States ranks 27th of 31 in the OECD social justice index; 17th of 24 on adult literacy; with 15 year olds' math scores closer to those of Kazakhstan than Germany or South Korea; gets a D+ from the American Society of Civil Engineers on its infrastructure; closes museums while others build them.[15] Even its vaunted Horatio Alger social mobility lags, not leads, most other industrial democracies.[16] The special interest-ism of the U.S. model, which runs deeper than partisanship to such systemic structural issues as divided power and interest group capture, has brought worrisome policy paralysis.[17] Much of Europe has been mired in economic crisis. Right-wing hate groups have been gaining political traction. The great European Union experiment has been under attack. Even trying not to over-react to current problems, there is serious questioning whether the stresses we are seeing in the social compacts underpinning so many advanced industrial societies are just marginally worse than at other points in history, or are now capable of undermining fundamental bases of states' political authority and associated policy capacity.[18] I'm not arguing that the answer is yes, but am arguing that the question is real.

The "end of history" and other prognostications of a democratic century are increasingly questionable. In China, as Bruce Dickson argues, contrary to the "conventional wisdom ... that there *should* be support for democracy in China, given the litany of problems we see

---

[15]Bertelsmann Stiftung, *Social Justice in the OECD—How Do the Member States Compare?* http://www.sgi-network.org/pdf/SGI11_Social_Justice_OECD.pdf (2011); *OECD Skills Outlook 2013*, http://skills.oecd.org/OECD_Skills_Outlook_2013.pdf; American Society of Civil Engineers, *Report Card for America's Infrastructure*, http://www.infrastructurereport-card.org/

[16]Jacob Hacker and Paul Pierson, *Winner-Take-All Politics* (Simon and Schuster, 2010).

[17]This goes back to James Madison's *Federalist #10*: "warning about the danger of "factions": a "minority of the whole, who are united and actuated by some common impulse of passion, or of interest, adverse to the rights of other citizens, or to the permanent and aggregate interests of the community." What would Madison think of K Street? If he read *Politico*? See also Theodore J, Lowi, *The End of Liberalism: The Second Republic of the United States* (New York: W.W. Norton, 1979) and Mancur Olson, *The Rise and Decline of Nations: Economic Growth, Stagflation and Social Rigidities* (New Haven: Yale University Press, 1982).

[18]Louis W. Pauly and Bruce W. Jentleson, eds., *Power in a Complex Global System* (London: Routledge, 2014).

in the popular media . . . more often, however, these protests are aimed at making the state govern better, not govern differently."[19] State-building in post-conflict societies is proving to be best as "hybrid" models that "rely on local customs, politics and practices" that may take time to move towards democracy, or not.[20] There isn't much "spring" left to the Arab Awakening amidst revanchist counter-revolution in Egypt, brutal repression in Syria, and Gulf monarchies buying off what protest they can and seeking to quash the rest. Mixed models may develop that establish claims to legitimacy that the likes of Mubarak and Ben Ali lacked but may not fit classical democratic models.

Rather than democracy/non-democracy, the debate is over what constitutes a capable state. A capable state meets two criteria: It has internal legitimacy in the eyes of its own people. It has the policy capacity to deliver on the crucial challenges its national society faces. This conception is both less than and more than democracy. It is less than democracy in allowing for the possibility that a people may deem its political system and government legitimate even if it is not based on elections. This does NOT include peoples cowed into submission. But it does acknowledge that for countries with mass poverty, endemic injustice, and other pressing human needs—that is to say, much of the world today—people are looking not just to be protected *from* government, but also to be protected *by* government. That never has and never will justify repressiveness, but it does recognize that in many societies political legitimacy is a function of performance not just process. It cannot be just about freedom from; it also has to be about the capacity to. In this sense capable states entail more than democratic practices like elections in stressing policy capacity in going beyond the "input" side—elections, legislative processes, lawmaking—to policy "outputs".

Economically, the fundamental state-market balance, which according to the prevalent modernization-development model limited the former and maximized the latter, is being challenged. Not by neo-protectionism, or neo-mercantilism, or authoritarian capitalism: these are

---

[19]Bruce J. Dickson, "Updating the China Model," *Washington Quarterly* 34 (Fall 2011), p. 53.

[20]Jon Western and Joshua S. Goldstein, "Humanitarian Intervention Comes of Age," *Foreign Affairs* 90 (November/December 2011), p. 59.

too dichotomous to capture current debate and practices. It is more about "purposive state intervention to guide market development and national corporate growth," both internationally (e.g., in currency markets) and as more sophisticated versions of the "developmental state."[21] China's unprecedented economic growth has not been about conversion to Western-style capitalism so much as its particular blending of the state and the market. Others such as Brazil and India offer their own variants, each with greater market forces than earlier decades but also with the state playing a significant ownership, planning and strategic investing role. Given whose economies are growing faster and whose financial sector plunged the world into crises, it's not hard to understand the appeal of such alternative models.

While the West still dominates rankings of economic competitiveness and scientific and technological innovation, the snapshots are more encouraging than the trend lines. Europe and the United States still dominate the World Economic Forum Global Competitiveness rankings, with economically Western-ish Japan, Singapore and Hong Kong filling out the top 10.[22] But the U.S. National Academy of Sciences study of innovation-based change from 2000-2010 ranked US 40th globally. The high tech sector, which ran a $15 billion favorable balance as recently as 1999, has been consistently in deficit in recent years. The conception of China as just a low technology, mass labor economy is belied by any number of major companies, including Siemens, Google and Microsoft, opening well-resourced research and development operations there. Even in genomic sciences, which began with the British scientists Francis Crick and James Watson and in which the American Craig Venter was the first to sequence the human genome, the Beijing Genome Institute is becoming a leader in the field, already doing cloning "on an industrial scale."[23] The West continues to have many innovation-conducive qualities in our culture and incentives, and to an extent in our policies, but there should be no complacency.

---

[21]Gregory Chin and Ramesh Thakur, "Will China Change the Rules of Global Order?" *Washington Quarterly*, October 2010, pp. 122-25.

[22]World Economic Forum, *Global Competitiveness Report 2012-13*

[23]Michael Specter, "The Gene Factory," *The New Yorker*, January 6, 2014, 34-43; David Shukman, "China Cloning on an Industrial Scale," BBC, January 13, 2014, http://www.bbc.co.uk/news/science-environment-25576718

Marketplace, not War, of Ideas

The "war" of ideas formulation had much currency in the wake of 9/11. It went along with the "why do they hate us" reaction that underlying the security threat was an ideological threat that ran deeper and was more sweeping than even Samuel Huntington's original clash of civilizations. But this approach was much too focused on the "September 11" agenda and not enough on the "September 10" one. The sense that "the whole world changed on September 11," while understandable in the trauma of the moment, belied all that was on the international agenda when we all went to bed on the night of September 10: the changing geopolitics of the end of the Cold War; the dispelling of euphoric notions of globalization; the politics of identity fueling ethnic cleansings and genocides. To a greater extent than any time since the immediate post-World War II period, big questions had been opened and new ideas needed on a number of fronts, not just in regard to terrorism-Islamist fundamentalism.

Moreover, the "war" metaphor itself was deeply flawed. Ideas don't fight wars against each other. There's no such thing as overwhelming force or unconditional surrender in the realm of ideas. The dynamic is more like a market than a battlefield, with quite intense competition of its own kind but for which the goal is to persuade more than pummel. The rules of engagement are much closer to those set out by social and economic thinkers, ranging from John Stuart Mill to Milton Friedman than those of a Clausewitz. The measure of success is market share, not body count.

With information technology making for exceedingly low barriers to entry, innumerable non-governmental players globally are in the game. All it takes is a website, a blog, a Twitter handle, a Facebook page, a YouTube channel. We can call these Western or non-Western, but their ideas may or may not align with their respective governments. They function as creators of ideas, disseminators, advocates, opponents, distorters, many other roles, and often with a technological nimbleness that makes them impactful well beyond their limited resources in using the internet as a "force multiplier." In some respects these are "liberation technologies" empowering citizens to confront, contain and hold accountable authoritarian regimes—and even to liberate societies from autocracy."[24] Efforts by repressive governments to block these transmissions have had much less success than when evaders had to rely on carbon paper and Xerox machines. The global digital infrastructure provides largely unmediated reach. But they also can be used destructively, as with 9/11 and other examples.

Demographic changes also are a factor. By 2030 at 1.2 billion, a 200% increase since 2005, the developing world's middle class alone will be greater than the total populations of Europe, the United States and Canada. Within that is the huge rural to urban migration flow by which urban sub-Saharan Africa will double, China will be 75% urban, India possibly as much as 55%. And within that the enormous youth bulge: about half the population of Pakistan is below the age of twenty-five; Lagos is a city dominated by children and teenagers; the median age in the Arab world is 26. The global competition of ideas will play out more within the political economy and sociology of chaotic, vibrant, pulsing cities of developing Asia, Latin America, and Africa than in the familiar cities of Western Europe or the mythic frontier communities of the American West.

Winning for Losing?

It is not that Western ideas and values can't compete in this 21st century marketplace. But this is not about winning in the sense of its traditional ideas prevailing and propagating. Adaptations of the international system to better fit the power diffusion and new nationalism of this Copernican world, and the need to forge a Sun-equivalent for this global age, must be pursued pro-actively not ceded begrudgingly. So too at the nation-state level there needs to be greater openness to a range of political-economic models beyond traditional Western ones so long as they do have genuine legitimacy in the eyes of their own people.

None of this is to be any less proud or positive on what the West has to offer. But it is to be more open to the benefits of reverse flows and ways in which non-Western ideas and practices may have strengths that ours do not for prosperity, justice, security and peace, and ourselves doing the learning and adapting.

---

[24]Larry Diamond and Marc F. Plattner, eds., *Liberation Technology: Social Media and the Struggle for Democracy* (Johns Hopkins University Press, Baltimore, 2012), p. xi.

Chapter 12

Transnational Revolutionary Ideologies and Movements

Mark N. Katz

In his chapter for this volume, Tomas Ries identified transnational revolutionary networks as one of two "black" actors (the other being global organized crime) with an agenda "actively threatening the interests of the lead states and alpha actors." In this chapter, I will discuss how transnational revolution can be understood as a flow, how the transnational revolution flow interacts with other flows, what sort of transnational revolutionary ideologies and movements are likely to be active between now and 2030, what challenges they will they pose for Europe and America, and how the European Union and the United States might respond to them. First, though, something first needs to be said about what transnational revolutionary ideologies and movements are as well as about their life spans.

Historical Background

Transnational revolutionary movements are political movements that arise in several countries either at the same time or in relatively close proximity to one another. They often gain strength through being motivated by a transnational revolutionary ideology: a set of ideas which gains transnational appeal through identifying a common set of problems, adversaries, and allies, and proposing a common solution to them which includes bringing about the downfall of incumbent regimes and their replacement by what the leaders of these movements promise will be better ones. When a movement advocating such an ideology gains power in one country, it often magnifies the appeal of the transnational revolutionary ideology and movement in others.

Transnational revolutionary movements that were powerful during the Cold War era included ones that espoused anti-European colonialism, Marxism-Leninism, Arab Nationalism, Islamic fundamentalism, and (toward the end of this period) democratization. (Some of these overlapped each other. For example, some anti-colonial revolutions were Marxist-Leninist, some were Arab Nationalist, and some were neither.) Since the end of the Cold War, transnational revolutionary movements that have been active include the continuation of the democratic revolutionary movement that arose at the end of the Cold War, the Bolivarian movement (essentially a Marxist revival in Latin America), the "color" revolutions (which sought to democratize former communist states where authoritarianism continued after the Cold War), and—most recently—the "Arab Spring" which has sought to wed democratization with an Islamic political orientation.

From just the above listing alone, it should be evident that some transnational revolutionary ideologies and movements have been more successful than others. For example, the anti-European colonial revolutionary wave not only achieved the goal of bringing about the independence of European colonies in Asia and Africa, but has also maintained this goal as well (i.e., the countries that gained independence have not been re-colonized). Others still—such as the Marxist-Leninist and the Arab Nationalist revolutionary waves—spread to several countries in a relatively short period of time, but most of the revolutionary regimes they brought to power sooner or later accommodated themselves to the world market economy and to the West, or were overthrown sometimes by another transnational revolutionary movement. Democratic revolutions succeeded in establishing democracy in some countries—but not in others. Other, especially more recent, revolutionary waves are still a work in progress whose final outcome is unclear.

In some cases, a transnational revolutionary ideology became popular with many people years or even decades before its adherents were able to seize power anywhere. This was true both of Marxism and of Arab nationalism. But with the extraordinary improvements in communications technology—especially in recent years with the penetration of mobile telephones and the internet (which together allow anyone with access to both to make videos and disseminate them instantly), transnational revolutionary ideologies and movements have been able not just to arise in an instant, but to lead to successful revolutions in a very short period of time as well.

Transnational revolutionary ideologies and movements are usually strongest from immediately before to immediately after they seize power somewhere. It is then that a state of euphoria emerges over the much anticipated and subsequently achieved downfall of the hated old regime and great optimism bursts forth about how better life now will surely be under the new regime. Such high expectations, however, usually cannot be met fully—or sometimes even partially—thus resulting in disillusionment with the new regime and perhaps even the revolutionary ideology it espouses. Of course, revolutionary regimes (like non-revolutionary ones) can remain in power for an extended period of time even without popular support. How they fare over the long-term, however, depends very much both on the success or failure of their domestic policies, the degree of support or opposition they receive from external powers (especially the great powers), and the degree of loyalty and cohesion they are able to maintain within the leadership ranks of the regime.

Transnational revolution possesses what Tomas Ries identified as the three essential characteristics of a flow: cyclicality (or circularity), transformation, and integration with other flows. In discussing the future of transnational revolution here, its integration with other flows will be discussed first, then cycles of transnational revolution, and after that the transformation of transnational revolution.

The Integration of Transnational Revolution with Other Flows

In her seminal book *States and Social Revolutions*, Theda Skocpol argued that social revolution occurs not so much as a result of the actions of revolutionaries but as a result of state breakdown, which creates opportunity for revolutionaries to seize power which they otherwise would not have. And state breakdown is the result of forces that that are far more powerful than revolutionary movements which neither states nor their revolutionary opponents create or control, but which strongly affect the balance of power between them.[1] Her

---

[1] Theda Skocpol, *States and Social Revolutions: A Comparative Analysis of France, Russia, and China* (Cambridge: Cambridge University Press, 1979).

insight is critically important for understanding how the transnational revolution flow is integrated with other flows.

Elsewhere in this volume, six global trends likely to impact global flows to 2030 are identified. These trends are 1) "G-Zero World" (changing distribution of global power); 2) "Liquid World" (diffusion of state power to transnational actors); 3) "More Human Power" (global technological diffusion); 4) "Shrinking World" (growing population and resource scarcity); 5) "Global Awakening" (empowerment of individuals and social vulnerabilities); and 6) "Extreme World" (climate change and environmental degradation). Each of these will be (all too) briefly discussed here in terms of their likelihood on the prospects for revolution between now and 2030.

Changing distribution of global power has been identified by several leading scholars as giving rise to revolution. Theda Skocpol saw defeat in war as contributing to state breakdown in the losing country,[2] while Fred Halliday theorized that war among the major powers (such as World War I and World War II) led to a weakening of their control over the international system and hence to revolution.[3] John Foran did not see war as being necessary for this, but a more broadly defined "world systemic opening" (which could occur through the great power patron of the regime in a particular country simply not paying sufficient attention to events there) as an essential ingredient for successful revolution.[4] Certainly since the beginning of the Cold War, waves of revolution have occurred in several countries when great powers became unwilling, for whatever reason, to continue costly efforts to maintain influence there. Thus, the withdrawal of European colonial powers weakened by World War II from the developing world led to revolution in many countries. Similarly, the U.S. withdrawal from Indochina in 1973 led to an upsurge of Marxist revolution in what was then known as the Third World during the 1970s. When Gorbachev signaled Moscow's unwillingness to remain militarily engaged in Afghanistan or back up hard-line communist regimes in Eastern

---

[2] *Ibid.*

[3] Fred Halliday, *Revolution and World Politics: The Rise and Fall of the Sixth Great Power* (Durham: Duke University Press, 1999).

[4] John Foran, *Taking Power: On the Origins of Third World Revolutions* (Cambridge: Cambridge University Press, 2005).

Europe, a wave of democratic revolution swept through the latter. It would not be surprising, then, that the American withdrawal from Iraq and Afghanistan could lead to another revolutionary upsurge. Indeed, the fact that "Arab Spring" revolutions overthrew governments long allied to Washington in Tunisia, Egypt, and Yemen in the same year that the U.S. was completing its withdrawal from Iraq may be an indication that this process has begun. The impending American withdrawal from Afghanistan combined with American and European reluctance to undertake major military interventions could lead to another upsurge of revolutionary activity lasting for several years.

Diffusion of state power to transnational actors may contribute to the perception that states are becoming weaker, and thus more susceptible to revolution. On the other hand, it may not make sense to overthrow the state if doing so will not lead to a decline in the power of transnational actors. Still, some revolutionary movements may simply aspire to free one or more countries they are concerned with from the influence of transnational actors they object to by replacing existing governments that cooperate with them with ones that will not. It is also possible that the growing influence of transnational actors may result in new types of revolutionary movements that focus their efforts not on overthrowing the state, but damaging or destroying the transnational actors that they find particularly objectionable.

Global technological diffusion, especially in the realms of communications technology and social media, has already provided revolutionary movements with highly important advantages. Through the use of mobile phones, Facebook, Twitter, and similar tools, revolutionary movements have been able to gather enormous crowds as well as publicize their actions to the rest of the world in an extremely short period of time. The rapidity of the Arab Spring revolutions in Tunisia and Egypt in particular are examples of this trend—which is only likely to grow stronger in the coming years. Still, the ability of technically-capable counter-revolutionary regimes such as China to limit or deny their opponents access to these new technologies while at the same time taking advantage of them should not be underestimated.

Growing population and resource scarcity, where these occur, are highly likely to contribute to the occurrence of revolution. Indeed, Jack Goldstone has argued that rapid prolonged demographic growth combined with fiscal incompetence has been the foremost cause of state breakdown leading to revolution in Europe and Asia since the 17th century.[5] This combination of factors is strongly present today in many Muslim countries in particular, and so Goldstone's theory would indicate that the Muslim world in particular is likely to experience revolutionary activity over the next several years. Still, the fact that democratic revolutionary movements have risen up in countries with low growing or even declining populations such as Eastern Europe in 1989 and Ukraine in both 2004 and 2013 shows that revolutionary activity in them cannot be ruled out (and also that it might be time for a new theory to explain this phenomenon). Resource scarcity may contribute to the fiscal problems which both beleaguer existing regimes and provide impetus for revolutionary movements. But while successful revolutions lead to a change in government, they cannot alter the fact of resource scarcity. Although they can (and usually do) drastically reduce the preferential access of groups favored by the ousted regime to these resources, all too often new (especially authoritarian) revolutionary regimes do not distribute these scarce resources equitably either—thus sowing the seeds of future discontent.

Empowerment of individuals can be expected to contribute to revolution while **social vulnerabilities** may both contribute to as well as result from revolution. Over four decades ago, political scientist Ted Robert Gurr observed that revolution does not occur either in the richest or the poorest countries, but in ones in between where conditions may actually be improving—but not fast enough to satisfy the growing expectations of the population.[6] Increased levels of education, connection to the outside world, and even affluence, then, may not contribute to stability, but to a heightened awareness of what one lacks compared both to elites at home and to people generally in other countries, and to a keener sense of the unfairness of this state of affairs. Increased education, connectedness, and/or affluence may not only increase the demand for democratization (a positive trend), but can also intensify feelings of nationalist, ethnic, and/or sectarian solidarity as well as conflict among different such groups (a negative trend). The growth

---

[5]Jack A. Goldstone, *Revolution and Rebellion in the Early Modern World* (Berkeley: University of California Press, 1991), and Jack A. Goldstone, "Population Growth and Revolutionary Crises," in John Foran (ed.), *Theorizing Revolutions* (London: Routledge, 1997), pp. 102-120.
[6]Ted Robert Gurr, *Why Men Rebel* (Princeton: Princeton University Press, 1970).

in nationalist, ethnic, and sectarian awareness as well as large numbers of conflicts in which they are an important factor in recent years combined with the lack of countervailing forces seeking to mitigate them suggest that they will play an important role in the unfolding of revolutionary conflict going forward. Further, prolonged violent revolutionary conflicts (such as is taking place in Syria) give rise to massive refugee flows that can destabilize neighboring countries and contribute to the growth in intolerant, anti-immigrant nationalist movements both in them and in Western countries.

Climate change and environmental degradation have not been at the forefront of causes that revolutionary movements espouse. However, climate change and environmental degradation that cannot be ameliorated by incumbent governments can contribute to state breakdown by demonstrating state incapacity and undermining incumbent government legitimacy, thus contributing to revolution against it. Of course, revolutionary movements that succeed in seizing power may have no more capacity to ameliorate the problems for their country caused by climate change and environmental degradation that the regimes which they have ousted. Climate change and environmental degradation may then work to demonstrate their incapacity.

With this discussion of larger global trends at work and how they might integrate with transnational revolution between now and 2030 in mind, we turn now to a discussion of the cycles of transnational revolution likely to be active during this period.

Transnational Revolutionary Cycles

The cyclicality of transnational revolution can be seen in the periodic rise, fall, and re-emergence of transnational revolutionary ideologies and movements. Those transnational revolutionary ideologies and movements that have shown a proclivity to re-emerge even after seeming to fail or dissipate in the past, then, may be ones that are likely to persist at least until 2030. These include persistent cycles of transnational revolution include authoritarian Marxist, Islamist, democratic, and nationalist ones.

Authoritarian Marxist revolutionaries who first came to power in Russia were disappointed that their movement was unable to quickly seize power in other countries. But in the wake of World War II, authoritarian Marxism did spread—and not just via the Red Army—to parts of Eastern Europe and East Asia. Primarily indigenous forces brought authoritarian Marxism to power in Yugoslavia, Albania, China, and North Vietnam during these years. Interestingly, it was indigenous communist parties in three of these countries (Yugoslavia, Albania, and China) that would break with the Soviet Union. Another wave of authoritarian Marxism arose in many developing countries including Cuba in 1959, South Yemen in 1967, and several others in the 1970s. This revolutionary wave, though, experienced a collapse in the late 1980s and early 1990s when authoritarian Marxist regimes fell in Eastern Europe, the Soviet Union, and the developing world. Authoritarian Marxist regimes in China and Vietnam survived and even prospered, but did so through adapting to the global economy. Only North Korea and Cuba survived as authoritarian Marxist regimes that adhered largely (if not completely) to autarchic communist economic models.

Yet despite the apparent collapse of communism in 1989-91, semi-authoritarian Marxism experienced a revival in the early 21st century in four Latin American countries: Venezuela, Bolivia, Ecuador, and Nicaragua. "Maoist" movements have been active both in India and Nepal, and have even played a role in governance in the latter. This Marxist revolutionary inclination appears likely to persist in Latin America and South Asia and may even arise elsewhere between now and 2030. On the other hand, this inclination does not appear any more likely than in the past to extract Marxist-ruled countries from the international market economy or construct a more successful Marxist economic model in them (much less the rest of the world). The best they may hope for is to replicate what China and Vietnam have done: increase domestic prosperity through embracing the world market under the rule of ostensibly Marxist parties.

The modern **Islamic revolutionary wave** began with the Iranian revolution of 1979. Historian Nikki Keddie, though, traced the Islamic revolutionary movement back to 1700 since when it has repeatedly risen and fallen.[7] The modern Islamic revolutionary movement is not

---

[7]Nikki R. Keddie, "The Revolt of Islam 1700-1993," *Comparative Studies in Society and History* 36:3 (1994), pp. 463-487.

monolithic, but is divided between Sunni and Shi'a branches, and among authoritarian tendencies (including al-Qaeda and its affiliates), more democratically-oriented ones (including some Islamist elements within the "Arab Spring"), and hybrids such as the Islamic Republic of Iran which combines authoritarian and democratic features. Before the Arab Spring, the modern Islamic revolutionary movement came to rule over three countries: Iran beginning in 1979, Sudan beginning in 1989, and Afghanistan from 1996 to 2001.

Islamists have played a role in all of the Arab Spring revolutions (whether successful or not). Islamist revolutionary activity, though, is widespread. With the withdrawal of American and allied military forces from Iraq and Afghanistan, it is possible that such groups might gain influence in all or part of these two countries. In fact, in both Iraq and neighboring Syria, we have already witnessed the rise of the Islamic State (IS) during 2014. Far more than the Marxist one, the Islamist transnational revolutionary movement is highly likely to be active through 2030 and beyond. On the other hand, it seems doubtful that this movement will be able to overcome sectarian differences between Sunni and Shi'a, resolve differences within it between authoritarian and democratic leanings, and succeed in persuading powerful non-adherents (such as secular Arab military establishments) to coexist with it.[8]

Democratization has sometimes occurred via **democratic revolution** and sometimes via other means, including more evolutionary ones. Samuel Huntington argued that democratization occurred in waves, but that these democracy waves were followed by reverse waves in which many of those that attempted democratization reverted to authoritarianism.[9] Non-violent democratic revolutionary movements burst forth in a number of countries since the latter part of the Cold War—most notably in 1989-91. But true to Huntington's warning, only some of these succeeded in instituting democracy (most notably in Eastern Europe) while others either failed to come to power (China 1989) or appeared to do so but then reverted to authoritarianism under elected leaders (Russia under Yeltsin and Putin).

---

[8]For an elaboration of this argument, see Mark N. Katz, *Leaving without Losing: The War on Terror after Iraq and Afghanistan* (Baltimore: Johns Hopkins University Press, 2012).

[9]Samuel P. Huntington, *The Third Wave: Democratization in the Late Twentieth Century* (Norman: Oklahoma University Press, 1991).

The "Color Revolutions" in Georgia (2003), Ukraine (2004), and Kyrgyzstan (2005) again showed that the seeming triumph of democracy could prove short-lived. The hopes for democratization that the Arab Spring gave rise to have also been largely disappointed. But as the recent resurgence of the Ukrainian democratic movement after then-President Yanukovych reneged on his decision to sign an association agreement with the EU demonstrated, attempts at democratic revolution in response to popular disappointment can burst forth quite suddenly. Whether as a result of unpopular decisions or contested election results, authoritarian regimes can be counted upon to supply numerous such opportunities for democratic revolutionary movements to arise. It is highly likely, then, that more democratic revolutionary efforts will occur between now and 2030 (and beyond). Some will succeed and some will fail—but even the failure of a democratic revolution or experiment does not preclude a successful effort from being made later.

The cycle of **nationalist movements** (both revolutionary and non-revolutionary) seeking independence for the colonies of West European countries in the developing world came to an end in 1975 when the Portuguese colonial empire collapsed. At the end of the Cold War, though, another cycle of nationalist movements (again, both revolutionary and non-revolutionary) aimed at the secession of regions from already independent states became strong. There were, of course, many secessionist movements during the Cold War era, but very few of them actually achieved independence. (The one major exception was Bangladesh's secession from Pakistan.) In the post-Cold War era, however, there has been a considerable amount of secession. It began with the breakup of the USSR into fifteen independent states. This was followed shortly thereafter by the breakup of Yugoslavia, Czechoslovakia, and Ethiopia. Kosovo became independent from Serbia, and, more recently, South Sudan seceded from Sudan. In addition to all these cases of generally recognized independence, there have also been other cases where de facto independence has been achieved despite not being officially recognized by many—or any— governments. Examples of this include the Somaliland Republic (which has effectively seceded from Somalia), Kurdistan (from Iraq), and—with Russian help—Abkhazia and South Ossetia (from Georgia). Although many other secessionist movements have not achieved independence even after years of trying, neither have they been eliminated by governments which have earnestly sought to do so—as in the North Caucasus, East Turkestsan (Xinjiang), Tibet, Kashmir, Mindanao, and many other instances in Asia, Africa, and elsewhere. Strong secessionist movements are also active inside some of the former imperial states of Western Europe, including ones in Scotland, Catalonia, and Northern Italy.

As noted earlier, many of the post-Cold War instances of successful secession—such as the breakup of the USSR—were not the result of revolutionary movements. Indeed, secessionist movements in the West (such as those in Western Europe and Canada) have sought to achieve their goals largely through legally-sanctioned elections. Others instances of secessionist nationalism, though, can be considered revolutionary (whether operating peacefully or violently). Secessionist nationalists have not acted under the influence of a transnational revolutionary ideology seeking secession generally. Instead, secessionists almost always justify their claim to independence as an exception needed for their specific nation. But the more that secession occurs or even seems likely to occur, the more that secessionists elsewhere are likely to believe that they too can achieve it. In other words, despite the disparities in the manner in which it is sought and achieved, increased instances of successful secession could give rise to new international norms more approving of secession and disapproving of violent efforts to suppress it.

We turn now to a discussion of how these cycles of transnational revolution might be transformed between now and 2030.

Transformation of Transnational Revolution

Tomas Ries notes that flows evolve dynamically. Revolution is a phenomenon that has evolved, and which can be expected to continue doing so. Three potential transformations in particular need to be discussed: 1) transformation in how revolution occurs; 2) transformation in the relationship between democracy and revolution; and 3) the evolution of revolutionary regimes.

There has long been variation in how revolution occurs. The "great revolutions" of the past—such as the French revolution in the 18th century and the Russian and Chinese revolutions in the 20th century—were prolonged, violent, and included significant peasant involvement. Especially since the fourth quarter of the 20th century, though, numerous revolutions (including the East European revolutions of 1989, the color revolutions in Georgia and Ukraine in 2003-04, and the Arab Spring revolutions in Tunisia and Egypt in 2011) were short, non-violent, and predominantly urban-based. These quick, non-violent revolutions were democratic in aspiration, if not always in achievement. It would not be surprising if more such revolutions occurred between now and 2030. As the Arab Spring of 2011 showed, they can both arise quite unexpectedly and topple incumbent regimes very quickly. But as Syria has shown, prolonged, violent attempts at revolution may also occur. The case of Syria suggests that the more prolonged and violent an attempt at revolution becomes, the more likely it is that authoritarian forces will dominate the revolutionary opposition.

The relationship between democracy and revolution is not just affected by whether revolution is short and non-violent or prolonged and violent. Even authoritarian revolutionary movements have long claimed to be democratic or reflecting the "will of the people." In recent years, though, there has been a degree of genuine ambivalence about whether transnational revolutionary movements are democratic or authoritarian. While Marxist revolutions during the Cold War gave rise to highly authoritarian regimes, the Bolivarian revolutions of the post-Cold War era have combined elements of authoritarianism with elements of democracy. The elected leaders of the self-declared revolutionary governments of Venezuela, Bolivia, Ecuador, and Nicaragua have all acted to limit the ability of their opponents to contest their rule, but have also allowed some space for their political opponents as well as private enterprise to operate in. While these regimes might evolve in more authoritarian directions, they could also evolve in more democratic ones. Similarly, just as the Iranian revolution of 1979 resulted in a regime combining both authoritarian and democratic elements, the 2011 Arab Spring revolutions in Tunisia, Egypt, and Yemen have combined both authoritarian and democratic elements. Their final outcome is still not clear. While the democratic revolutions in Eastern Europe in 1989 all resulted in democratization (albeit more rapidly in some countries than in others), the color revolutions in Georgia, Ukraine, and Kyrgyzstan resulted in partially democratic, partially authoritarian regimes. Finally, the desire for democracy combined with the desire for nationalist secession can (and has) led to democratically-elected but intolerantly nationalist leaders both favoring and opposing secession. The continuation of this trend suggests that even though revolutions themselves may be occurring increasingly quickly and peacefully, there may well be prolonged ambiguity about their outcomes.

Past patterns in the long-term evolution of revolutionary regimes, though, suggest that even highly expansionist authoritarian transnational movements that come to power violently can evolve into non-revolutionary, status quo powers. This is because, once in power, the main goal of these revolutionary leaders tends to focus on remaining in power. Attempting to spread revolution, they find, is either a costly failure—or worse—a pyrrhic victory because it leads to the installation either of weak revolutionary regimes elsewhere that are much costlier to defend than to bring to power or to strong revolutionary regimes that become their rivals. By contrast, remaining in power, revolutionary leaders often conclude, is much easier to do through cooperation with the West rather than continued hostility toward it. A recent example of this occurring is Iran, where President Ahmadinejad's belligerence only served to isolate and impoverish that country while the moderation of his successor, President Rouhani, has brought forth the prospect of easing sanctions and improving relations with the West. Further such transformations hold out the prospect that other anti-Western transnational revolutionary movements that have come to power more recently –or may yet come to power—will also become less revolutionary and more willing (even if just for the sake of their own self-preservation) to cooperate with the West in the long-run.

Challenges for Europe and America in 2030

Just as in the past, transnational revolution is highly likely to be something that occurs and thus poses a challenge to Europe and America between now and 2030 (and beyond). The discussion above about the integration of transnational revolution with other flows suggests that 1) as a group, these other flows work to encourage revolution; 2) advances in communications technology and social networking in particular increase the prospects for revolutionary movements to arise suddenly and surprisingly; and 3) the flows encouraging transnational revolution are so strong that Europe and America probably have little capacity to restrain them even if they tried to do so. The discussion of transnational revolutionary cycles suggests that Islamic, democratic, nationalist secessionist, and even authoritarian Marxist revolutions are the most likely varieties of revolution to occur between now and 2030, though the possibility of other types cannot be ruled out. And the discussion of the transformation of transnational revolution suggests that even though revolution may arise and topple regimes quickly, 1) their outcomes may take a considerable period of time to unfold, and 2) even initially anti-Western revolutionary regimes may eventually come to regard cooperation with the West as being in their interests.

Recognizing that their ability to do so is limited, what can Europe and America do to meet the challenges to them from transnational revolutionary movements that they will undoubtedly confront?

Europe and America are fortunate that since the latter part of the Cold War, democratic revolutionary movements that seek cooperation—or even integration—with the West have been especially active. This was in contrast to most of the Cold War era when so much revolutionary activity was led by non-democratic movements that were hostile to the West.

Even pro-Western, democratic revolutionary movements, though, can pose serious challenges for Europe and America. It is wonderful when such movements come to power quickly and peacefully. Often, however, the authoritarian regimes they seek to overthrow act to suppress them violently. What should Europe and America do in such cases? Intervention, or even lesser forms of active assistance, can be costly and frustrating—especially when the democratic revolutionary movement proves to be poorly organized and divided. Yet doing little or nothing risks the defeat of democratic opposition movements by authoritarian regimes that might have been more restrained if the democratic opposition they faced was receiving serious Western support and protection. A longer term risk is that people disappointed by not receiving Western support for a democratic revolution against an authoritarian regime may turn to some form of non-democratic revolutionary ideology as the "only way" to get rid of a dictator whom they have come to believe that the West actually supports. Western indifference to the democratic aspirations of religiously-minded Arabs, for example, could result in the latter turning to the anti-democratic jihadists whom they previously rejected.

Of course, it is not always clear how democratic a revolutionary movement actually is before it comes to power, or even afterward. Transnational revolutionary movements and ideologies, as was noted earlier, usually claim to be democratic and to represent "the will of the people." But the definition of democracy is often contested. Should it be secular liberal as in the West, or should it be informed by religious values in societies (such as Muslim ones) where these are especially strong? To what extent should the new democratic regime embrace majority rule, and to what extent should the rights of minorities (however defined) be protected from the majority? These are questions that are currently affecting those countries where Arab Spring revolutions have either taken place or are being attempted. Part of the problem is that while different political groupings may genuinely see themselves as committed to democracy, they often do not see their rivals as being so. As the situation in Egypt is demonstrating now, such situations pose serious challenges for Europe and America.

So do nationalist secessionist movements. What these are often about is competing images of democracy. Is the existing state the most desirable locus of democracy, or would its division be preferable? If a referendum on the matter were held, the majority in an existing state might well vote to keep it intact, while a minority that is a majority in a region of it might instead vote for secession. How should such a situation be decided? When the government of the existing state is authoritarian and the movement seeking secession is (or claims to be) democratic, then the latter often succeeds in attracting sympathy and support from Europe and America—as occurred with Kosovo and South Sudan. But is the best solution to these situations allowing the region seeking independence to secede, or the democratization of the existing state? And if secession occurs without the consent of the state that loses a region, what impact will this have on the prospects for democratization in the remaining "rump" state? There are no easy answers to these questions. Something that Europe and America do need to understand, though, is that every time they support secession out of exceptional and/or humanitarian considerations, they fuel the demand for secession elsewhere by others who see their cause as being at least as equally deserving.

In addition, just as Europe and America need to be alive to the possibility that democratic revolution can yield an authoritarian outcome, they also need to be alert to the possibility that authoritarian revolutionary regimes can democratize. This may especially be true in cases where the revolutionary regime already allows some degree of electoral contestation (as in Iran, Venezuela, Bolivia, Ecuador, and Nicaragua), and where popular disillusionment with them has grown.

Europe and America may not be able to do much of anything to spark democratization, democratic revolution, or political change of any kind in the two authoritarian great powers, Russia and China. Should political change occur in either or both of them, however, Europe and America should act to encourage it in a democratic direction as well as to prevent change in Russia and/or China from disrupting their neighbors' security.

Policy Recommendations

As discussed here, transnational revolutionary movements and ideologies are highly varied phenomena. They will require varied policies on the part of Europe and America in order to deal with them effectively. Here are several suggestions:

Toward anti-democratic movements: Do not just focus exclusively on defeating them militarily, but also on discrediting them. While authoritarian movements have shown that they can survive the former, their own bad behavior makes them unwitting allies in the latter.

Toward democratic revolutionary movements: There are actions short of costly intervention that Europe and America can undertake to help them, including:

- Proclaim Western support for resolving confrontations between democratic opposition and authoritarian regime through free, internationally-monitored elections;
- Impose European and American sanctions on regimes that resist doing so (i.e., don't wait for authoritarian Russia and China to

approve Security Council sanctions, or use their unwillingness to do so as an excuse not to impose Western ones);

- Encourage authoritarian leaders to surrender power through arranging for their safe flight into exile (while many of their democratic opponents will demand that they be tried and punished, arranging for their exile can lead to a speedier end to the crisis and fewer casualties);
- Facilitate discussions between the regime's security force commanders and the democratic opposition leadership with a view to bringing about defections from the former to the latter.

Toward democratic revolutions with ambiguous results:

- Proclaim Western support for democratic processes as preferable to the use of force;
- Be willing to work with whatever politicians and parties are elected, but urge them to compromise with their opponents;
- If the military ends up ousting an elected leader and even if such a move is broadly popular (as in Egypt in 2013), call upon the military to hold free and fair elections that are open to those whom it ousted as soon as possible, and urge the ousted party to participate in them.

Toward old and tired authoritarian revolutionary regimes:

- Recognize that the prospects for democratization in these countries could be improved when their relations with Europe and America are improving;
- Seek to alter their behavior not just through applying sticks, but also through offering carrots.

Toward nationalist secessionism:

- Seek to reduce the demand for what can be the highly disruptive process of breaking up a country through democratic and federal solutions;
- When this clearly won't work, help negotiate a peaceful divorce, and work to integrate both governments into Western-backed economic and security architectures in order to give them both a powerful incentive not to engage in hostilities with each other;

- Anticipate that their new common border and other issues might still divide them. Work pro-actively to prevent these differences from degenerating into conflict, and move quickly to resolve them if and when they do.

About the Authors

Mika Aaltola is Program Director of the Global Security research program at the Finnish Institute of International Affairs. He has been a visiting Senior Research Fellow at the Center for Transatlantic Relations at Johns Hopkins University SAIS as well as visiting Professor at Tallinn University and the University of Minnesota. He holds a Ph.D. from the University of Tampere. Among his recent publications is *The Challenge of Global Commons and Flows to U.S. Geostrategy: The Future of Transatlantic Relations*, published by Ashgate in 2013.

Peter Andreas is a professor in Brown University's Department of Political Science, and a professor of international studies at the university's Watson Institute. He joined the Institute in the fall of 2001, and currently serves as associate director. Previously he served as an academy scholar at Harvard University, a research fellow at the Brookings Institution, and an SSRC-MacArthur Foundation Fellow on International Peace and Security. He holds an MA and Ph.D in government from Cornell University and a BA in political science from Swarthmore College. He is the author, co-author, or co-editor of nine books. These include *Blue Helmets and Black Markets: The Business of Survival in the Siege of Sarajevo* (Cornell University Press, 2008); *Policing the Globe: Criminalization and Crime Control in International Relations* (Oxford University Press, 2006); *Border Games: Policing the U.S.-Mexico Divide* (Cornell University Press, 2000, second edition 2009); and *Sex, Drugs, and Body Counts: The Politics of Numbers in Global Crime and Conflict* (Cornell University Press, 2010). He has also written for a wide range of scholarly and policy publications, including *International Security, International Studies Quarterly, Review of International Political Economy, Foreign Affairs, Foreign Policy, The New Republic*, and *The Nation*. Other writings include congressional testimonies and op-eds in major newspapers such as the *Washington Post*. His latest book, on the politics of smuggling in American history, is *Smuggler Nation: How Illicit Trade Made America* (Oxford University Press, 2013).

Raimund Bleischwitz joined University College London as BHP Billiton Chair in Sustainable Global Resources in August 2013. He was previously Co-Director of Material Flows and Resource Management at the Wuppertal Institute in Germany, and has been Visiting Professor at the College of Europe in Bruges, Belgium since 2003. An economist by training, he has more than twenty years experience in research on environmental and resource economics, resource efficiency, incentive systems and policies, raw material conflicts, industry and sustainability. He is often invited as a speaker, acknowledged as an influential policy adviser and cooperates with business in projects such as the EU Eco-Innovation Observatory and the RECREATE research network for forward-looking activities and assessment of research and innovation prospects in the fields of climate, resources efficiency and raw materials, a five-year EU Coordination and Support Action project. He spent a two-month fellowship at the American Institute for Contemporary German Studies (AICGS) at Johns Hopkins University Washington, DC in Spring 2013 and one academic year at the Transatlantic Academy in Washington DC from September 2011 until July 2012. He was involved in the Millennium Collaborations Projects on climate, energy and eco-efficiency conducted by the Japanese Economic and Social Research Institute (ESRI) from 2000–2005, fellow of the Japanese Society for the Promotion of Science in 2005, and has close relations with the Institute for Global Environmental Strategies (IGES) and other researchers and stakeholders in Japan. He supported Ernst Ulrich von Weizsäcker in establishing the Wuppertal Institute, inter alia as his permanent substitute in a National Committee on the Earth Summit preparations in 1992, and he was one of the lead authors of a report entitled "Sustainable Germany." He also had earlier engagements at the Max Planck Project Group on Collective Goods in Bonn (where he did his habilitation), at the Institute for European Environmental Policy (IEEP) and in the German Bundestag. A longer version of his chapter is part of a forthcoming book on the *Global Resource Nexus* (Earthscan Publisher).

Erik Brattberg is a Non-Resident Scholar at the Center for Transatlantic Relations at Johns Hopkins University SAIS and a Resident Fellow at the Atlantic Council's Brent Scowcroft Center on International Security. He is also a Research Associate at the Swedish Institute of International Affairs. He has published widely on European and transatlantic security issues.

Rob Edmonds is a senior consultant at Strategic Business Insights, a business research and technology consulting company with offices in Silicon Valley, Princeton, New Jersey, Croydon, England, and Tokyo, Japan. Rob helps organizations identify and map opportunities created by emerging developments in software and electronics. Prior to joining Strategic Business Insights, he worked in a consulting role at IBM and holds a M.Sc. in cognitive science from Birmingham University (England) and a B.A. in philosophy from Middlesex University (England).

Daniel S. Hamilton is the Austrian Marshall Plan Foundation Professor and Director of the Center for Transatlantic Relations at the Paul H. Nitze School of Advanced International Studies (SAIS), Johns Hopkins University. He also serves as Executive Director of the American Consortium for EU Studies, designated by the European Commission as the EU Center of Excellence Washington, DC. He has held a variety of senior positions in the U.S. Department of State, including Deputy Assistant Secretary for European Affairs; U.S. Special Coordinator for Southeast European Stabilization; Associate Director of the Policy Planning Staff for two Secretaries of State; Director for Policy in the Bureau of European Affairs; and Senior Policy Advisor to the U.S. Ambassador and U.S. Embassy in Germany. In 2008 he served as the first Robert Bosch Foundation Senior Diplomatic Fellow in the German Foreign Office. He has led international work for the Johns Hopkins-led National Center of Excellence in Homeland Security, and was co-director of Atlantic Storm, a Ministerial-level biosecurity exercise. Selected publications include *Transatlantic Homeland Security; Protecting the Homeland: European Approaches to Societal Security—Implications for the United States; The Geopolitics of TTIP; Transatlantic 2020: A Tale of Four Futures; Europe 2020: Competitive or Complacent?; Shoulder to Shoulder: Forging a Strategic U.S.-EU Partnership;* and *Humanitarian Assistance: Improving U.S.-European Cooperation.*

Paul A. Isbell is the CAF Atlantic Energy Fellow at the Center for Transatlantic Relations at Johns Hopkins SAIS and author of *Energy and the Atlantic: The Shifting Energy Landscape of the Atlantic Basin* (German Marshall Fund and OCP Foundation, 2012). At CTR he is exploring the implications of the emergence of the southern Atlantic. He is also consultant to the Inter-American Development Bank (IDB) on climate change issues. Previously he was visiting senior fellow for energy and climate change at the Inter-American Dialogue in Washington, DC and, until 2010, director of the Energy and Climate Change Program at the Elcano Royal Institute for International and Strategic Studies (Real Instituto Elcano) in Madrid. In 2002-04, he was the secretariat of the ASEM (Asia Europe Meeting) Special Task Force on Closer Economic and Financial Partnership between Asia and Europe. Prior to that, he was Emerging Markets and Currencies analyst—with a focus on Latin America—at the Madrid-based investment bank of Banco Santander. He has also been a professor of economics and international political economy at a number of Spanish and American universities, including the University of Alcala de Henares, ICADE, CUNEF, Syracuse University, and George Washington University. Currently he teaches energy economics and geopolitics at ICADE (Universidad Pontificia Comillas) in Madrid, and emerging market economies at the Instituto Tecnológico de Buenos Aires (ITBA). His areas of work and interest have included international economy, currency and monetary politics, and energy and climate economics, as well as the political economy of emerging market countries. He completed undergraduate studies at Georgetown University in Washington, D.C. and Sussex University in the UK, and his graduate work at the University of Dar es Salaam.

Bruce Jentleson is Professor of Public Policy and Political Science at Duke University, where he served from 2000-2005 as Director of the Terry Sanford Institute of Public Policy. He served as a Senior Advisor to the U.S. State Department Policy Planning Director, 2009-2011. Other policy experience includes serving as a foreign policy aide for Senator Dave Durenberger (1978-79) and Senator Al Gore (1987-88); Special Assistant to the Director of the State Department Policy Planning Staff (1993-94); and as a foreign policy advisor to Vice Presidential candidate Gore (1992) and a senior foreign policy advisor to the Gore presidential campaign (1999-2000). He currently is serving as a member of the Responsibility to Protect Working Group co-chaired by Madeleine Albright and Rich Williamson, and as co-Director of Amidst the Revolutions: U.S. Strategy in a Changing Middle East, a project of the Center for a New American Security. Prior to coming to Duke, he was Professor at the University of California-Davis and Director of the UC Davis Washington Center. He has held research appointments at the U.S. Institute of Peace, the Brookings Institution, Oxford University, the International Institute for Strategic Studies (London), and as a Fulbright Senior Research Scholar in Spain. He has published numerous books and articles, including *American Foreign Policy: The Dynamics of Choice in the 21st Century*, a leading university text now in its 4th edition (W.W. Norton, 2010) and *The End of Arrogance: America in the Global Competition of Ideas*, co-authored with Steven Weber (Harvard University Press, 2010). He holds a Ph.D. from Cornell University, and was recipient of the American Political Science Association's Harold D. Lasswell Award for his doctoral dissertation; a Master's from the London School of Economics and Political Science; and a Bachelor's degree also from Cornell.

Mark Katz is Associate Professor of Government and Politics at the School of Policy, Government, and International Affairs at George Mason University. He earned a BA in international relations from the University of California at Riverside, an MA in international relations from the Johns Hopkins University School of Advanced International Studies, and a PhD in political science from M.I.T. He writes on Russian foreign policy, the international relations of the Middle East, transnational revolutionary movements, and other subjects. He has been a research fellow at the Brookings Institution, held a temporary appointment as a Soviet affairs analyst at the U.S. Department of State, was a Rockefeller Foundation international relations fellow, and was a Kennan Institute research scholar and research associate. He has also received a U.S. Institute of Peace fellowship and grant, and several Earhart Foundation fellowship research grants. Recently, he was a visiting scholar at the Hokkaido University Slavic Research Center, and at the Kennan Institute. He is the author of *The Third World in Soviet Military Thought* (Johns Hopkins University Press, 1982), *Russia and Arabia: Soviet Foreign Policy toward the Arabian Peninsula* (Johns Hopkins University Press, 1986), *Gorbachev's Military Policy in the Third World* (Center for Strategic and International Studies, 1989),

Revolutions and Revolutionary Waves (St. Martin's Press, 1997), and *Reflections on Revolutions* (St. Martin's Press, 1999). He is also the editor of *The USSR and Marxist Revolutions in the Third World* (Wilson Center/Cambridge University Press, 1990), *Soviet-American Conflict Resolution in the Third World* (U.S. Institute of Peace Press, 1991), and *Revolution: International Dimensions* (CQ Press, 2001).

Barry Lynn directs the Markets, Enterprise, and Resiliency Initiative, and is a senior fellow at the New America Foundation. He is author of *Cornered: The New Monopoly Capitalism and the Economics of Destruction* (Wiley 2010) and *End of the Line: The Rise and Coming Fall of the Global Corporation* (Doubleday 2005). His groundbreaking writings on interdependence among nations and the growing fragility of complex industrial systems have attracted wide attention, and he has presented his work to high officials in China, Japan, Germany, Britain, France, Taiwan, and the European Commission, as well as in the White House and U.S. Treasury Department. His work has been profiled on CBS and in the New York Times, and his articles have appeared in publications including *Harper's, the Financial Times, Harvard Business Review*, and *Foreign Policy*. He has appeared on *CBS, PBS, CNN, the BBC, NPR, MSNBC, C-Span*, and the *Christian Broadcasting Network*, among others. Prior to joining New America, Lynn was executive editor of *Global Business Magazine* for seven years, and worked as a correspondent in Peru, Venezuela, and the Caribbean for the Associated Press and Agence France Presse.

Joseph P. Quinlan is a Non-Resident Fellow at the Center for Transatlantic Relations at the Paul. H. Nitze School of Advanced International Studies of Johns Hopkins University. Together with CTR Director Daniel Hamilton he is the award-winning author of a series of publications on the transatlantic economy and its strategic importance to the United States, Europe and the world. He is a seasoned Wall Street economist and currently the Chief Market Strategist at Bank of America Merrill Lynch. Prior to that, he served as a Senior Global Economist for Morgan Stanley from 1994 to 2002. Prior to joining Morgan Stanley, he worked as Director of Economic Research at Sea-Land Services, a $3 billion global transportation firm. He has also been an International Management Consultant. He lectures on global finance at New York University, where he has been on the faculty since 1992. In 1998, he was nominated as Eisenhower Fellow and studied China-Taiwan cross-straits relations for a month in Taiwan. He has published over 125 articles on international economics and trade, with publications appearing in such venues as *Foreign Affairs*, *The Financial Times*, *The Wall Street Journal* and *Barron's*.

Bill Ralston is vice president and board director of Strategic Business Insights, a business research and technology consulting company with offices in Silicon Valley, Princeton, New Jersey, Croydon, England, and Tokyo, Japan. He advises multinational corporations and government organizations on emerging issues and strategy. He is the author of *The Scenario Planning Handbook: Developing Strategies for Uncertain Times*, published by Thomson South Western in 2006, and numerous articles on technology management, scenario planning, and strategic planning. He has a BS in civil engineering from Stanford University and an MBA from Harvard University.

Tomas Ries is a s senior lecturer at the Swedish National Defence College in Stockholm. and former Director of the Swedish Institute of International Affairs. His main area of interest is the global security environment. He was Senior Researcher at the National Defense College in Finland from 1997-2004, focusing on globalization and security and EU and NATO affairs. From 1992-1997 he was Director of the International Training Course in Geneva, Switzerland. He has also worked as Researcher and then Senior Researcher at the Norwegian Institute of International Affairs and the Institute for Defense Studies in Oslo where his focus was Nordic security and defense policies. He has written two books and over one-hundred articles and research studies. He holds a B.Sc. (Econ) from the London School of Economics and Political Science and a Ph.D. from the Graduate Institute of International Studies at Geneva University.

Louise Shelley is a University Professor at George Mason University. She is in the School of Public Policy and directs the Terrorism, Transnational Crime and Corruption Center (TraCCC) that she founded. She is a leading expert on the relationship among terrorism, organized crime and corruption as well as human trafficking, transnational crime and terrorism with a particular focus on the former Soviet Union. She also specializes in illicit financial flows and money laundering. She received her undergraduate degree cum laude from Cornell University in Penology and Russian literature. She holds an

M.A. in Criminology from the University of Pennsylvania. She studied at the Law Faculty of Moscow State University on IREX and Fulbright Fellowships and holds a Ph.D. in Sociology from the University of Pennsylvania. She held a Fulbright and researched and taught on crime issues in Mexico. She has also taught on transnational crime in Italy. She is the recipient of the Guggenheim, NEH, IREX, Kennan Institute, and Fulbright Fellowships and received a MacArthur Grant to establish the Russian Organized Crime Study Centers. In 1992, she received the Scholar-Teacher prize of American University, the top academic award of the university. Her most recent book, *Dirty Entanglements: Corruption, Crime and Terrorism* will be published by Cambridge University Press in 2014. She is the author of *Human Trafficking: A Global Perspective* (Cambridge 2010), *Policing Soviet Society* (Routledge, 1996), *Lawyers in Soviet Worklife and Crime and Modernization*, as well as numerous articles and book chapters on all aspects of transnational crime and corruption. She is also an editor (with Sally Stoecker) of *Human Traffic and Transnational Crime: Eurasian and American Perspectives*. She has testified before the House Committee on International Relations Committee, the Helsinki Commission, the House Banking Committee and the Senate Foreign Relations Committee on transnational crime, human trafficking and the links between transnational crime, financial crime and terrorism. She is presently serving on the Global Agenda Council on Illicit Trade and Organized Crime of the World Economic Forum (WEF) and was the first co-chair of its Council on Organized Crime where she continues to serve. She presently co-chairs a group on human trafficking within the Global Agenda Councils of the WEF.

Carl Telford is a senior consultant and program manager for Strategic Business Insights' Scan™ Service. Scan is a continuous process to detect changes impacting the business environment, giving clients a head start in identifying emerging threats and opportunities. He has doctoral and bachelor's degrees in materials engineering from Brunel University (England) and the University of Surrey (England) respectively.

Robert Thomas is a principal consultant at Strategic Business Insights, a business research and technology consulting company with offices in Silicon Valley, Princeton, New Jersey, Croydon, England, and Tokyo, Japan. He specializes in helping companies with their strategic planning, technology foresighting and commercialization activities. Robert has doctoral and bachelor's degrees in physics from Imperial College, London and Jesus College, Oxford respectively and an executive finance certificate from the Grenoble Ecole de Management.